# Currencies and Crises

# Currencies and Crises

Paul R. Krugman

The MIT Press
Cambridge, Massachusetts
London, England

Seventh printing, 1999

First MIT Press paperback edition, 1995

This book was set in Palatino by Asco Trade Typesetting Ltd., Hong Kong, and was
printed and bound in the United States of America.

Library of Congress Cataloging-in-Publication Data

Krugman, Paul R.
    Currencies and crises / Paul R. Krugman.
        p.   cm.
    Includes bibliographical references and index.
    ISBN 0-262-11165-9 (HB), 0-262-61109-0 (PB)
    1. International finance.   2. Foreign exchange.   3. Debts, External.   I. Title.
HG3881.K77   1991
    332'.042—dc20                                                    91-39568
                                                                        CIP

# Contents

## IV  The International Monetary System

# Preface

This is my second book of collected papers. The first, *Rethinking International Trade*, was a collection built around a single theme: the reconstruction of international trade theory to take account of increasing returns and imperfect competition. My work on international monetary economics, the subject of this collection, has often involved the construction of analytical models, but it has been motivated less by the desire to reconstruct theory than by the attempt to make sense of a rapidly changing world. So this is a book of less intellectual coherence but perhaps more immediate real-world relevance.

This kind of work cannot be done in isolation. My ideas about international monetary economics have emerged out of countless bleary-eyed discussions on the 6:40 AM flight to Washington, heated exchanges at Cambridge blackboards, and unplanned seminars that spontaneously developed over bitter coffee drunk from paper cups. So every one of these papers in a way has several coauthors. Since my graduate student days Rudiger Dornbusch, whose intellectual sharpness has been reinforced by ever-growing policy reach and acumen, has been a crucial source of ideas and advice. My colleague and coauthor Julio Rotemberg has been an invaluable sounding board over the years. Another colleague and coauthor, Ken Froot, played a key role in the development of several of the papers in this book. And all of my work has benefited immensely by the intellectual environment provided both by MIT and by the National Bureau of Economic Research.

Finally, as always, it is family—my parents and my wife—who provide the bedrock on which everything else depends.

# Introduction

When the Bretton Woods system of fixed exchange rates broke up in the early 1970s, most international economists were not dismayed. Not only did they believe that greater flexibility of exchange rates was a good thing; they also believed that they understood reasonably well how the new system would work.

They were wrong. The last 20 years of the international monetary system have involved one surprise after another, most of them unpleasant, all of them forcing economists to scramble to keep up with new issues and unexpected turns in old ones.

The 11 papers collected in this book record my own international monetary scramblings from the late 1970s to the beginning of the 1990s. They come from a period in which all economists writing on international money and macro, myself very much included, were repeatedly getting it wrong: making incorrect predictions, or simply failing to perceive the imminent importance of a new issue and thus being caught flat-footed by events. It was also, however, a period of great intellectual excitement. For it is paradoxically true that times of radical change, in which economic theory is most likely to go wrong, are also the times in which such theory is most useful and interesting. In calm times the theorist mostly gets it right, but he has little to offer the experienced practitioner and may find it hard to come up with new ideas. In crazy times the theorist mostly gets it wrong; but the experienced practitioner, who has never seen anything like what is happening, hasn't a clue; and new ideas are virtually forced upon the researcher by each day's newspapers. And although one might expect that research that responds to events would quickly come to look dated, my own experience has been that papers written in an effort to understand current issues are often the ones that best stand the test of time.

It would be nice to go even further, to say that all of these pieces represent steps on the road to a unified theory of international money and macroeconomics. Unfortunately, they don't. Partly this is because they were written not in pursuit of a general theory but in response to specific issues as they arose. Mostly, however, it is because a unified monetary theory (domestic or international) is a goal that seems to recede further every year. So this volume is more like a song cycle than a sonata. Yet there are some unifying themes, both those that apply to all the papers and those that link the papers into specific groups.

## General Unifying Themes

The main overall unifying theme in this volume is methodological. All of the papers use the same basic approach: take a real-world problem that is a source of puzzlement or dispute, and construct a small theoretical model that in some simplified way seems to get at the essence of the problem. While some of the papers try to be quantitative as well as conceptual, the essential purpose of this kind of economic analysis is to build intuition. Success in the effort is measured by the "aha" index: A paper has achieved something if the informed reader feels that she has gained a significantly greater insight into an important problem, an insight whose major content is often that of providing a language to discuss that problem. This is the kind of economics that Robert Solow did when he introduced the basic concepts of growth theory, that James Tobin did when he introduced the idea of $q$, that Robert Lucas did when he introduced the concept of a rational expectations business cycle.

This kind of economics is not universally popular, to say the least. On one side, many contemporary economists now believe that economic analysis is valid only if it is built on microeconomic foundations from the ground up, that there is no room for models that start somewhere in the middle; an alarmingly large number of academics also tend to dismiss simple models on the ground that if they are easy to understand they must also be trivial. On the other side, some economists and many practical people see little utility in abstract theorizing of any sort; they want to see quantitative results ready for immediate application.

Obviously I disagree with both positions. The growing demand for rigor and mathematical difficulty in economics has, I would argue, gone much too far; if we refuse to think about anything until we can base our thoughts rigorously on the axioms of microeconomics, we will abandon most of what makes economics interesting and useful. In any case supposedly rigorous analysis is not necessarily actually reliable. To take the most glaring example, many economists have rejected the idea that nominal prices are sticky because they believe that such stickiness is inconsistent with fully rational behavior. But there is abundant evidence that prices are in fact sticky, and no evidence at all that people are fully rational, so an economist who assumes sticky prices may well be on more solid ground than the purist who condemns her. Eventually economics may become a truly integrated structure in which it is possible to address all issues using a consistent set of assumptions. But that millenium is nowhere near, and meanwhile I refuse to give away the insights that a little ad hockery can bring.

On the other side, in the real world there is little patience for economists who want to offer insights rather than produce specific predictions, and a general preference for the judgment of people who have experience and look prosperous over academics who base their ideas on models. Yet in times of radical change this preference is exactly wrong. An anecdote may make the point. I once helped prepare a background report for a Third World debtor country, which, among other things, was critical of plans for a repurchase of part of that country's debt on the secondary market. (The reasons for that critical position are discussed in chapter 9). The country's central bank, with advice from its bankers, dismissed the criticism, with some waspish remarks about the silliness of relying on abstract arguments rather than the experience of practitioners. But of course there are no experienced practitioners in the area of Third World debt reduction—nothing remotely like the current experience has happened since the 1930s. Guesswork is all that we have to go on, and those who discipline their guesses with models are more reliable than those who fly by the seat of their pants, no matter how well tailored. In fact, in the particular area of market-based debt reduction, the bankers have persistently been wildly impractical, arguing that a little financial engineering will produce perpetual motion machines, while the economic theorists have correctly pointed out the limitations of clever financial schemes.

So the papers in this volume are linked by a methodological approach that uses abstract models but is willing to cut corners on rigor in order to gain insight. This methodology brings with it a natural attitude toward modeling style: a very strong preference for maximum simplicity. For economists who believe that maximization and equilibrium are unchallengeable axioms rather than frequently convenient metaphors, simplicity and elegance are less important than Truth. For economists who are actually building empirical models, complexity may be necessary in order to save the phenomena. If one is trying to build insight, however, it is essential to clear away as much clutter as possible. That means looking for the simplest, cleanest model that makes the point.

Simplicity does not mean an absence of technique. Sometimes one needs to introduce fancy mathematics in order to express an idea simply. For example, the analyses of the J-curve and adjustment in chapter 2, and of speculative attack in chapter 4, use the idea of saddle-path instability to describe succinctly the key role of expectations; the analysis of exchange rate target zones in chapters 5 and 6 relies on stochastic calculus to simplify an otherwise messy description of speculative behavior; the discussion of exchange rate regimes in chapter 11 implicitly appeals to the idea of subgame perfection to pin down the nature of the credibility problem. The point, however, is to wear one's technique lightly, to use it to make things easier, not harder. One should not fall into the trap of assuming that only papers with lots of theorems and lemmas are sophisticated, when often the truest sophistication is finding a way to express novel ideas with no more than a diagram or a numerical example.

The common ground of all of these papers then is one of method and style. The papers also, however, fall into four groups organized around particular substantive themes. The subthemes of the book are, first, the role of exchange rates in balance of payments adjustment; second, the role of speculation in the functioning of exchange rate regimes; third, the problem of Third World debt; and finally, the problem of constructing an international monetary system.

Within each group the papers use related models so that each group of papers at least gropes toward a unified approach to its particular subject. Thus the three papers on balance-of-payments adjustment focus on the role of the real exchange rate and move from a static toward a dynamic description of that role; the three papers on speculation use the same stripped-down monetary approach, and the third of the papers essentially integrates the first two; the three papers on debt share the common theme that debt reduction represents a trade-off of option value against incentives and build toward an increasingly policy-oriented statement of that framework; and the two papers on the international monetary system share an emphasis on the microeconomics of money. Any suggestion of small-minded consistency within each set of papers is, however, dispelled by the nearly complete absence of common assumptions between sections.

## Exchange Rates and International Adjustment

The first three chapters in this volume examine an old issue: the relationship between currency devaluation and the trade balance.

It may seem surprising that this issue could still be a subject of dispute. After all, during the 1940s and 1950s there were a series of classic papers on the theory of devaluation by Joan Robinson, Gottfried Haberler, Sidney Alexander, and above all James Meade. By the beginning of the 1980s there had also been extensive empirical work on the short- and medium-run determinants of trade flows, whose conclusions have mostly stood up fairly well over the past decade. One might have thought that little new was left to say.

Yet the rise and fall of the dollar during the 1980s turned the topic of exchange rates and trade adjustment into an area of heated dispute. One major reason was that influential economists—represented in particular by Ronald McKinnon and Robert Mundell—fiercely denounced the traditional view that a country could most easily reduce a trade deficit by allowing its currency to depreciate. Their view, which was echoed by policymakers and journalists, was that the growing international mobility of capital had ended any useful role for exchange rate adjustment. Changes in national savings-investment balances could now, they claimed, be translated directly into changes in trade balances, with depreciation playing no useful role. This was more than an analytical point. The McKinnon-Mundell argument was a key debating point for those who argued for a return to fixed exchange rates. Remarkably, few international economists rose to the defense of the conventional wisdom, perhaps because the mundane issue of trade balance adjustment had attracted so little research attention in the previous decade that the simple things had been forgotten.

Somebody needed to argue forcefully that this challenge to standard views was wrong both conceptually and empirically. In chapter 1, originally written for the unofficial advisory Group of 30, I took on that task. The chapter confronts the widely held idea that high mobility of financial capital somehow allows changes in saving or investment to influence imports or exports directly, rather than via a mechanism in which the exchange rate plays a crucial role. John Williamson has felicitously called this the doctrine of "immaculate transfer"; it is a misconception pure and simple. The chapter also shows that as an empirical matter, reducing a trade deficit requires substantial real depreciation by the deficit country and that there is over-whelming evidence that real depreciation is most easily accomplished by devaluing the nominal exchange rate. In other words, the chapter was an effort to defend the (hard-won) conventional wisdom on the usefulness of exchange rate adjustment against fashionable but misguided criticism.

When chapter 1 was written (in summer 1987), its defense of the useful-ness and effectiveness of currency depreciation sounded a bit hollow. At the time the falling dollar had not yet had any noticeable effect in reducing the U.S. trade deficit, while the capital inflow that was the counterpart of the deficit was increasingly taking the form of foreign purchases of U.S. corporations. This led to charges both by global monetarists and by protectionists that the fall in the dollar, instead of reducing the trade deficit, was leading to a "fire sale" of U.S. assets at distress prices. In chapter 2, written a year later, I tried to show that the perception of a fire sale was both misleading and a natural part of the adjustment process, that precisely because of long lags in the response of trade flows to the exchange rate, it was to be expected that during an interim period the United States would attract capital via a perceived low value of its currency.

Both chapter 1 and chapter 2 were essentially conservative intellectually, arguing that traditional views about short- and medium-run trade adjustment were still right in spite of trendy intellectual challenges and a few years of disappointing trade figures. Chapter 3 argues, however, that the demand-side framework that continues to work fairly well at explaining trade flows in the medium run is badly misleading for the long run. The standard framework sees each country as facing a fairly inelastic downward-sloping demand curve for its exports. This suggests that countries with rapidly growing exports, like Japan or Korea, should have rapidly falling relative export prices over time. Yet this is manifestly not the case, a fact that is explained in the standard model by a coincidental correlation between high growth and favorable income elasticities.

What chapter 3 argues with the aid of a simple illustrative model is that no coincidence is involved, that long-run trends in exports and imports reflect supply-side effects which conventional estimates mistakenly pick up as income elasticities. The main implication of this argument is that purchasing power parity is a much better guide to equilibrium exchange rates in the long run than the abject failure of PPP in the short run might have suggested.

### Speculation and Exchange Regimes

Before the 1970s balance-of-payments analyses focused on flows: on the trade balance and on what were perceived as sustained, gradual movements of capital. Indeed, for a time it was standard for economists to gauge a country's position by a so-called basic balance that added the current account and long-term capital flows; this basic balance was assumed to be what really mattered, with short-term capital flows more of a nuisance than a really important issue.

With the growing international mobility of capital after 1970, however, it became increasingly clear that there were substantial stocks of capital that were prepared to move en masse from one currency to another. Countries that tried to fix their exchange rates could find their reserves (or, in the case of surplus countries, their patience) quickly exhausted by massive speculative attacks; countries with floating exchange rates found that those rates fluctuated with the expectations of speculators. At the same time the rational expectations revolution in economics made it possible to say more interesting (if not always true) things about speculative behavior than had been possible before.

Chapter 4, which is the oldest paper in this volume, addresses the role of speculation in forcing the collapse of a fixed rate regime. When I wrote it early in 1977, I had in mind the collapse of Bretton Woods and the short-lived Smithsonian agreement that followed. But the model really came into its own a few years later with the huge capital flight from Argentina, Venezuela, and Mexico on the eve of the debt crisis. Building on a classic analysis of the gold market by Stephen Salant and Dale Henderson, the chapter shows that sudden runs on a country's currency need not be the result of irrational herd behavior on the part of speculators. On the contrary, when a country attempts to peg its exchange rate without following domestic policies consistent with that goal, a speculative attack that exhausts the country's foreign exchange reserves in a very short time is actually predictable. The concept of speculative attack has now become a standard tool of international monetary analysis. Unfortunately, policymakers continue to give us opportunities to apply it.

Chapter 5 addresses the role of speculation in a seemingly very different context. During the 1970s and 1980s the unexpected volatility of exchange rates created considerable dismay; yet many people were reluctant to contemplate a return to fully fixed rates. When European countries formed the European Monetary System, they allowed exchange rates to fluctuate within considerably wider bands than under Bretton Woods. Influential economists who advocated stabilization of all major currencies called for still wider bands, which John Williamson (again) felicitously dubbed "target zones." Advocates of target zones hoped that they would preserve some flexibility, while curbing the speculative instability that they felt was playing a destructive role under floating rates.

As late as 1987, however, despite widespread discussion and even half-hearted implementation of the target zone idea, there were no clear models of how such zones would work. Some economists even claimed that target zones would destabilize exchange rates by offering speculators fixed targets to shoot at. What chapter 5 (initially presented at a 1987 conference) did was to introduce a simple approach to modeling target zones, showing that rational speculation under such a zone would in fact be stabilizing. The interest of the paper was not only in its practical application but in the novelty of its technique (which was simultaneously and independently brought into international economics in a different context by Avinash Dixit): It was followed by scores of papers that applied the idea of "regulated Brownian motion" to more complex models, both in international economics and elsewhere.

Chapter 6 represents a different kind of extension; it links the target zone analysis to the speculative attack analysis in chapter 4. The model was at least partly motivated by concerns that target zone arrangements, like fixed exchange rates, would often fail to be backed up by adequate domestic policies. It also turns out that allowing for the possibility of speculative attacks helps to demystify some of the technical apparatus that has grown up around the original target zone model.

## Third World Debt

In 1982 bank lending to developing countries dried up, and more than a dozen countries found themselves unable to service the debt they had accumulated over the previous decade. The debt crisis has been an enduring source of policy anxiety—some of which I shared in the early stages, as a staffer at the Council of Economic Advisers. It has also been, to be honest, a source of much intellectual fascination.

Chapters 7, 8, and 9 date not from the early stages of the crisis but from the period from 1986 on when the initial strategy for coping with the crisis began to unravel. In 1982 and 1983 most analysts—myself included—thought that if the principal on Third World debt were rescheduled and some of the interest recycled through "concerted lending," economic growth would allow most debtors to work their way back into creditworthiness. By 1986 this was starting to look unrealistic, and there were growing calls for a shift to debt forgiveness. Yet there seemed to be a lack of clear thinking about how to decide what debt strategy was appropriate.

Chapter 7 was an effort to clarify that issue. At the time it was written (during the winter of 1986–87, when I was visiting at the IMF), the discussion on debt strategy was marked by absolutism. That is, bankers and U.S. officials insisted that debt should never be forgiven under any circumstances; some economists argued, on the contrary, that whenever countries are unable to service their debt it is in everyone's interest to "recognize reality" and reduce the debt burden. Chapter 7 suggested that both positions were wrong because there is a trade-off involved. Creditors want to keep claims high in order to benefit if the debtor happens to do better than expected, but reducing claims offers the hope that a lower debt burden will enhance a country's ability to service the remaining debt.

From 1986 to 1989, while official policy opposed any concerted debt reduction, there were widespread hopes that ingenious financial schemes, such as debt-equity swaps, could be used to engineer a decentralized solution to the debt problem. The point of chapter 8, written early in 1988, was to argue that these hopes were largely misguided. The paper offered a compressed summary of the trade-off discussed in chapter 7, the "debt relief Laffer curve." It then used this organizing device to show that the conditions under which financial engineering could benefit both debtors and creditors were essentially the same as those under which concerted debt reduction was in everyone's interest, so there was no magic in market-based approaches.

A year later the scene had changed again. Early in 1989 the U.S. Treasury Secretary Nicholas Brady declared himself in favor of an effort to reduce developing country debt and indicated that at least some resources from the World Bank and other sources would be made available to help finance such reductions. The actual content of the "Brady Plan" was, however, unclear. Initially, at least, U.S. officials seemed to believe that clever financial packages would allow them to leverage small outside contributions into large debt reductions, without any kind of coercion of private creditors. Chapter 9, which was presented that summer at the Latin American Econometric Society, was intended as a sort of primer. Using the same framework as chapter 8, and avoiding algebra as much as possible, it tried to lay out the case for concerted rather than market-based debt reduction. (The only really major Brady deal so far has been for Mexico. Although banks were given a menu of options, they were not given the option of not participating, so the principle of voluntarism was in effect abandoned.)

## The International Monetary System

The Bretton Woods system, a system of fixed exchange rates in which the United States effectively dictated world monetary policy, ended in the early 1970s. Yet the new system (or nonsystem) that followed has never really settled down.

Despite the collapse of the dollar-centered exchange rate system, the U.S. dollar has continued to play a special international role. During the early years of floating exchange rates, however, there was considerable speculation about whether the dollar's key currency status would survive, and whether a collapse of that role would pose dangers to the system. Chapter 10, written in 1980, argued that the self-perpetuating aspects of the key currency role could allow the dollar to retain its special role for the foreseeable future. A main purpose of the paper was to point out the importance of increasing returns, circular causation, and multiple equilibria in the international monetary system. These were unpopular themes at the time but have more recently become the cutting edge of theory in a number of fields.

Finally, at the end of the 1980s, when we thought that we had seen everything, Europe surprised us all with a sudden drive toward monetary union. Chapter 11 is an interpretive survey of the cases for and against monetary areas. Like the first two chapters of this volume, it is in large part a defense of a conventional wisdom that has come under so much attack that it now seems almost radical. The traditional analysis of currency areas stressed the painful trade-off between microeconomic efficiency and macroeconomic adjustment, a trade-off that could not be avoided but that could be best met by a world carved up into optimal currency areas. In the new enthusiasm for fixed rates and monetary union, however, many economists have come to deny the existence of that trade-off. They deny that exchange rate flexibility conveys any macroeconomic advantages (echoing some of the issues discussed in chapter 1) and invoke new issues, like the need to achieve inflation-fighting credibility. The chapter argues that the old trade-off view remains valid. It also offers the unpopular suggestion that there is little real evidence to back the current enthusiasm for European monetary union and that the case for EMU is essentially political rather than economic.

## What Comes Next?

International money is the oldest field in economics: David Hume's "Of the Balance of Trade," published in 1753, was the first real example of an economic model as we now understand it. It is also one of the most innovative and rapidly changing fields because the best analysis in this area is driven not by deference to established theory but by the need to make sense of an ever-changing world.

It is always risky to predict where interesting areas of research will lie in the future, especially given the incredible succession of surprises over the past 20 years. My guess, however, is that the focus of international monetary economics over the next few years will shift from macroeconomics to microeconomics. As always, interesting work will be driven to an important extent by real world events, in this case the growth of regional trading blocs. The EC has been reinforced by enlargement and 1992, the U.S.-Canada free trade area will probably be enlarged by the addition of Mexico, and (some would argue) a characteristically unlegislated but still de facto East Asian trading area centered on Japan is starting to emerge. The obvious next question is how these new trading arrangements will affect monetary arrangements. The Europeans think they know the answer: A recent EC document is called *One Market, One Money*. But does this mean that Canadian and Mexican currency must turn green if they are to realize the full benefits of free trade?

To answer this question, it will be necessary to examine the microeconomics of international money, a subject that has been largely avoided by formal theory until recently. Events now make the subject important, while new techniques may make it more tractable than before. So this may be another case of that happy marriage of new technique and real-world relevance that has led to the best international monetary economics in the past.

I do not expect to see a grand unified theory of international money emerge in my lifetime. What I do expect is that events will continue to provoke research, that this research will continue to yield important insights, and that in its messy but exciting way the field will continue to progress.

# I

**Exchange Rates and the Balance of Payments**

# 1    Adjustment in the World Economy

There is widespread, though not universal, agreement that the large imbalances in industrial-country accounts that emerged in the 1980s should be narrowed. Among those who want a reduction of current account imbalances, however, there is considerable disagreement over what medicine will cure the ailment. Now that the dollar has declined to roughly its 1980 effective exchange rate, should we focus on correcting fiscal divergences, while stabilizing currency values? Should the dollar be driven still lower, since its decline so far has had disappointing results in turning trade around, or should nations focus fiscal and monetary policy on domestic targets, adopting at least for the time being a position of benign neglect toward exchange rates?

Like most policy debates, the debate over exchange rate policy stems in part from conflicts of interest and in part from legitimate disagreements over empirical parameters. However, it also appears to stem to an important degree from confusion, pure and simple, about how the *mechanism* of international adjustment works. This chapter cuts through as much of this confusion as possible, clearing the way for debate over the truly disputable issues.

The current discussion of the international adjustment mechanism is an unusually murky one because it is not a debate between two coherent positions. Instead, what we have is a coherent, though not necessarily correct, standard view that is under attack from a number of directions. This standard view holds in brief (1) that current account imbalances are the result of divergent fiscal policies, (2) that this fiscal divergence led to current account divergences via a rise in the relative price of U.S. goods and factors

Originally published as NBER Working Paper No. 2424. Reprinted with permission from *Group of Thirty Occasional Papers* 24 (1987), pp. 1–40. Copyright © 1987 by the Group of Thirty. All rights reserved.

of production (i.e., a real appreciation), and (3) that narrowing the imbalances requires both reversal of the fiscal divergence and a *nominal* depreciation of the dollar against other industrial-country currencies. Challenges to this view deny that fiscal policy drives the current account, that real exchange rates have anything to do with current accounts, or that nominal exchange rate movements have anything to do with real exchange rates. These challenges to the standard view do not add up to a coherent alternative; indeed, some of them are mutually contradictory. That is why attempts to squeeze the debate into a Keynesian-monetarist or supply-side/demand-side mold only add to the confusion.

The chapter is in five sections. Section 1.1 elaborates on the standard view of the sources of, and cure for, current account imbalances, and suggests that challenges to this view can be viewed as originating in negative answers to any one of three key questions that the standard view answers in the affirmative. Section 1.2 examines the rationale and empirical evidence bearing on the question, Does fiscal policy drive the current account? Section 1.3 similarly evaluates the proposition that real exchange rate changes are a necessary part of balance-of-payments adjustment, and the counterargument that in the modern integrated world economy this linkage is gone. Section 1.4 asks whether the orthodox view that real exchange rate changes are most easily achieved through nominal exchange rate adjustment is valid. Section 1.5 draws the arguments together for an assessment of what we know about the international adjustment mechanism, and what our knowledge says about policy.

To preview the conclusions: The weakest link in the standard view is actually the part that has achieved the most public acceptance, the link from budget imbalances to trade imbalances. While a plausible case for this link can be made, there is enough contrary evidence to give us pause. But the other challenges to the standard view are as close to being just plain wrong as any positions in economic debate can be. The view that real exchange rates have nothing to do with trade balances is, in the form in which it is often stated, a confusion between accounting identities and behavior. There are certain cases where, in principle, balance-of-payments adjustment need not be accompanied by relative price changes, but these cases can be empirically rejected. Similarly the view that relative price changes would not be facilitated by nominal exchange rate adjustment is often stated in a way that misstates the issue, and a logically coherent statement of the view can be rejected on the basis of the evidence.

## 1.1   The Standard View of the Adjustment Mechanism

The standard view of the source of the current account imbalances of the 1980s takes as its starting point the famous identity

$$S - I = Y - E = X - M,$$

where $S$ and $I$ are national savings and investment, $Y$ and $E$ national income and expenditure, and $X$ and $M$ national exports and imports of goods and services. An external deficit *must* have as its counterpart an excess of domestic investment over domestic savings, which makes it natural to look for the sources of a deficit in an autonomous change in the national savings rate. The identity may be further rewritten as

$$S_P + S_G - I = X - M,$$

where $S_P$ and $S_G$ are private and government savings, respectively. This immediately suggests how the budget deficit gets into the story. A rise in the budget deficit—that is, a fall in government saving—must, unless offset by a rise in private saving, be reflected either in a decline in investment or in a rise in the external deficit. It seems plausible to expect the external deficit to bear part of the burden, so a budget deficit can lead to a trade deficit.

Although an economy must respect accounting identities, looking at these identities can never be the full analysis. We must ask how the accounting identity is translated into incentives that affect individual behavior. The standard view of how a budget deficit translates into a trade deficit emphasizes the channel that runs through interest rates and the exchange rate. This view was most influentially expounded by Martin Feldstein during his tenure as chairman of the U.S. Council of Economic Advisers.[1] Subsequent expositions, such as that of Branson (1985), have refined the analysis but not changed the essential character of the story.

In the standard view a budget deficit is not offset by an increase in private savings. Instead, it leads to a reduction in aggregate national savings relative to investment demand. This fall in savings leads to a rise in the real interest rate. The rise in the real interest rate in turn, by making claims on the deficit country attractive to foreign investors, leads to a rise in the real exchange rate. With home production more expensive relative to foreign, imports rise and exports fall, leading to an external deficit. The counterpart of this external deficit is a capital inflow that fills the gap between domestic investment and savings.

**Table 1.1**
United States: Savings, investment, and the external balance

|  | 1979 | 1985 |
|---|---|---|
| **Percent of GNP** | | |
| Gross investment | 18.2 | 16.5 |
| Gross private savings | 17.8 | 17.2 |
| Government savings | 0.5 | −3.4 |
| Net foreign investment | 0.1 | −2.9 |
| **Real exchange rate**[a] | 98.9 | 142.8 |
| **Real interest rate**[b] | −1.3 | 7.0 |

Sources: *Economic Report of the President*, 1987, and IMF, *International Financial Satistics*.
a. IMF index of normalized relative unit labor costs.
b. Government bond yield less previous year's CPI increase.

This standard analysis has achieved remarkably broad acceptance. It was also remarkably successful at accounting for U.S. external economic developments up until about two years ago. By abstracting from the intervening business cycles, we have in table 1.1 a summary of how the savings-investment identity held in 1979 and 1985. The sharp decline in government saving was essentially matched one for one by a decline in national savings. The decline in national savings was primarily reflected in a rise in the external deficit rather than in domestic crowding out. The external deficit was accompanied by, and therefore presumably largely caused by, a huge real appreciation of the dollar, and a sharp rise in U.S. real interest rates was in turn associated with this rise.

The match between theory and experience seemed almost too good to be true, and since 1985 several puzzling developments have spoiled the perfection of the picture. As table 1.2 shows, since early 1985 the U.S. exchange rate has fallen sharply, to roughly its pre-Reagan level, and the real interest rate has also fallen considerably. These changes have taken place with little change either in the presumed source of the original disequilibrium, the U.S. budget deficit, or in the external deficit itself. As the predictive power of the standard view has seemed to erode, advocates of alternative views have become increasingly vocal. However, the challenges come from several different and often contradictory directions, so the net effect of the discussion has been confusing to lay audiences and even to many professionals. To clarify this discussion, we need to systematize challenges to the standard view around several key questions.

The standard view explains the U.S. external deficit as the result of a budget deficit that operated through a real appreciation effected by a

**Table 1.2**
United States: Experience since the dollar's peak

|  | Exchange rate[a] | Real interest rate[b] | Government savings | Net foreign investment |
|---|---|---|---|---|
| 1985:1 | 160 | 7.0 | −96.6 | −83.8 |
| 1985:2 | 156 | 6.3 | −155.6 | −112.0 |
| 1985:3 | 148 | 5.9 | −138.0 | −121.2 |
| 1985:4 | 137 | 5.8 | −155.1 | −143.8 |
| 1986:1 | 129 | 6.0 | −125.1 | −128.6 |
| 1986:2 | 124 | 5.9 | −173.3 | −143.0 |
| 1986:3 | 119 | 5.5 | −133.3 | −148.3 |
| 1986:4 | 118 | 5.0 | −129.4 | −147.7 |
| 1987:1 | 111 | 4.2 | −122.9 | −145.7 |

Source: *Survey of Current Business*, and IMF, *International Financial Statistics*.
a. IMF MERM index, 1980 = 100.
b. Government bond yield less previous year's CPI increase.

nominal exchange rate change. Challenges to this view question one or more of the links in this process. Thus the debate over the international adjustment process is really three debates over three separate questions.

1. *Does fiscal policy drive the current account?* While the budget identity linking savings, investment, and the external balance cannot be denied, a decline in government savings need not always be reflected in a corresponding change in the current account. One influential school of thought holds that changes in government savings will be offset by equal and opposite changes in private savings. In this view, national savings fell for reasons independent of the budget deficit. An alternative view—backed by considerable, albeit controversial, evidence—holds that the normal effect of a change in national savings is primarily a change in national investment, not a change in the external deficit, so the apparent one-for-one effect in the first half of the 1980s was an aberration that needs a special explanation. Finally, some commentators have blamed both the decline in U.S. national savings and the external deficit on tight monetary, rather than loose fiscal, policy.

2. *Does the real exchange rate have anything to do with the trade balance?* There is a widespread, though not formalized, view among policymakers that fiscal policy affects the trade deficit directly, rather than through the channel of real exchange rate changes. Indeed, this view often stands Feldstein on his head. Where the standard view holds that the U.S. budget deficit caused

the strong dollar and hence the trade deficit, one often now hears the view that correction of the U.S. budget deficit is an *alternative* to further dollar decline. This practical men's view overlaps at its edges with two quite distinct alternative views, one that sees faster growth in export markets as the only cure for the trade deficit and another that denies any need for relative price adjustment as a counterpart to trade adjustment.

3. *Does nominal exchange rate adjustment help smooth the path of real adjustment?* In a world of perfectly flexible prices, nominal exchange rate changes could neither produce nor facilitate changes in relative goods prices, and thus could have no role in the international adjustment mechanism. The apparent lack of real effects from the dollar's depreciation so far has led monetarist advocates of fixed exchange rates to reemphasize the neutrality of money, and thus the uselessness of exchange rate changes.

It should be dear from this brief presentation that the various critiques of the standard view do not add up to a common alternative vision. Clearly the right way to proceed is to address each of the individual questions separately, and then try to draw together what we have learned.

## 1.2    Does Fiscal Policy Drive the Current Account?

Challenges to the presumed role of the U.S. internal deficit in causing its external deficit are not central to the current debate, where the challenges to the standard view mostly go the other way—namely, independent of the exchange rate, the budget deficit is given a direct role in causing the trade deficit. However, criticism of the emphasis on the budget deficit has been a steady rumble since 1982 and adds to the atmosphere of uncertainty about how the international adjustment mechanism works. Thus it is important to be clear about the valid grounds for questioning the conventional view, as expressed by Branson's (1985) often cited remark that "the budget deficit did it!"

One challenge here comes from the supply-side/new classical camp, the other from a more traditional viewpoint that questions the closeness of world capital market integration. We consider each in turn.

### Do Budget Deficits Affect National Savings?

An extensive debate within the economics profession has swirled around the issue of whether government deficits reduce the national savings rate.

This debate is far too elaborate to summarize here; however, the key issues are fairly simple. Against the prima facie case that government dissaving reduces national savings an influential "Ricardian" view argues that government deficits will be offset by increases in private savings. Suppose that the government cuts taxes without any prospect of future reductions in spending. Then households should know that in the future the government will have to raise taxes again, both to restore the original cuts and to service the increase in its debt. In present value the total expected tax liabilities of the private sector will not have changed. Thus the private sector will not increase its consumption. and all of the tax cut will be saved.

The theoretical rejoinder to this argument has several strands. First, some of the tax liability resulting from a temporary tax cut will fall on unborn generations; those currently consuming will therefore experience some reduction in their lifetime tax burden. Second, some households may be liquidity constrained. Unable to borrow at the same rate at which they can lend, they prefer a marginal dollar of consumption to a marginal dollar of savings but are not willing to borrow to spend more than their income. For these households an increase in current income will be spent even if the present value of their lifetime income has not changed. Third, the assertion that tax cuts will be fully saved requires a high degree of sophistication on the part of all households; they must understand the future tax implications of the current budget. If a sizable fraction of households behaves in a less sophisticated way using some rule of thumb rather than a careful calculation of future government fiscal prospects, much of a tax cut will similarly be spent rather than saved.

The facts of the 1980s certainly do not provide any support to the Ricardian view. As table 1.1 showed, the U.S. fiscal deficit was reflected fully in a decline in national savings, with no offset from the private sector. This could of course be a coincidence. National savings might have fallen for other reasons, such as expectations about future cuts in government spending on goods and services or a future surge in productivity and output. I find such explanations wildly unconvincing, and the continuing popularity of the Ricardian view a triumph of theoretical nicety (of a kind that happens to serve a political purpose as well) over both macroeconomic evidence and any plausible description of individual behavior. However, the Ricardian challenge need not occupy much space in this chapter, because it is not, as we have noted, central to the international debate.

National Savings and the Current Account

Whether or not the budget deficit is responsible for the fall in the U.S. national savings rate, there is a legitimate question over whether the equal and opposite movement of U.S. savings and the current account was a normal occurrence, and whether a reversal of the budget deficit should be expected to lead to an unwinding of the trade deficit. Changes in budget deficits can in principle be reflected in changes in domestic investment rather than in changes in the external account. Was it just chance that the U.S. budget deficit spilled over entirely into the trade deficit? There are several pieces of evidence that might lead one to suspect this.

First, even with perfect capital mobility one should not expect the U.S. budget deficit to crowd out only the trade balance, with no effect on domestic investment. The United States forms roughly a third of the world market economy. Even in a world in which crowding out is completely global, we would expect U.S. investment to absorb about one-third of the fall in national savings, with the external balance absorbing the other two-thirds. In fact much of the world is not open to free capital mobility, so the external side should absorb less of the deficit. Furthermore, if the appreciation of the dollar is perceived as temporary, it must be sustained by a rise in U.S. real interest rates relative to those abroad. This further concentrates the crowding out on U.S. rather than foreign investment (a point made by Frankel 1986). A back-of-the-envelope calculation suggests that something less than half of a change in the U.S. budget deficit should be reflected in the trade balance and that correspondingly something more than half should be reflected in domestic crowding out (Krugman 1985a).

To explain why virtually all of the deficit was reflected in the external balance, it is necessary to invoke special factors. The effect of U.S. fiscal expansion on the current account was reinforced by nearly equal fiscal contraction in the rest of the OECD (see Blanchard and Summers 1984). There may have been an increase in investment demand in the United States as a result of tax cuts and increased optimism. Finally, "safe haven" motivations may have helped push the dollar up. While these additional factors are plausible and do not contradict the basic conventional view about the way the world works, they do indicate that the perfect correlation between budget and external deficits was indeed too good to be true, and in part a coincidence.

A deeper criticism of the fiscal-external link is that the apparent link for the United States in the 1980s is pretty much unique for industrial countries. Historically the link between national savings rates and the current account has been at best weak, and the link between national budget positions and the current account virtually nonexistent.

Feldstein and Horioka (1980) showed that there was little correlation between the national savings rates of OECD countries and their current accounts, or equivalently that differences in savings rates seem to have been reflected primarily in differences in investment. While these results have been extensively criticized and elaborated (see Frankel 1986), the basic point still stands: The cross-sectional evidence suggests that capital mobility among industrial countries is fairly limited. As for the link between budgets and trade, the cross-sectional evidence is not present at all: Japan during the first half of the 1980s combined the largest current account surplus of the G7 countries with the largest inflation-and-unemployment corrected budget deficits (see Gordon 1986).

Again, this cross-sectional evidence can be rationalized. High savings rates and high investment rates might arise from the same causes. Further, since saving is measured by investment plus external balance, a bias in the measurement of investment would weaken the apparent correlation between savings and the external balance. However, it must be recognized that the assumption that capital markets are virtually perfectly integrated, which has become conventional wisdom in much discussion of international issues, is a view maintained in the face of substantial contrary evidence rather than an established fact.

Did Monetary Policy Do It?

Some supply-side defenders of the U.S. tax cuts of 1981, such as Roberts (1987), argue that the U.S. current account deficit is the result not of the fiscal deficit but of excessively tight monetary policy. This argument can actually be rationalized within a perfectly standard demand-side macroeconomic view.[2] In the standard Mundell-Fleming model with high capital mobility and sticky prices, a monetary contraction will lead to a real appreciation and a trade deficit. The savings-investment identity will hold because the fall in net exports produces a contraction of national income, leading to a fall in both government revenues and private income. Hence both private and government savings fall.

Many economists would agree that this is a good story for the early stages of the rising dollar and the emerging external imbalances in 1981 and 1982. However, it is a difficult story to maintain for the persisting imbalances of 1984 and after. The reason is that an unavoidable side implication of the story is that the country experiencing a monetary contraction must also be experiencing a decline in output—if not in absolute terms, at least relative to the rest of the world. This flies in the face of the fact that the widening of external imbalances continued during the U.S. recovery of 1982–85, which wag dramatically more rapid than that of other industrial countries and has brought the United States close to most estimates of the minimal unemployment rate consistent with stable inflation.

In the standard view of the sources of the U.S. external deficit it sometimes seems as if economists have forgotten about money and monetary policy. It would be more accurate, however, to say that what proponents of the standard view assume is that monetary policy in each economy is targeted on keeping the economy near what the monetary authority believes is its full-employment level, so the analysis of fiscal policy can proceed as if the economy were in fact continually at full employment. This seems to be a reasonable description of the situation in the mid-1980s, though not of the early years of the decade. Monetary policy of course *could* have been different, but to say that "monetary policy failed fully to accommodate fiscal expansion, and therefore the dollar rose," is very far from assigning monetary policy per se an independent role in causing the external imbalances.[3]

Significance of the Critique

The view that monetary policy was responsible for the U.S. external deficit in the mid-1980s can be rejected as inconsistent with the basic facts. However, this does not demonstrate that fiscal policy did it. There is an important debate over the relationship between the budget deficit and saving, and an equally important debate over whether savings rates normally spill over into trade balances. Thus it is important to acknowledge the uncertainties over these links, which have become closely identified with the standard view about the sources of, and cure for, current account imbalances. However, it is important to notice that *critiques of the fiscal-external linkage have no bearing on the puzzling trade developments since 1985*. The point is that the U.S. fiscal deficit has not changed much since 1985, nor has the U.S. national savings rate. The puzzle is how it was possible, given the lack of change in these factors, for the dollar to move so much—and how it was possible for the dollar to decline so much without much effect on external imbalances.

## 1.3   Do Real Exchange Rates Have to Change?

We next turn to the key issue of the current debate over the process of international adjustment: the role of real exchange rates in the adjustment process. In the standard view fiscal imbalances work *through* the real exchange rate: A budget deficit leads to a real appreciation, which reduces the competitiveness of a country's industry and thus leads to a trade deficit. American critics of the conventional wisdom, however, have argued that no real exchange rate change is necessary and that a shift in savings rates can change the trade balance at constant relative prices. European and Japanese commentators often go further, seeming to argue that deficit correction is an *alternative* to real depreciation and that the deficit needs to fall in order to keep the dollar from declining further. Thus in a recent article Wakasugi (1987) writes:

The fundamental causes of the dollar's depreciation are the U.S. budget deficit and an unfavorable balance of payments which shows no sign of improving. Only the U.S. itself can recover the dollar's status as an international key currency. Therefore, in the long run, decreasing the budget deficit and enhancing productivity are vital steps.

The fact that the United States advocates of the view that real depreciation is unnecessary are more or less monetarist in their views on macroeconomic policy, and that their scepticism of the need for *real* depreciation is tied to a denial of real effects of *nominal* depreciation, makes it seem to casual observers that this dispute is yet another monetarist-Keynesian argument that hinges on the issue of price flexibility. However, this is a misperception. This is a replay of an old debate, but it is Keynes versus Ohlin, not Tobin versus Friedman. It is the old question of the relative price effects of an international transfer of resources.

To see the nature of the issue, it is useful to consider a rudimentary model that reveals the conditions under which a real depreciation is or is not necessary as part of current account adjustment. (A more formal treatment of this model is given in appendix A at the end of this chapter.) We can then examine the empirical evidence that bears on the question.

Redistributing Expenditure and the Real Exchange Rate

Suppose that the world consists of only two countries, *US* and *ROW*. *US* is assumed initially to be running an undesirable current account deficit. We initially suppose that each of the countries produces only a single good, so that the real exchange rate may be defined as the price of the *US* good relative to the *ROW* good. Finally, suppose for the sake of argument that both countries are initially at full employment so that a balance-of-payments adjustment cannot involve an expansion in either country's output.

Now let us try to reduce *US*'s current account deficit. Can we do this at a constant real exchange rate? It is useful here to write the balance-of-payments identity in its alternate form

$$X - M = Y - E;$$

that is, the external balance is the difference between income and expenditure. Since the real exchange rate is being held constant, we can measure the terms in this equation in terms of either good. More conveniently still, it does no harm to suppose that nominal prices are held constant, so we can simply measure income and expenditure in nominal terms.

The first point to notice is that there is no channel that links the budget deficit to the trade deficit other than through its effect on expenditure. A shift in fiscal policy reduces *US*'s expenditure and raises *ROW*'s expenditure, and that is all. There is no direct way in which it makes the *US* good more competitive. The issue then is whether it is possible to reduce *US*'s expenditure and raise *ROW*'s expenditure, while keeping the relative price of the *US* and the *ROW*'s goods constant.

Suppose that through fiscal contraction *US* reduces its expenditure by $100 billion, while *ROW* increases its expenditure by the same amount. The fall in *US*'s expenditure will directly reduce spending on the *US* good by $100(1 - m)$ billion dollars, where $m$ is the fraction of a marginal dollar of *US*'s spending that is spent on imports. On the other hand, the rise in *ROW*'s spending will raise spending on the *US* good by $100m^*$ billion dollars, where $m^*$ is the fraction of a marginal dollar spending that falls on imports. The net change on spending on the *US* good is therefore $100(m + m^* - 1)$ billion dollars. If $m + m^* < 1$—which we will see below is certainly the case in practice—then the redistribution of world expenditure will reduce the demand for the *US* good and increase the demand for the *ROW* good. To correct the excess supply of the *US* good and the excess demand for the *ROW* good, the relative price of the *US* good must fall: The correction of the current account deficit must be effected via a real depreciation.

The key criterion here is a familiar one: It is the criterion for a terms-of-trade effect of a transfer. A redistribution of world expenditure must be accompanied by a change in relative prices unless the marginal spending pattern of the countries increasing their expenditure is the same as that of the country reducing its spending. If the United States has a higher marginal propensity to spending on its own goods than other countries do, which is the case where $m + m^* < 1$, then a fall in the U.S. share of world spending must be accompanied by a fall in the U.S. real exchange rate.

It is important to avoid two confusions that can obscure this point. First is the idea that the issue is somehow tied to the degree of capital mobility. McKinnon (1984) has argued strongly that the real exchange rate needs to change to adjust the trade balance only when an economy is "insular," that is, closed to capital movement. He argues that when capital is mobile, savings-investment gaps are directly reflected in trade balances, with no need for relative price changes. "With smoothly functioning capital markets, little or no change in the 'real' exchange rate is necessary to transfer saving from one country to another" (1984, 14).

What is wrong with this argument should be immediately clear. It confuses the question of whether a change in the savings rate will be reflected in a change in the distribution of world expenditure with the question of whether a change in that distribution necessitates a change in relative prices. The latter question is a question about goods markets, not capital markets. No matter how mobile capital may be, if Japanese residents spend much less on U.S. goods at the margin than do U.S. residents, a redistribution of world spending from the United States to Japan will reduce the demand for U.S. goods at constant relative prices.

The other confusion that can obscure the issue is to mix up the necessity for a change in relative prices with the question of whether changes in nominal exchange rates help produce such changes. If prices are flexible, a currency depreciation by itself has no relative price effects, and a real depreciation can be achieved with a constant nominal exchange rate via deflation in one country and/or inflation in the others. However, this has nothing to do with the question of whether the real exchange rate needs to change.

Empirical Evidence

We have now seen that external adjustment requires real exchange depreciation to the extent that the marginal propensity to spend on a country's goods is higher for domestic than foreign residents. Casual observation certainly suggests that this must be the case: *Average* consumption has a very strong domestic bias in every country, so that marginal spending would have to be radically different in order to make $m + m^* = 1$.

**Table 1.3**
Estimates of $m$ and $m^*$ implied by some recent studies

| Study | Implied $m$ | Implied $m^*$ | Sum |
|---|---|---|---|
| Krugman-Baldwin | 0.33 | 0.12 | 0.45 |
| DRI | 0.14 | 0.05 | 0.19 |
| NIESR | 0.19 | 0.05 | 0.23 |
| OECD | 0.23 | 0.05 | 0.28 |
| EPA | 0.24 | 0.11 | 0.35 |
| MCM | 0.28 | 0.11 | 0.39 |
| Taylor | 0.33 | 0.11 | 0.44 |
| Marris | 0.24 | 0.11 | 0.35 |

Sources: See appendix B.

This conclusion may be confirmed by looking at econometric evidence. Econometric estimates of trade flow equations are not usually presented in this form, but it is possible to recast them in such a way as to yield estimates of $m$ and $m^*$. (Appendix B explains how this is done.) Table 1.3 presents a number of recent estimates of the demand effects of redistributing world expenditure from the United States to the rest of the world. While there is considerable divergence among estimates, all estimates show $m + m^*$ much less than one. That is, a fall in U.S. expenditure matched by a rise in rest of world expenditure would represent a net decline in the demand for U.S. goods; a rise in Japanese expenditure matched by a fall in the rest of the world's spending would represent a rise in the demand for Japan's goods.

Consider, for example, the estimate from Krugman and Baldwin (1987), which actually gives the highest estimate of $m + m^*$ reported. According to this estimate, a fall in U.S. expenditure of $100 billion would reduce spending on U.S. goods by $67 billion, while a corresponding rise in rest-of-the-world expenditure would provide an offsetting increase in export demand of only $12 billion. The remaining $55 billion would show up as an excess supply of U.S. goods, which would have to be eliminated by a fall in their relative price.

Why should this be the case? The answer presumably lies in the still highly imperfect integration of markets for goods and services. Much of the expenditure of even very open economies falls on goods and services that are nontradable due to perishability or prohibitive transport costs. Trade restrictions turn potentially tradable goods into de facto nontraded ones. And there are also probably significant Linder effects, in which countries tend even within the set of traded goods to produce goods most suitable for domestic tastes. Thus, while it is possible in principle that a redistribution of world expenditure could eliminate a trade deficit without any need for a change in the real exchange rate, the reality of world markets for goods and services that are far from perfectly integrated makes this observation purely academic.

## Some Caveats

The argument just presented shows that the view that integrated capital markets somehow eliminate the need for real exchange rate adjustment to accompany a reduction of current account imbalances is misconceived. There is a valid argument that given sufficiently integrated *goods* markets, no real exchange rate changes would be needed, but this argument can be decisively rejected on the basis of both casual observation and econometric evidence. Before closing this discussion, however, it is necessary to tie up some loose ends.

The first caveat is that even with $m + m^* \ll 1$, little real exchange rate change would be necessary if goods produced in different countries were very close substitutes. However, like the alternate argument for a lack of necessity for real exchange rate change, this can be rejected both on the basis of casual observation and on econometric evidence. The casual observation is that the huge swings in real exchange rates since 1980 would have been impossible if goods from different countries were close substitutes. The econometric evidence is that estimated price elasticities in trade are fairly low, typically between 1 and 2 (see Goldstein and Khan 1985; Brookings 1987). The fall in the relative price of imports to the United States from 1980 to 1985 provides a natural experiment: Although import volume soared, the share of imports in GNP actually fell slightly, from 11.7 to 11.2 percent. While lags and special factors complicate the picture, this clearly indicates a demand elasticity that cannot be much more than one.

The second caveat is that countries do not in fact produce only a single good, and relative price changes may take place among goods that a country produces. In particular, a reduction in the U.S. current account deficit will to some extent require a fall in the price of tradables relative to nontradables as well as a fall in the price of U.S. exports relative to U.S. imports. Empirical evidence for the United States suggests that in the long run the United States is more like the one-good economy of our simple model than the "small open economy" whose terms of trade may be taken as given. However, even if the tradable/nontradable price alters significantly in the adjustment process, there is no question that a country that reduces its external deficit must reduce its wages relative to those of trading partners. Since many competitiveness indicators focus on unit labor costs rather than export prices, and since the appropriate role of nominal exchange rates may hinge more on wages than on prices (see below), this wage adjustment is important whether or not it is reflected in a change in the terms of trade.

The Role of Growth in Surplus Countries

A more important objection to the view that real depreciation by deficit countries is necessary to reduce imbalances is that the necessity of real depreciation may be avoided if the surplus countries start from a position of excess capacity. In that case it is possible for expenditure to rise more in the surplus countries than it falls in the deficit countries, which could permit a reduction in external deficits without any real depreciation.

A continuation of our numerical illustration may make the point. I previously noted that according to the Krugman-Baldwin estimate a fall in U.S. expenditure by $100 billion would reduce spending on U.S. goods by $67 billion. Now suppose that instead of rising by only $100 billion, expenditure in the rest of the world were to rise by enough so that this reduction in U.S. demand for its own products were offset by export demand. Given an $m^*$ of 0.12, this would require that rest-of-world spending rise by $558 billion. Of this spending, $67 billion would full on U.S. goods, exactly offsetting the decline in domestic U.S. demand. The other $491 billion would fall on rest-of-world goods, far exceeding the $33 billion fall in U.S. import demand.[4]

This increase in foreign expenditure is possible only if there is enough excess capacity in the rest of the world to accommodate the required increase in production. Specifically, to reduce the U.S. external deficit by $100 billion in this way would require that rest-of-world output rise by $458 billion (= 491 increase in domestic demand less the 33 fall in U.S. imports).

If surplus countries have excess capacity, then it becomes possible in principle to reduce the current account deficit without any real depreciation. However, the numerical example also makes it clear how limited the prospects for doing this are in practice. The income of market economies outside the United States is approximately $8 trillion. Thus an increase in output of $458 billion would represent a 5.7 percent increase in output. To eliminate the whole 1986 U.S. current account deficit of $140 billion at constant relative prices would require an even larger output increase, approximately 8 percent. Few, if any, countries believe that they have that much excess capacity,[5] and it is hard to believe that the world as a whole outside the United States would be willing to risk a demand-led expansion of output of more than, say, 2 percent. This means that a willingness of surplus countries to risk faster growth can play at best a distinctly secondary role in correcting external imbalances.

In contrast to the debate over whether fiscal policy drives external imbalances, the debate over the role of real exchange rate adjustment has a clear resolution. Those who deny the need for real exchange rate adjustment are wrong—many of them wrong at a basic logical level, the rest wrong in their arithmetic. The view that since capital is mobile, changes in saving and investment can somehow move the trade balance without moving the real exchange rate, is based on a fundamental conceptual confusion, and the case in which this view could nonetheless turn out to be correct can be decisively rejected empirically. If surplus countries have excess capacity, a willingness on their part to grow faster can substitute for real exchange rate adjustment, but in practice only limited help can be expected from this source.

There remains of course the puzzle of why the real exchange rate changes since 1985 have thus far produced such modest results. What this discussion shows is that the trade puzzle cannot be resolved by arguing that the savings-investment balance somehow directly determines the trade balance, without a role for the real exchange rate. There is a real puzzle, but its resolution must be sought in the behavior of markets for goods and services, not in the fact of capital market linkages.

Adjusting external deficits then requires real exchange rate adjustment. The remaining question is whether nominal exchange rate changes have a valuable role to play in this process.

## 1.4   The Role of Nominal Exchange Rate Adjustment

Although the key analytical debate about the international adjustment mechanism is probably about the role of the real exchange rate, the immediate policy concern is with nominal exchange rates—whether the dollar should be encouraged, or at least allowed, to decline further, while the yen rises higher. The idea of promoting exchange rate movements in pursuit of external balance has come in for extremely sharp criticism from advocates of a return to some form of fixed rates. For example, Mundell (1987, 3) writes:

The claim that [favorable consequences] will follow from depreciation is sheer quackery. It is closer to the truth to say that a policy of appreciating the yen and the European currencies relative to the dollar will cause deflation abroad, inflation at home, a larger dollar deficit, and vast equity sales to foreign investors. Ownership of factories, technology, and real assets will be exported to finance an even larger trade deficit without there being much, if any, real expansion in exports or reduction in the dollar value of imports. U.S. assets will be sold abroad at bargain-basement prices. If the American dog gets fed better, it will be by eating its own tail.

Is this negative assessment at all justified? To make sense of the dispute, we need to consider two issues. First, the question of whether nominal exchange rate movements are intended to produce real exchange rate changes that would not have happened otherwise, or to facilitate real exchange rate changes driven by other forces. Second, the question of whether it is indeed easier to adjust relative prices via exchange rate changes than via inflation and deflation.

The Facilitating Role of Exchange Rate Changes

Suppose that the world economy started from a position of equilibrium and that a sudden depreciation of the dollar was somehow engineered. Nearly all economists would agree that in the long run the effect of this depreciation would be some combination of inflation in the United States and deflation abroad, with the original real exchange rate being eventually restored and no long-run effect on external balances. To the extent that prices and wages adjust slowly, there would be a temporary period of higher U.S. output and a larger U.S. trade surplus, but few would view this transitory effect as worth seeking through an exogenous depreciation.

Suppose, however, that the world economy does *not* start from a position of equilibrium. In particular, suppose that an adjustment of U.S. and rest-of-world fiscal policies requires a real U.S. depreciation against the rest of the world. Then the situation is very different. If the dollar does *not* depreciate, there will have to be some mix of *deflation* in the United States and *inflation* abroad. To the extent that prices are slow to adjust, this need to change internal price levels will lead both to a delay in the adjustment of external imbalances and a period of unemployment in the United States. An exchange rate adjustment can facilitate the process of adjustment by eliminating this need for changes in internal price levels.

The critics of dollar depreciation, such as Mundell, have portrayed the situation as being our first case, where exchange rate changes are simply imposed on an equilibrium situation. This view in turn goes back to the argument that current account adjustment does not require any real exchange rate changes. However, we have seen that this argument is fallacious. There is no reasonable quarrel with the view that narrowing current account divergences requires a fall in the relative prices of goods produced in deficit countries. A depreciation of the dollar and appreciation of the currencies of surplus countries looks much more favorable when it is viewed, not as an attempt to conjure up a real exchange rate change out of thin air, but as an attempt to achieve more rapidly, and with less cost, a relative price change that would have happened anyway.

While there may be some in the United States who expected dollar depreciation to somehow solve the trade problem without any change in domestic expenditure, the standard view has always been clear on this point. The underlying problem is to narrow the gap between investment and savings. However, dollar depreciation is supposed to facilitate the adjustment of the real exchange rate to its new equilibrium level. To reject this role for the exchange rate out of hand, on the ground that exchange rate changes are neutral in the long run, may not be "sheer quackery," but it is a misrepresentation of a carefully thought-out position.

Now there are some reasonable practical doubts about the current situation: Has the exchange rate adjustment that has already taken place been enough? Should exchange rates be encouraged to fall ahead of fiscal policy instead of waiting for fiscal action? We turn briefly to these questions in the last part of the chapter. Meanwhile there is the general question of how important it is to adjust nominal exchange rates. If it is almost as easy to change real exchange rates with fixed as with flexible exchange rates, then one might argue against exchange rate adjustment on ground of monetary stability even if real exchange rates do need to change.

How Useful Is Exchange Rate Adjustment?

Even if prices were perfectly flexible, there would be a good case for preferring exchange rate changes to general deflation in deficit countries and/or inflation in surplus countries. The classic case in defence of using exchange rate adjustment was that of Milton Friedman (1953), who made the analogy with changing to daylight saving time; it is easier to change one price, the exchange rate, than to change the prices of everything an economy produces, just as it is easier for everyone's clocks to be set back an hour than for everyone to change his or her schedule.

However, it is hard to credit the case that prices of goods, and especially wage rates, are so flexible that the huge real exchange rate changes needed to eliminate current external imbalances could have been accomplished quickly through inflation and deflation. The problem is essentially one of coordination within an economy. Although the discussion of this problem is familiar in macroeconomics, it is perhaps less familiar in the international context, and so will bear one more discussion.

Suppose that, as typical estimates suggest, to balance the U.S. current account it was necessary that US wages fall 30 percent relative to foreign wages from their 1985 peak. For an individual worker a 30 percent wage cut is very drastic; one would imagine that bringing wages down by that much would require a protracted and bitter struggle between employers and employees. However, if all U.S. wages fall by 30 percent, the real wage rate will fall much less, say, only 3 percent, since the bulk of U.S. consumption is domestically produced. This means that if all wages could change simultaneously, and each worker could know that other workers would take the same wage cut, it might be possible to get such an adjustment fairly quickly and painlessly. However, this would happen only in a world of hyperrational agents, with no long-term contracts. In the real world nominal wages never fall that much except in the face of a collapsing economy.

What a currency depreciation does is to solve the coordination problem by lowering all domestic wages relative to foreign wages at the same time. Figure 1.1 shows the behavior of U.S. unit labor cost relative to its competitors and of the nominal dollar effective exchange rate, both as calculated by the IMF. The figure surely shows that there is a prima facie case that exchange rate changes do produce short-run changes in relative labor cost, and thus can facilitate such a change when one is necessary. The figure also shows the huge magnitude of the fall in U.S. relative wages that has already occurred since the dollar's peak. If one believes that a relative wage change of this magnitude was necessary, it is worth imagining what it would have required to achieve this with a fixed exchange rate.

As years of debate in closed-economy macroeconomics have shown, someone committed to the belief that prices are perfectly flexible cannot be convinced of the existence of some inertia on the basis of evidence, since evidence can always be rationalized away. However, for those less committed the prospect of attempting to achieve large real exchange rate movements without changing nominal exchange rates must surely look unappealing.

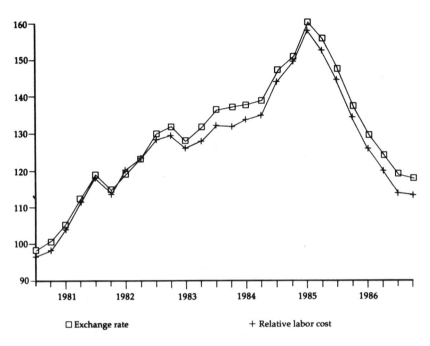

**Figure 1.1**
U.S. exchange rate and labor cost (1980 = 100)

## Exchange Rates and Capital Flows

A final point that needs to be discussed regarding nominal exchange rate changes is their effect on capital flows. The quotation from Mundell (1987) given earlier puts the case in purple prose, but there is fairly widespread concern among the financial community that a cheap dollar leads to a "sell-off" of U.S. assets at bargain prices.

The first point to notice about this argument is that it contradicts the basic premise of the critique of nominal depreciation, namely, that it only produces inflation with no real effects. It makes no sense to argue that dollar depreciation cannot do anything to reduce the relative price of U.S. goods and services but that it makes U.S. stocks, capital and real estate cheap on world markets—unless one has an implicit model in which goods prices and wages are perfectly flexible but asset prices are sticky!

Second, the argument that devaluation leads to excessive selling off of assets to foreigners must be made consistent with the accounting identity that capital inflows have as their counterpart current deficits. If depreciation leads to capital inflows, it must lead to a widened trade deficit—as Mundell recognizes. However, we have seen that there is no direct channel by which the savings-investment balance somehow gets translated into the trade balance without affecting the real exchange rate. A foreign transfer of savings to a deficit country must be associated with a rise in the relative price of that country's goods and services.[6] One doubts whether the claim is actually being made that nominal depreciation leads to real appreciation. In any case the facts clearly contradict this, since the depreciation of the dollar and the rise of the yen have, as figure 1.1 showed, been associated with approximately equal real exchange rate changes in the same direction.

## 1.5 Conclusions and Implications for Policy

This chapter has arrived at one definite conclusion, one strong presumption, and one probability. These are the following:

1. *Reducing external imbalances requires real depreciation by deficit countries, real appreciation by surplus countries.* The only exception is where there is large excess capacity in the surplus countries, and this caveat is of only modest importance in the current situation. The widespread belief that integrated world capital markets somehow bypass the need for real exchange rate adjustment is a misconception pure and simple.

2. *Nominal exchange rate changes can help facilitate necessary real exchange rate adjustment.* One hesitates to say that evidence demonstrates conclusively that prices are imperfectly flexible—there are too many economists committed to undermining such evidence. Nonetheless, it is true. As a practical precautionary stance, in any case, it seems hard to argue with the view that countries should rely on changing currency values rather than deflation and inflation to achieve the real exchange rate changes that are needed to correct external imbalances.

3. *Fiscal imbalances contributed to the widening of external imbalances in the 1980s, and fiscal policy can contribute to narrowing these imbalances.* As we have seen, there are some reasonable grounds for scepticism about the standard view that the U.S. deficit is the root of the whole international imbalance. However, focusing on the U.S. budget deficit remains the best game in town, and it is likely that fiscal correction would make a significant contribution to narrowing current account imbalances.

The purpose of this chapter is primarily to discuss how the international adjustment mechanism works rather than to prescribe policy. However, it is important to discuss at least briefly the policy implications of this discussion, since it might seem that the chapter gives a clear-cut case for further dollar depreciation and yen appreciation. While I do in fact believe that such exchange rate movements are likely and desirable, it is worth pointing out several important sources of uncertainty.

One source of uncertainty is that we do not know what the equilibrium pattern of world current account imbalances really is. In particular, there is a reasonable case for arguing that high-saving Japan has a structural current account surplus of 2 to 3 percent of GNP that will endure for many years, just as Britain's 5 percent surplus did for 40 years before World War I. Thus we cannot be sure that the real exchange rate adjustment that would undoubtedly be needed to eliminate Japan's surplus will take place any time in the foreseeable future.

A second source of uncertainty is the fact that real exchange rates have changed sharply already since the dollar's 1985 peak. Almost surely the current account imbalances of 1986 will narrow over time even at present real exchange rates, as lagged effects work their way through the pipeline. Almost all econometric analyses of the trade position suggest that the real dollar depreciation from 1985 to the summer of 1987 was still not enough to move the United States anywhere close to current account balance,[7] but one cannot definitely rule out the possibility that the econometrics are wrong and that a sharp narrowing of external imbalances is just around the corner.

Finally, to the extent that fiscal adjustment is the key to correcting the external imbalances, the apparent paralysis of action on fiscal policy in the United States and elsewhere poses a problem. There is a reasonable case that given the long lags in the effects of exchange rates on trade, exchange rate adjustment should precede fiscal change. If fiscal action is still six years away, however, one would not want to anticipate it with exchange rate adjustment now.

Does this mean that nothing can be said about policy? On the contrary, on the basis of what we do know about the international adjustment mechanism, one quite clear piece of advice can be given: *We should not lock ourselves into potentially unsustainable exchange rates.* It is highly likely that when fiscal policy finally is fixed, further real depreciation by the United States and further real appreciation by the surplus countries will be required. If would therefore be a mistake if exchange rates were to be fixed at current levels, on the basis of a misguided belief that fiscal policy somehow fixes trade imbalances without real exchange rate changes.

## Appendix A: The Trade Balance and the Real Exchange Rate

In the text the conditions under which a redistribution of world expenditure requires a change in the real exchange rate were explained verbally and through a numerical example. This appendix briefly presents an algebraic model, first presented in Krugman and Baldwin (1987), that makes the same point in a more rigorous way.

Consider a world economy consisting of two countries, US and ROW. Each country will be assumed to produce a single good that is both consumed domestically and exported. We let ROW's output be numéraire, and define $p$ as the relative price of the US good. Initially let us assume full employment so that US produces a fixed output $y$ and ROW produces a fixed output $y^*$. We also leave the determination of expenditure in the two countries in the background, simply treating US's expenditure in terms of its own good as a parameter $a$. For the world as a whole income must equal expenditure. Thus if $a^*$ is ROW's expenditure, measured in terms of the ROW good, it must be true that

$$pa + a^* = py + y^*$$

or (A1)

$$a^* = y^* + p(y - a).$$

Now it is certainly true as an accounting identity that the trade balance is equal to the excess of income over expenditure, so the US trade balance, in terms of the US good, is simply

$$t = y - a, \tag{A2}$$

an expression in which the relative price of US goods does not directly appear.

This does not, however, allow us to forget about relative prices. There is still a requirement that the market for US output clear (in which case the market for ROW output clears as well, by Walras's law). Each country will divide its expenditure among the two goods. For simplicity let us make the Cobb-Douglas assumption that expenditure shares are fixed, with the US spending a share $m$ of its income on imports and $1 - m$ on domestic output, ROW spending $m^*$ on imports and $1 - m^*$ on domestic goods. Then we can write the market-clearing condition as

$$py = (1 - m)pa + m^*a^*$$

or

$$p[y - (1 - m)a] = m^*a^*$$

$$= m^*[y^* + p(y - a)],  \tag{A3}$$

implying that

$$p = \frac{m^*y^*}{D},  \tag{A4}$$

where

$$D = (1 - m)y - (1 - m - m^*)a.$$

The implications of this small model are illustrated in figure 1.2, which is much more general than the example. On the horizontal axis is the US level of real expenditure $a$, and on the vertical axis is the relative price of US output $p$. The line $TT$ is an *iso-trade-balance* line; that is, it represents a locus of points consistent with some given trade balance in terms of US output. The accounting identity that equates the trade balance to income minus expenditure, regardless of relative prices, is reflected by the fact that $TT$ is vertical. Meanwhile, the line $UU$ represents points of market clearing for US output. It is here drawn with a positive slope, which will be the case if $(1 - m) > m^*$, that is, if US residents have a higher marginal propensity to spend on US output than ROW residents do. Point $E$ is the equilibrium for a given trade balance.

If the picture is as we have drawn it in figure 1.2, a reduction in the US trade deficit will necessarily be accompanied by a decline in the relative price of US output. A reduction of US real expenditure shifts $TT$ inward to $T'T'$. This requires that the equilibrium shift from $E$ to $E'$, which involves a fall in the relative price $p$.

Now there are two circumstances in which this relative price adjustment need not take place. First is the case where US and ROW goods are perfect substitutes; that is, we are effectively living in a one-good world. The other is the case where spending patterns are identical between the countries so that $(1 - m) = m^*$. In either case, the effect is to make $UU$ horizontal (figure 1.3) so that a reduction in US expenditure need not be accompanied by a decline in the relative price of what the US produces.

It is also possible for the trade deficit to fall without real depreciation if foreign output expands. From (A4) an increase in foreign output $y^*$ will shift $UU$ up. Thus, if there is excess capacity in ROW, it is possible

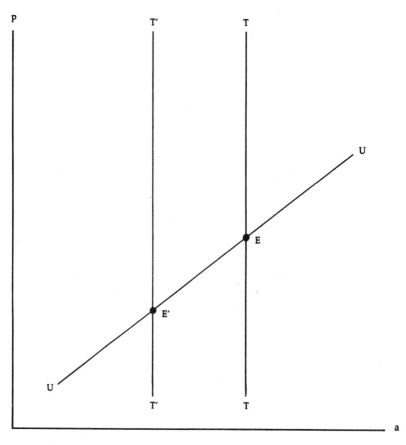

**Figure 1.2**
The trade balance and the real exchange rate: Case 1

to have a scenario in which *US* expenditure falls without any real depreciation (figure 1.4).

### Appendix B: Deriving Estimates of *m* and *m*\*

The text and appendix A showed that the need for real exchange rate
change as part of world payments adjustment depends crucially on the
fraction of a marginal dollar of expenditure that goes to imports in surplus
and deficit countries. Econometric trade flow equations, however, rarely
produce results in this form; instead, they yield elasticities of imports with
respect to expenditure or more usually income. To extract the key parameters *m* and *m*\*, we need to perform a transformation on these results.

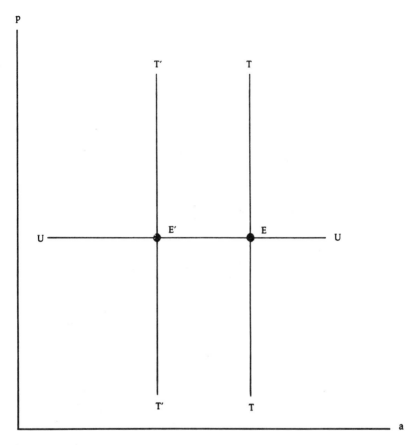

**Figure 1.3**
The trade balance and the real exchange rate: Case 2

First, consider the case of an estimate of the elasticity of imports with respect to expenditure. Let $M$ denote total imports, and $E$ and $Y$ expenditure and income. Then for changes in $E$, we have

$$dM = mdE$$

or, by multiplying and dividing, we obtain

$$m = \frac{(M/E)(dM/M)}{dE/E}.$$

But $(dM/M)/(dE/E)$ is the elasticity of imports with respect to expenditure. Thus $m$ may be derived by multiplying an estimate of this elasticity by the share of imports in expenditure.

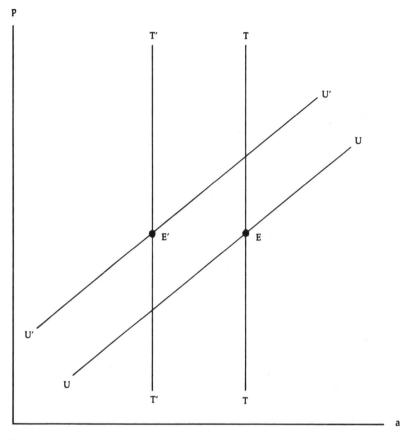

**Figure 1.4**
The trade balance and the real exchange rate: Case 3

If the estimated elasticity is instead with respect to income, this poses difficulties of interpretation, since in general there need not be a unique relationship between output and imports even at a constant relative price. In particular, an increase in output to meet increased export demand need not bring with it an increase in imports (except of intermediate goods, which pose a further complication). However, if output fluctuations and changes in domestic expenditure are closely correlated (as they have usually been), we can view output as a proxy for expenditure. Note that, other things equal, an increase in domestic expenditure will be reflected in an increase in income:

$$dY = (1 - m)\, dE.$$

**Table 1.4**
Derivation of $m$ and $m^*$

| | Elasticity of U.S. import demand | Implied $m$ | Elasticity of U.S. export demand | Implied $m^*$ |
|---|---|---|---|---|
| **Expenditure-based estimates** | | | | |
| Krugman-Baldwin | 2.9 | 0.33 | 2.4 | 0.12 |
| DRI | 1.2 | 0.14 | 1.0 | 0.05 |
| NIESR | 1.6 | 0.19 | 1.0 | 0.05 |
| OECD | 2.0 | 0.23 | 1.0 | 0.05 |
| **Output-based estimates** | | | | |
| EPA (Japan) | 1.8 | 0.24 | 1.2 | 0.11 |
| MCM (Federal Reserve Board) | 2.1 | 0.28 | 2.1 | 0.11 |
| Taylor | 2.5 | 0.33 | 1.3 | 0.11 |
| Marris | 1.8 | 0.24 | 1.5 | 0.11 |

Sources: Krugman and Baldwin (1987); Marris (1985); Brookings (1987); and author's calculations.

At the same time it is still true that $dM = mdE$. By substituting out $E$ and rearranging, we eventually arrive at the formula

$$m = \frac{e(M/Y)}{1 - (M/Y)},$$

where $e = (dM/M/(dY/Y)$, the elasticity of imports with respect to income.

Table 1.4 reports elasticities of U.S. exports and imports with respect to expenditure or income from eight recent studies. Six of these studies were presented at a Brookings Workshop on the U.S. current account deficit in January 1987 (Brookings 1987); the estimates from Krugman and Baldwin (1987) and Marris (1985) are included.

To convert elasticities into marginal propensities to import, values of $E$ and $Y$ for 1984 were taken for all market economies from the World Bank *World Development Report* of 1986. Values of $m$ and $m^*$ were the 1984 values of imports and exports of goods and services from the 1987 *Economic Report of the President*. These were then used, together with estimated elasticities, to construct the table. For example, Krugman and Baldwin (1987) estimate a U.S. expenditure elasticity of import demand of 2.9. Since the share of imports in U.S. expenditure in 1984 was 0.115, this yields a marginal propensity to import of 0.33.

# 2

## The J-Curve, the Fire Sale, and the Hard Landing

The dollar peaked almost four years ago. The subsequent era of dollar decline, which has now lasted longer than the era of the strong dollar, has confounded the expectations of both optimists and pessimists. Optimists believed that a return of the dollar to historical levels would quickly bring about a restoration of U.S. external balance. Yet, although the dollar is now by any measure below its previous low point in the late 1970s, the United States continues to run current account deficits that would have been inconceivable a decade ago. Pessimists feared that a declining dollar would lead to capital flight, cutting off the supply of foreign savings on which the U.S. economy has become dependent. Yet capital inflows have remained large, and there has so far been little sign of financial crisis due to a loss of foreign confidence.

The failure of a declining dollar to produce either good news about trade or bad news about financial markets has led to a recasting of the debate. There are still optimists, but their optimism no longer takes the form of cheerful predictions of a rapid decline in the trade deficit. There are still pessimists, but they no longer predict a "hard landing" in which a cutoff of capital creates a dramatic economic crisis.

The new optimists, instead of predicting fast improvement in trade, ask what is so bad about a trade deficit. They point to the fact of continuing capital inflow and conclude that the United States will not have any problem with financing its investment for many years. Of course the budget deficit needs to be brought down, and the national savings rate increased, but there is no urgency: Foreigners have been willing to cover the gap between savings and investment for the last seven years and will surely be willing to do so for some while longer, while a "flexible freeze" slowly reduces the federal deficit and private savings spontaneously recover.

Originally published in *AEA Papers and Proceedings* 79, 2 (May 1989), pp. 31–35.

The new pessimists look at the same facts, and reach a different conclusion: that dollar depreciation has failed, and indeed been disastrous. The trade deficit remains huge; meanwhile foreigners have bought up large quantities of U.S. assets at bargain prices, thanks to the weak dollar. The problem, as now seen by the pessimists, is not that the United States is on the verge of sudden crisis but that it is selling its birthright for a mess of pottage.

This chapter argues that both the new optimism and the new pessimism on the dollar are off the mark. The optimists, in looking at the continuation of capital inflows, have failed to notice that this continuation results from the sluggish response of trade flows, not from continued foreign confidence. The pessimists are correct in their observation of a "fire sale" in which the United States has been able to continue to attract capital inflows only by making its assets much cheaper through dollar depreciation. They are wrong, however, in decrying this fire sale as a great mistake; it is in fact an inevitable part of the adjustment process. And both optimists and pessimists have been too quick to dismiss the possibility of a hard landing for the U.S. economy: A financial squeeze due to a cutoff of foreign capital is not only a live possibility, it is arguably already in process.

## 2.1   Capital Inflows and the Fire Sale

When the dollar was at its peak, economists who warned of trouble ahead feared that once the bubble burst there would be a cutoff of the supply of foreign capital, leading to a financial hard landing. Experience has thus far belied this fear. Even though the current account deficit actually widened in nominal terms until recently, the United States has continued to finance this deficit without any obvious strain. This absence of crisis has led to a new consensus among many economists: that the external deficit is a problem only because of its long-run implications for living standards, not because of prospective problems of financing.

The combined persistence of the current account deficit and of capital inflows—which are of course equal—has led to a reversal of opinions among many about the wisdom of allowing the dollar to decline. A few years ago the orthodox view that the strong dollar was a key factor in the plunge of the United States into net debtor status was generally accepted. Now, however, a growing body of opinion holds that the strategy of weakening the dollar has actually worsened rather than improved the U.S. position as a debtor. In this view, which we may describe as the fire sale theory, the main effect of a cheap dollar is not to make U.S. goods more competitive, but to make U.S. assets cheap. Foreigners in general, and the Japanese in particular, therefore are more, not less, able to buy up U.S. assets.

The fire sale view is sometimes expressed in melodramatic terms, as something that will turn us all into paupers within a few years. This is an overdrawn picture. Yet there is clearly some truth here. Those who look only at the flow of foreign capital into the United States since 1985, and not at the decline in the dollar needed to attract that capital, are missing an important aspect of the situation.

Yet there is also something wrong with the fire sale view. Many of its advocates treat the dollar's decline as if it were some kind of exogenous event, foisted upon the country by Secretary of State James Baker. They also treat the sale of U.S. assets at bargain prices as if it represents a pure windfall to foreign investors. This cannot be right. If U.S. assets are such a good buy, then why is it that their prices do not get bid up? And if it is now so attractive to invest in the United States, should not the desire to keep investing here drive up the value of the dollar? The point is that neither asset prices nor the value of the dollar (which is an asset price itself) can be regarded as given.

In order to make sense of what has been happening to the United States in recent years, it is necessary to tell a more complete story. In this story the key element is the sluggish response of trade flows to the exchange rate.

## 2.2   Confidence, the J-Curve, and the Exchange Rate

Suppose that international investors were suddenly to lose confidence in the United States. What it means to "lose confidence" is a slightly problematic issue; perhaps investors start to demand a risk premium on U.S. assets, perhaps they revise downward their views about the long-run equilibrium real exchange rate, or perhaps they start to have a "peso problem," viewing a catastrophic fall in the dollar as a possibility though not a probability. Whatever the precise nature of the loss of confidence, the important point is that we suppose that investors become unwilling to hold claims on the United States at their current rates of return.

What happens next? Investors cannot simply pull their money out of the United States, since there would be nobody on the other side of the transaction. When everybody wants to sell, the result is not a lot of sales but a fall in the price. The immediate result of a loss of confidence in the United States then is not a sudden flight of capital but a sudden fall in the dollar.

The textbook view of what happens next is that the fall in the dollar leads to a reduction in the U.S. current account deficit. This deficit reduction has as its counterpart a decline in the rate of capital inflow, so this is the channel through which a decline in confidence leads to a cutoff of capital flows. The move toward current account balance also reduces the supply of savings domestically, driving up the interest rate. Equilibrium is reached when the interest rate is driven up sufficiently to make investors willing to hold U.S. assets again.

This textbook view is consistent and correct as a description of the medium run. As a short-run story, however, it overlooks a crucial point: the sluggishness with which the trade balance responds to the exchange rate. As recent experience has confirmed, the response of trade flows to the exchange rate takes years because consumers are slow to change habits and, more important, because many changes in supply and sourcing require long-term investment decisions. As a result of this sluggishness, a fall in the dollar does not lead to any immediate reduction of the U.S. trade deficit, and indeed probably leads to a temporary rise in that deficit. Since the rate of capital inflow is by definition equal to the current account deficit, we have a paradoxical result: Capital markets cannot determine the rate of capital inflow. All they can do is determine the value of the dollar, which itself can influence the rate of capital flow only with a long lag.

This may at first sight appear to leave the dollar with no bottom. As the dollar drops, however, it falls relative to its expected long-run level and thus offers foreign investors a higher expected rate of return. At some point this will be enough to induce these investors to hold onto U.S. assets. And since the current account deficit remains, foreign investors will actually continue to put funds into the United States. Indeed, thanks to the J-curve, they may be putting capital in at a greater rate than before.

Only over time does a textbook answer emerge, as the weak dollar *gradually* reduces the trade deficit. Eventually the result is a smaller external deficit on one side and a rise in interest rates on the other. But this result takes time, and meanwhile foreigners continue to finance the deficit.

In this not entirely hypothetical story we see some aspects of the U.S. story of the past few years emerge. The loss of confidence by foreigners is initially reflected in a decline in the currency, not in a decline in the rate of capital inflow. Someone who looks only at the current account financing would conclude that foreigners are as willing to invest here as ever. What attracts the foreigners is precisely the fire sale of U.S. assets: The fall in the dollar makes the assets cheap, thus presenting foreigners with a higher expected rate of return. This fire sale is not, however, a windfall presented to foreigners by a arbitrary decline in the dollar. Both the decline in the dollar and the fire sale result from the unwillingness of foreigners to keep investing in the United States, which requires that they be offered a higher expected rate of return.

Finally, notice that a hard landing—a financial squeeze brought about by the cutoff of foreign financing—does occur in this story, but not immediately. Since the loss of confidence by foreign investors cannot immediately show up in a reduced capital inflow, the hard landing takes time to develop. It would clearly be a mistake, however, to look at the absence of financial strain in the immediate aftermath of dollar decline and conclude that there will never be a financial problem.

### 2.3 A Formal Model

The story told above is a simple one, yet it is not a familiar one among economists. Thus it may be worthwhile to state it in a formal model. The model is essentially the full employment real exchange rate model suggested by William Branson (1985), with one new feature: the addition of lags in trade adjustment, borrowing a convenient formulation originally introduced by Rudiger Dornbusch (1976).

I begin with the savings-investment identity, expressing both savings and investment in terms of domestic goods:

$$S(r) - I(r) = X(E_P) - \frac{M(E_P)}{E_S}. \tag{1}$$

Here savings and investment are assumed to depend on the real interest rate in terms of domestic goods. Trade *volumes* are assumed to depend not on the current price of domestic goods relative to foreign $E_S$ but on a "permanent" real exchange rate $E_p$ that is a distributed lag of past real exchange rates. Specifically,

$$\dot{E}_P = \lambda(E_S - E_P), \tag{2}$$

where $1/\lambda$ is the mean lag. Let us assume that although in (1) the exchange rate has a perverse short-run effect on the trade balance, the long-run effect via $E_P$ is sufficient to insure that a depreciation eventually reduces the trade deficit. That is, there is a J-curve.

Finally, suppose that expectations are rational. Then, except when there are surprises, the rate of return on domestic assets (including real appreciation) must equal the rate of return on foreign assets, plus any required risk premium:

$$r(E_S, E_P) + \frac{\dot{E}_S}{E_S} = r^* + \rho, \tag{3}$$

where $\rho$ is the risk premium. Notice that I have written $r$ as a function of $E_S$ and $E_P$; from (1) it is apparent that a rise in the current real rate raises the domestic real interest rate because it reduces the trade deficit, while a rise in the permanent rate reduces $r$. We must have $r_1 + r_2 < 0$.

The dynamic system defined by (2) and (3) may be illustrated by figure 2.1. The line $\dot{E}_P = 0$ is simply the 45-degree line; the line $\dot{E}_S = 0$ represents all points where the domestic interest rate equals the foreign plus the required risk premium. It is straightforward to determine that the relative slopes are as shown and that there is a downward-sloping stable arm, shown by $SS$.

Suppose now that the economy is initially in equilibrium at point 1 and that there is a foreign loss of confidence, which I model as a rise in the risk premium $\rho$. Then the result is a sudden drop in the real exchange rate to point 2, followed by gradual convergence to the new steady state. The initial effects of this loss of confidence are perverse: The trade deficit, and hence the rate of capital inflow, *widen*, while the domestic interest rate *falls*. What attracts continuing inflows of foreign capital is the fire sale, represented by the fact that $E_S$ at point 1 has actually overshot its long-run level.

This is simply a formalization of the verbal story in section 2.2. As in that story the fire sale is not an arbitrary windfall but something required

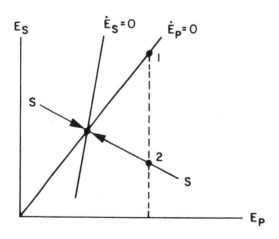

**Figure 2.1**

by the foreign loss of confidence in the face of sluggish trade response. And the eventual cutoff of foreign financing, and the corresponding rise in $r$, is only postponed, not avoided.

## 2.4   Policy Implications

The analysis presented here suggests that a loss of foreign confidence in the United States is not something that might happen in the future; it is something that has already happened. Foreign investors are continuing to finance the U.S. current account deficit only because they regard U.S. assets as cheap, due to a weak dollar. If they are right, and the dollar really is cheap, then there will eventually be serious crowding out of domestic investment as the current account deficit narrows. Thus raising national savings is a more urgent matter than optimists, who think the United States has no financing problem, have imagined.

It is of course possible that the markets are wrong, that only modest further narrowing of the trade gap will occur at the current value of the dollar. If that turns out to be the case, however, the markets will drive the dollar down still further: If they are not now getting assets at fire sale prices, they will insist on doing so in the future.

It is a mistake, however, to decry the fire sale as some kind of mistake of exchange rate policy. If foreigners are no longer willing to invest money here without a high expected rate of return, this is not something that could have been avoided if only the U.S. Treasury had supported the dollar. The only way to avoid a fire sale is not to need one—that is, to provide enough domestic saving so as to avoid reliance on foreign capital inflows.

So the policy moral of this analysis is one that has become boring through repetition but is still as true as ever. The United States needs to restore its national savings rate to historical levels as soon as it can. International investors have signaled that they are not willing to continue financing massive current account deficits, not by cutting off capital flows suddenly but by driving the dollar down to unprecedented lows. Putting aside the alarmist or conspiratorial views of some fire sale theorists, the point remains that the growing complacency about perpetual foreign borrowing will lead us to a rude awakening, sooner than most economists think.

# 3

# Differences in Income
# Elasticities and Trends
# in Real Exchange Rates

What determines equilibrium real exchange rates? In the practical attempt to determine equilibrium rates, international economists generally exhibit a kind of schizophrenia. When we analyze short- and medium-run balance-of-payments developments, we use an income-and-price-elasticity framework that presumes that the exports of different countries are imperfect substitutes for one another—and indeed empirical implementation of this framework suggests fairly low price elasticities, implying that goods produced by different countries are not close substitutes. However, such a framework seems to imply that there should be substantial changes in equilibrium real rates over time, due to either differences in income elasticities or differences in growth rates. This is an implication that somehow we are unwilling to accept: When we do long-run analysis, we all seem to reveal a deep-seated belief in some form or purchasing power parity.

The purpose of this chapter is twofold. First, I want to point out an empirical regularity; second, I want to argue that this empirical regularity lends support to a particular view of international trade that reconciles the seemingly contradictory views of many international economists about the short and long runs.

The empirical regularity is that the apparent income elasticities of demand for a country's imports and exports are systematically related to the country's long-term rate or growth. Fast-growing countries seem to face a high income elasticity of demand for their exports, while having a low income elasticity of demand for imports. The converse is true for slow-growing countries. The result of this difference in income elasticities is, it turns out, just about sufficient to make trend changes in real exchange rates unnecessary. That is, although an income-and-price-elasticity framework in

Originally published in *European Economic Review* 33 (1989), pp. 1031–1054. Copyright ©
1989 by Elsevier Science Publishers B.V. (North-Holland).

principle should give rise to substantial shifts in equilibrium real exchange rates over time, in practice the income elasticities turn out to be just right to make this unnecessary. I will refer to this empirical regularity as the "45-degree rule."

The theoretical point that follows from this is more questionable. I argue that the results on income elasticities are unlikely to be a coincidence. Instead, estimated income elasticities probably reflect a confounding of income effects with supply-side effects—a point that many authors have made. The new point here is that in order to explain the 45-degree rule, with its implication that there are not strong trends in real exchange rates, it is necessary to suppose that there is not much comparative advantage among industrial countries and that their specialization at any point in time is largely arbitrary specialization due to increasing returns rather than comparative advantage trade.

The chapter is in four sections. Section 3.1 considers the conventional income-and-price-elasticity analysis and shows that this analysis will normally imply substantial shifts in equilibrium real exchange rates over time. Section 3.2 reviews some historical estimates of income elasticities in world trade and shows that these show a characteristic pattern of correlation with rates of growth, such that countries in general need much less real exchange rate movement over time than one would have expected a priori—the 45-degree rule. Section 3.3 offers an explanation of this result that draws on the modern theory of trade based on increasing returns and imperfect competition. Section 3.4 then offers some updated results on income elasticities in the 1970s and 1980s, arguing that these new results support the general approach offered in this chapter.

## 3.1   The Significance of Income Elasticities

Although much theoretical literature in international economics is set in a general equilibrium framework with fairly complex production structures and many relative prices, the workhorse of practical trade balance analysis is still, as it was a generation ago, the partial equilibrium analysis of trade flows that are assumed to depend on real income and a single relative price. This framework can be defended as a pretty close approximation to a more carefully specified framework in which expenditure as well as income enters into import demand. In any case, since this framework is still the way most practical analysis is done, it will be used as the starting point here without much apology.

Consider then a two-country world in which we define $y$, $y^*$ as domestic and foreign real output, $p$, $p^*$ as the prices in local currency of these outputs, and $e$ as the price of foreign currency in terms of domestic. Define $r = ep^*/p$ as the real exchange rate, which is in this case the price of foreign relative to domestic goods. Then the standard trade balance model may be written as follows. Export volume depends on foreign output and the relative price of domestic goods:

$$x = x(y^*, r). \tag{1}$$

Import volume depends on domestic income and the relative price of imports

$$m = m(y, r). \tag{2}$$

The trade balance (in domestic currency) can be written

$$B = px - ep^*m$$
$$= p[x - rm], \tag{3}$$

so the trade balance in terms of domestic output is simply

$$b = x - rm. \tag{4}$$

Now it was pointed out in the 1950s by Johnson (1958) that if the framework (1)–(4) is a reasonable description of trade balance determination, then economic growth is likely to require secular changes in real exchange rates. To see why, define the following. Let

$\zeta_x$ = income elasticity of demand for exports,

$\zeta_m$ = income elasticity of demand for imports,

$\varepsilon_x$ = price elasticity of demand for imports,

$\varepsilon_m$ = price elasticity of demand for imports,

$\hat{y}$ = rate of growth of domestic output [i.e., $(dy/dt)/y$],

$\hat{y}^*$ = rate of growth of foreign output,

$\hat{r}$ = rate of real depreciation.

Now differentiate (4). We have

$$\frac{db}{dt} = x[\zeta_x \hat{y}^* + \varepsilon_x \hat{r}] - rm[\zeta_m \hat{y} + (1 - \varepsilon_m)\hat{r}]. \tag{5}$$

Suppose that initially $b = 0$ so that $x = rm$. Then, to keep a zero trade balance, we must have

$$\zeta_x \hat{y}^* - \zeta_m \hat{y} + (\varepsilon_x + \varepsilon_m - 1)\hat{r} = 0. \tag{6}$$

This implies a trend in the real exchange rate of

$$\hat{r} = \frac{\zeta_x \hat{y}^* - \zeta_m \hat{y}}{\varepsilon_x + \varepsilon_m - 1}. \tag{7}$$

Equation (7) immediately identifies two reasons why there may be a trend in the equilibrium exchange rate: Either countries may face different elasticities of import and export demand, or they may have different long-term rates of growth. More generally, there will be a trend in the real exchange rate unless

$$\frac{\zeta_x}{\zeta_m} = \frac{\hat{y}}{\hat{y}^*}, \tag{8}$$

which we would a priori imagine to be unlikely

Suppose in particular that income elasticities are assigned to countries randomly based on whatever happens to be their comparative advantage Then (7) would lead us to expect rapidly growing countries to experience secular depreciation on average, needing progressively to cut the relative prices of their goods in order to be able to sell ever increasing volumes on world markets.

Even without careful econometric analysis, it should immediately be clear to even casual observers that this assertion is not true. Japan has not experienced progressive real depreciation vis-a-vis the United States; if anything, the reverse has been true. Thus there must be something systematic about the relationship of relative growth rates to relative income elasticities. Let us now turn briefly to some old econometric evidence to pin that relationship down.

## 3.2 The 45-Degree Rule in the 1950s and 1960s

In 1969 Houthakker and Magee published a paper that remains a benchmark for comparative estimation of trade equations across a large number of countries. Their main conclusion was that there were large differences among countries in their relative income elasticities—specifically, that Japan faced the highly favorable combination of a high income elasticity of demand for its exports and a low income elasticity of import demand, while the United States and the United Kingdom faced the reverse. While Houthakker and Magee did of course notice that Japan was the fastest

**Table 3.1**
Income elasticities and growth rates in the 1950s and 1960s

| Country | Income elasticity | | | Growth rate, 1955–65 |
| | Imports | Exports | Ratio | |
| --- | --- | --- | --- | --- |
| United Kingdom | 1.66 | 0.86 | 0.52 | 2.82 |
| United States | 1.51 | 0.99 | 0.66 | 3.46 |
| Belgium | 1.94 | 1.83 | 0.94 | 3.77 |
| Sweden | 1.42 | 1.76 | 1.24 | 4.18 |
| Norway | 1.40 | 1.59 | 1.36 | 4.41 |
| Switzerland | 1.81 | 1.47 | 0.81 | 4.66 |
| Canada | 1.20 | 1.41 | 1.18 | 4.66 |
| Netherlands | 1.89 | 1.88 | 0.99 | 4.67 |
| Denmark | 1.31 | 1.69 | 1.29 | 4.74 |
| Italy | 2.19 | 2.95 | 1.35 | 5.40 |
| France | 1.66 | 1.53 | 0.92 | 5.62 |
| Germany | 1.80 | 2.08 | 1.56 | 6.21 |
| Japan | 1.23 | 3.55 | 2.89 | 9.40 |

Sources: Income elasticities from Houthakker and Magee (1969); growth rates from *International Financial Statistics.*

growing country in their sample and that the United States and the United Kingdom were the slowest, they did not explicitly consider the possibility that the differences in underlying growth rates were somehow systematically related to the differences in estimated income elasticities.

Yet is is difficult to escape this conclusion. Table 3.1 presents the Houthakker-Magee income elasticity results for industrial countries, together with the growth rates of those countries over the period 1955–65. The relationship is striking; it becomes even more so when the ratio $\zeta_x/\zeta_m$ is graphed against $\hat{y}$, a plot shown in figure 3.1.

Basically what the Houthakker-Magee results show is that (8) holds, that the ratio of income elasticities over their estimation period was such as to allow countries to have very different growth rates without strong trends in equilibrium real exchange rates. This may be confirmed more formally, by regressing the natural logarithm or the Houthakker-Magee elasticity ratio on the national growth rates[1]

$$\ln\left(\frac{\zeta_x}{\zeta_m}\right) = -1.81 + \underset{(0.208)}{1.210} \ln\left(\frac{\hat{y}}{\hat{y}^*}\right), \qquad (9)$$

$R^2 = 0.754, \quad SEE = 0.211.$

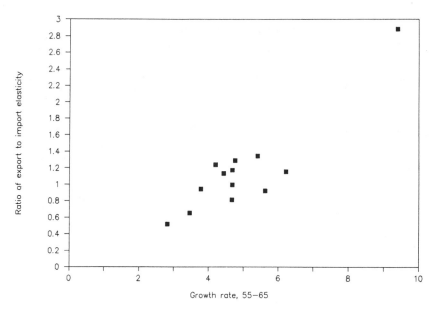

**Figure 3.1**
Growth versus elasticity ratio

In this regression we see that on average, if country $A$ grew twice as rapidly as country $B$ over the period 1955–65, then country $A$ turned out to have an estimated ratio of export to import elasticities that was twice that of country $B$.

The result of this systematic relationship between growth rates and income elasticities was to make relative purchasing power parity hold much better than one would have expected if one assumed that income elasticities were identical, or distributed randomly. One might have expected Japan to need to have rapidly falling relative export prices in order to accommodate its extremely rapid economic growth—but the combination of high export elasticity and low import elasticity took care of that. One might have expected the United Kingdom to receive compensation for its low growth rate by a secular appreciation of its real exchange rate—but the combination of low export elasticity and high import elasticity deprived it of that benefit.

Clearly something is going on here. It seems unlikely that the systematic association of growth rates and income elasticities is a pure coincidence. So our next step is to turn to potential explanations.

## 3.3   Explaining Apparent Income Elasticity Differences

The close association between growth rates and the favorableness of income elasticities could have two types or explanation. On one side, income elasticities could determine growth: Countries that happen to face unfavorable income elasticities could find themselves running into balance-of-payments problems whenever they try to expand. If this forces them into stop-go economic policies that inhibit growth, the result could be to limit growth to a level consistent with little real exchange rate change over time. The same result would occur if a wage-price spiral prevents effective real depreciation; then countries would not be able to achieve the real depreciation necessary to grow faster than the relative rate dictated by the income elasticities.

The other basic explanation is that differential growth rates affect trade flows in such a way as to create apparent differences in income elasticities. That is, we may conclude that there is a supply-side element in the apparent differences in demand that countries face.

I am simply going to dismiss a priori the argument that income elasticities determine economic growth, rather than the other way around. It just seems fundamentally implausible that over stretches of decades balance-of-payments problems could be preventing long-term growth, especially for relatively closed economies like that of the United States in the 1950s and 1960s. Furthermore we all know that differences in growth rates among countries are primarily determined in the rate of growth of total factor productivity, not differences in the rate of growth of employment. It is hard to see what channel links balance-of-payments problems due to unfavorable income elasticities to total factor productivity growth.

Thus we are driven to a supply-side explanation of the income elasticities It is important, however, to think about what kind of supply-side explanation is needed. Simply to posit a supply curve for exports for each country will not help: As a country grows, its supply curve will shift out, but this will simply move it *down* the demand curve, not shift the curve. Admittedly, if countries face upward-sloping supply curves for exports and imports, there will be some bias in empirical estimates that ignore this. However, this seems unlikely to explain the basic stylized fact that countries seem able to grow at different rates without the need for trend shifts in real exchange rates.

A more sophisticated view would draw on the traditional analysis of the effects of growth on the terms of trade, as developed by Johnson (1958) and Bhagwati (1958, 1961). That literature points out that when countries are not specialized in trade—that is, when they produce import-competing as well as exported products—growth can have ambiguous effects on the terms of trade. Growth that is biased toward exports will indeed require a secular deterioration in the terms of trade, but growth that is biased toward imports will actually improve the growing country's terms of trade. The key question is the effect of growth on the demand for imports: If growth reduces the demand for imports at a given terms of trade, as will be the case for sufficiently import-biased growth, then a growing country's terms of trade will improve over time.

There may be something to this. In the 1950s and 1960s the fast-growing country was Japan, while the slow-growing countries were the United States and the United Kingdom. Japan was clearly playing catch-up with the rest of the industrial world, which meant that it was becoming *more similar* to its trading partners. Now suppose that initially Japan had a competitive advantage in labor-intensive goods but a comparative disadvantage in capital-intensive goods. As it became more similar to other industrial countries, it would become relatively better at producing capital-intensive goods, so its growth would be biased toward the sectors in which it did not initially have a comparative advantage and away from those sectors in which it did. This is precisely import-biased growth and could explain why Japan did not need declining terms of trade. Conversely, the United States and the United Kingdom were being caught up to: The world was becoming more similar to them, which would, other things equal, tend to worsen their terms of trade.[2]

Although the argument that fast-growing countries were experiencing import-biased growth is appealing in many respects, I am doubtful about its relevance in explaining the data in figure 3.1, for three reasons. First, it explains why the apparent income elasticities could be favorable for fast-growing countries but not why they are favorable to almost precisely the extent needed to yield zero trend in the real exchange rate. Second, this story has an implication about the shares of trade in income. Suppose that an economy grows, while the rest of the world does not. If the growing economy is not to have a deterioration in its terms of trade, it must have no increase in its import demand. Hence the share of imports in national income must fall: The economy must become more closed over time. Admittedly this result can be softened by making ceteris not paribus (e.g., by imagining that global trade liberalization is taking place and that there is also some growth in other countries). However, the fact that stable terms of trade were in fact consistent with growing trade relative to income casts doubt on the view that import-biased growth in catch-up countries could explain the real exchange rate developments (or more to the point, the lack of them) in the 1950s and 1960s.

The third reason for scepticism about the traditional trade and growth explanation is that it is a contingent one: The 45-degree rule *could* happen, but there is no particular reason why it should. In particular, it should not be expected to be stable over time. As we will see, however, the 45-degree rule has generally been stable over time, persisting in the 1970s and 1980s despite a major shift in relative growth rates. Thus I at least am inspired to look for more unusual explanations.

In looking for a more fundamental explanation of the 45-degree rule, let me engage in a bit of professional self-psychoanalysis. Why do international economists mostly believe at a gut level that rough purchasing power parity should obtain among industrial countries over the long run? The answer, I would submit, is that it is because we believe that the industrial nations are basically all pretty much the same. Germany and the United States can produce pretty much the same things, and produce them about equally well. If costs and prices in either country were very far off those in the other for an extended period, all production would lend to move there. In the long run then we expect competition over the location of production to keep relative prices from moving too far apart.

But if Germany and the United States are pretty much alike, why do they trade at all? The answer has to be some arbitrary specializalion that is driven not by comparative advantage but by the inherent advantages of specialization itself, which is to say, by increasing returns. Thus (not surprisingly) I would argue that the 45-degree rule is best explained by appealing to the new theory of trade in which similar countries trade because of increasing returns rather than comparative advantage.

The story runs as follows. Fast-growing countries expand their share of world markets not by reducing the relative prices of their goods but by expanding the range of goods that they produce as their economies grow. What we measure as exports and imports are not really fixed sets of goods but instead aggregates whose definitions change over time as more goods are added to the list. What we call *Japanese exports* is a meaningful aggregate facing a downward-sloping demand curve at any point in time. But as the Japanese economy grows over time, the definition of that aggregate changes in such a way as to make the apparent demand curve shift outward. The result is to produce apparently favorable income elasticities that allow the country to expand its economy without the need for a secular real depreciation.

To make this point more concrete, let us consider a minimal formal model. No effort will be made at realism; instead, the purpose is simply to offer a suggestive example of how the 45-degree rule could arise out of an increasing returns model of international trade.

The model we consider is the "rock-bottom" model introduced in Krugman (1980), based on the Dixit-Stiglitz (1977) model of monopolistic competition. We suppose that there are two countries, Home and Foreign, and that each can produce and consume any of an infinite number of product varieties. These product varieties all enter symmetrically into consumption. with everyone sharing the instantaneous utility function[3]

$$U = \left\{ \theta^{-1} \sum_{i=1}^{\infty} c_i^{\theta} \right\}^{1/\theta}, \qquad 0 < \theta < 1. \tag{10}$$

We suppose that each country has only one factor of production, which we will call *labor* but which may be envisaged as an aggregate of resources. The key point is that we ignore any differences in relative factor endowments among countries or in factor intensities among goods that would give rise to comparative advantage. Instead, trade arises because of increasing returns, which enter the model through the assumption that the labor required to produce a good involves a fixed cost:

$$1_i = \alpha + \beta x_i \qquad \text{for all } i, \tag{11}$$

where $1_i$ is the quantity of resources used to produce any good with nonzero output, and $x_i$ is the output of the good

For each country there is a full employment constraint

$$L = \sum_i 1_i. \tag{12}$$

As pointed out in the work of Dixit and Stiglitz a closed economy with this utility and technology will have a monopolistically competitive equilibrium. Each good that is produced will be purchased by only one firm, since a firm could always choose to start a new good that is equally profitable, and thus has no incentive to contest markets with other firms. The firm producing any particular good will face an elasticity of demand

$$\phi = \frac{1}{1-\theta}. \tag{13}$$

Given this elasticity of demand, each firm will charge a price that is a markup over the wage rate

$$\frac{p}{w} = \frac{\beta}{\theta}. \tag{14}$$

The zero-profit condition then determines the output and employment per product

$$x\left(\frac{p}{w - \beta}\right) = \alpha \Rightarrow x = \frac{\alpha\theta}{\beta(1 - \theta)}, \tag{15}$$

and

$$1 = \frac{\alpha}{1 - \theta}. \tag{16}$$

It follows that the number of product varieties produced in a country is simply proportional to its labor force

$$n = \frac{L(1 - \theta)}{\alpha}. \tag{17}$$

Next consider trade between two such economies, with labor forces $L$ and $L^*$. If transport costs may be neglected, these trading economies simply constitute a world economy with labor force $L + L^*$; wage rates and the prices of representative goods will be equalized whatever the relative size of the economies. Trade will result from the desire of consumers in each country to diversify their purchases: with Home producing $n$ varieties and Foreign $n^*$, each consumer spends a fraction or his income $n/(n + n^*) = L/(L + L^*)$ on Home goods, a fraction $n^*/(n + n^*) = L^*/(L + L^*)$ on Foreign goods.

Now note that Home income deflated by the price or a representative product is

$$y = \frac{wL}{p} = \frac{L\theta}{\beta}. \tag{18}$$

The volume of Home imports is therefore

$$M = \left(\frac{n}{n + n^*}\right)y, \tag{19}$$

and the volume of Home exports analogously is

$$X = \left(\frac{n^*}{n + n^*}\right)y^*. \tag{20}$$

Now consider what happens if the Home and Foreign economies are growing over time. We may represent growth as increases in $L$ and $L^*$, recognizing that productivity gains can be represented as increases in the *effective* labour forces. Then we may immediately note that even if the labor forces grow at different rates, the prices of representative products in the two countries will still be equalized. That is, there will be no real exchange rate change. The reason is that the faster growing country will be able to increase its share of world expenditure by increasing the number of goods it produces faster than the other country, allowing it to sell more without a reduction in its relative price.

By differentiating (19) and (20), we find that

$$\hat{X} = \hat{M} = \hat{y}\left(\frac{y^*}{y + y^*}\right) + \hat{y}^*\left(\frac{y}{y + y^*}\right). \tag{21}$$

Now suppose a naive econometrician were to attempt to fit a conventional trade model to these data. He would find an apparent income elasticity of export demand equal to

$$\zeta_x = \frac{\hat{X}}{\hat{y}^*} = \left(\frac{\hat{y}}{\hat{y}^*}\right)\left(\frac{y^*}{y + y^*}\right) + \frac{y}{y + y^*}, \tag{22}$$

and similarly an apparent income elasticity or import demand equal to

$$\zeta_m = \frac{\hat{M}}{\hat{y}} = \frac{y^*}{y + y^*} + \left(\frac{\hat{y}^*}{\hat{y}}\right)\left(\frac{y}{y + y^*}\right). \tag{23}$$

We note immediately from (22) and (23) that the higher the relative growth rate of Home, the higher will be the apparent income elasticity of demand for its exports (other things equal) and the lower the apparent income elasticity of demand for imports. This of course simply reflects the effects of changing numbers of products that we have already alluded to. Furthermore the ratio of these apparent income elasticities will in fact precisely fulfill the 45-degree condition:

$$\frac{\zeta_x}{\zeta_m} = \frac{\hat{y}}{\hat{y}^*}.$$

We see then that a simple model in which trade arises because of economies of specialization rather than comparative advantage in effect predicts that an econometrician will find the 45-degree rule. The fundamental logic is that if countries are basically alike, the prices of their typical traded outputs should be the same, and apparent income elasticities will be such as to make continued price equality possible.

If the 45-degree rule is really a reflection of something fundamental about trade flows rather than something contingent on particular circumstances, we should expect to find that it holds over different time periods. In particular, we should find that if a country's relative growth rate changes, its apparent income elasticities should change as well, so as to preserve the 45-degree rule. Thus our next step must be to examine the validity of the 45-degree rule in the 1970s and 1980s.

## 3.4 The 45-Degree Rule in the 1970s and 1980s.

Tables 3.2 and 3.3 report the results of a set of standard export and import equations estimated for industrial countries on annual data for the period 1971–86. The dependent variables are

$X$ = manufactures exports in 1982 prices,

$M$ = manufacturers imports in 1982 prices.

**Table 3.2**
Estimates of export equations, 1971–86

| Country | Coefficients | | | | | | |
|---|---|---|---|---|---|---|---|
| | $Y^*$ | $RXP$ | $RXP(-1)$ | $SEE$ | $R^2$ | $D-W$ | $\rho$ |
| Austria | 3.05 | −0.56 | −0.04 | 0.03 | 0.992 | 2.11 | — |
| | (0.10) | (0.42) | (0.42) | | | | |
| Belgium | 1.24 | 0.39 | −0.58 | 0.02 | 0.971 | 2.18 | — |
| | (0.13) | (0.16) | (0.14) | | | | |
| Canada | 2.87 | 0.62 | 0.18 | 0.02 | 0.996 | 1.96 | — |
| | (0.09) | (0.20) | (0.18) | | | | |
| Germany | 2.15 | −0.32 | −0.23 | 0.03 | 0.987 | 2.11 | — |
| | (0.09) | (0.23) | (0.21) | | | | |
| United Kingdom | 1.30 | 0.00 | −0.54 | 0.03 | 0.963 | 2.01 | — |
| | (0.08) | (0.14) | (0.13) | | | | |
| Italy | 2.41 | 0.08 | −0.31 | 0.04 | 0.982 | 1.61 | — |
| | (0.11) | (0.19) | (0.20) | | | | |
| Japan | 1.65 | −0.35 | −0.53 | 0.06 | 0.978 | 2.19 | 0.81 |
| | (0.80) | (0.18) | (0.21) | | | | |
| Netherlands | 3.86 | −0.56 | −0.20 | 0.03 | 0.980 | 1.46 | 0.94 |
| | (0.66) | (0.22) | (0.29) | | | | |
| United States | 1.70 | −0.44 | −0.98 | 0.04 | 0.976 | 2.10 | — |
| | (0.08) | (0.16) | (0.16) | | | | |

Note: All equations estimated on annual data, 1971–86. Standard errors in parentheses.

**Table 3.3**
Estimates of import equations, 1971–86

| Country | Coefficients | | | | | | |
|---|---|---|---|---|---|---|---|
| | $Y^*$ | RMP | RMP(−1) | SEE | $R^2$ | D − W | ρ |
| Austria | 2.94 | −0.14 | 0.41 | 0.04 | 0.979 | 1.74 | 0.41 |
| | (0.99) | (0.43) | (0.75) | | | | |
| Belgium | 1.99 | −0.39 | −0.14 | 0.03 | 0.975 | 1.62 | — |
| | (0.10) | (0.16) | (0.15) | | | | |
| Canada | 1.66 | −0.79 | −0.66 | 0.07 | 0.916 | 1.66 | 0.40 |
| | (0.27) | (0.51) | (0.51) | | | | |
| Germany | 2.83 | −0.33 | 0.24 | 0.03 | 0.988 | 1.24 | 0.54 |
| | (0.26) | (0.20) | (0.26) | | | | |
| United Kingdom | −0.20 | 1.03 | −0.04 | 0.01 | 0.999 | 1.95 | 0.95 |
| | (0.09) | (0.05) | (0.04) | | | | |
| Italy | 3.65 | −0.51 | −0.17 | 0.04 | 0.981 | 1.69 | — |
| | (0.37) | (0.20) | (0.14) | | | | |
| Japan | 0.80 | 0.03 | −0.45 | 0.12 | 0.928 | 1.51 | — |
| | (1.19) | (0.29) | (0.38) | | | | |
| Netherlands | 2.66 | −0.11 | −0.11 | 0.02 | 0.987 | 2.13 | 0.79 |
| | (0.46) | (0.14) | (0.19) | | | | |
| United States | 1.31 | 0.11 | −1.04 | 0.08 | 0.957 | 1.62 | — |
| | (0.44) | (0.34) | (0.36) | | | | |

Note: All equations estimated on annual data, 1971–86. Standard errors in parentheses.

The explanatory variables are

$Y$ = GNP in constant prices,

$Y^*$ = foreign GNP in constant prices, calculated as a geometric average of GNP in 14 industrial countries, weighted by their 1978 shares of the exporting country's exports,

$RXP$ = OECD index of relative export prices of manufactures,

$RMP$ = relative price or manufactures imports, calculated as ratio or manufactures import unit value to GNP deflator.

All data are from OECD *Economic Outlook*. All equations were estimated in log-linear form; where severe serial correlation was evident, a correction was made.

By and large, these estimates look fairly decent; taken one at a time, they might suggest the need for more careful cleaning of data. addition or some extra variables, etc., but they would not discourage a researcher from using the income-and-price-elasticity framework. The major exception is the United Kingdom, whose import equation refuses to make sense. I have

**Table 3.4**
Income elasticities and growth rates, 1970–86

| Country | Growth rate of GNP | | | Income elasticity | | |
|---------|----------|---------|-------|---------|---------|-------|
|         | Domestic | Foreign | Ratio | Exports | Imports | Ratio |
| United States | 2.49 | 2.91 | 0.86 | 1.70 | 1.31 | 1.30 |
| Netherlands | 1.96 | 2.17 | 0.90 | 3.86 | 2.66 | 1.45 |
| Germany | 2.10 | 2.23 | 0.94 | 2.15 | 2.83 | 0.76 |
| Belgium | 2.15 | 2.19 | 0.98 | 1.24 | 1.99 | 0.62 |
| Italy | 2.56 | 2.37 | 1.08 | 2.41 | 3.65 | 0.66 |
| Austria | 2.63 | 2.08 | 1.26 | 3.06 | 2.60 | 1.18 |
| Canada | 3.59 | 2.55 | 1.41 | 2.87 | 1.66 | 1.73 |
| Japan | 4.15 | 2.37 | 1.75 | 1.65 | 0.80 | 2.06 |

Sources: Tables 3.2 and 3.3.

not been able to resolve this puzzle and will drop the United Kingdom from subsequent discussion.

What we may note, however, is that there is still, as in the Houthakker-Magee results, a systematic tendency for high-growth countries to face favorable income elasticities. Table 3.4 presents a summary of estimated income elasticities, their ratios, and growth rates (calculated by fitting trends to domestic and foreign GNP). When these results are plotted in figure 3.2, the result is less striking than for the Houthakker-Magee data in figure 3.1—partly because the spread of growth rates is smaller—but the upward-sloping relationship is still apparent. On average the 45-degree rule continues to hold, although with much less confidence:

$$\ln\left(\frac{\zeta_x}{\zeta_m}\right) = -0.00 + \underset{(0.609)}{1.029}\ln\left(\frac{\hat{y}}{\hat{y}^*}\right),$$

$R^2 = 0.322, \quad SEE = 0.41.$

Perhaps a more illuminating test is to look at the way in which estimates changed from the earlier period to the later period. In the 1950s and 1960s, as Houthakker and Magee noted, Japan was the country with highly favorable income elasticities, while the United States and the United Kingdom were the countries disfavored. In the 1970s and 1980s there was a general convergence of growth rates. European growth rates declined more than those of the United States, so the United States grew almost as rapidly as its trading partners. Japan, though still fast growing, was not as far out of line as before. If the preceding analysis is right, we should expect to find

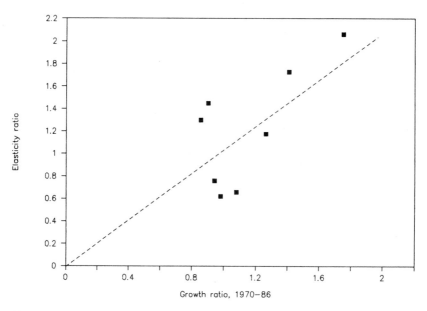

**Figure 3.2**
Growth ratio versus elasticity ratio

a decline in Japan's $\zeta_x/\zeta_m$ ratio and a rise in that of the United States. And indeed we do find this: According to the estimates made here, Japan's ratio of elasticities, while still high, is lower in my estimates than in the Houthakker-Magee results, while the United States actually is estimated to have a $\zeta_x/\zeta_m$ greater than one.

## 3.5   Conclusions

This chapter has suggested that the surprising thing about long term trends in real exchange rates is their absence. That is, over the long run relative purchasing power parity for the manufactures outputs of industrial countries holds better than we would expect given the fairly low price elasticities usually estimated. The way that conventional econometrics justifies this is by finding that countries with high growth rates face high income elasticities of demand for their exports while having low income elasticities of import demand, with the result being that their faster growth is accommodated without a need for secular real depreciation. I have offered this as a stylized fact in the data, and dubbed it the 45-degree rule. Like most stylized facts, this needs a little squinting to see in the charts, but

I would argue that there is enough evidence for a systematic association between apparent income elasticities and relative growth rates to be regarded as something that needs explaining.

The best explanation, I would argue, is that trade among industrial countries largely does not reflect country-specific comparative advantages, leading countries to face long-term downward-sloping demand for their unique products. Instead, countries specialize to take advantage of scale economies at different levels. As countries grow, they can expand their range of outputs, and hence increase their share of world markets without the necessity of secular real depreciation.

It should be clear that this is only a preliminary study. Ideally we would like to go beyond the simple regressions and simple model presented here to develop a model that explicitly links the long-run to the short- and medium-run dynamics in which the conventional income-and-price-elasticity framework remains a crucial tool. However, the chapter draws attention to what I believe is an important if fuzzy empirical regularity.

# II

# Speculation and Exchange Rates

# 4

# A Model of Balance-
# of-Payments Crises

A government can peg the exchange value of its currency in a variety of ways. In a country with highly developed financial markets it can use open-market operations, intervention in the forward exchange market, and direct operations in foreign assets to defend an exchange parity (see Girton and Henderson 1976 for an analysis of central bank operations and their effects on the exchange rate); the list could be extended to include such other instruments as changes in bank reserve requirements. But all of these policy instruments are subject to limits. A government attempting to keep its currency from depreciating may find its foreign reserves exhausted and its borrowing approaching a limit. A government attempting to prevent its currency from appreciating may find the cost in domestic inflation unacceptable. When the government is no longer able to defend a fixed parity because of the constraints on its actions, there is a "crisis" in the balance of payments.

This chapter is concerned with the analysis of such crises. Although balance-of-payments crises have not received much theoretical attention, there are obviously features common to many crises, and the empirical regularities suggest that a common process must be at work. A "standard" crisis occurs in something like the following manner: A country will have a pegged exchange rate; for simplicity, assume that pegging is done solely through direct intervention in the foreign exchange market. At that exchange rate the government's reserves gradually decline. Then at some point, generally well before the gradual depletion of reserves would have exhausted them, there is a sudden speculative attack that rapidly eliminates the last of the reserves. The government then becomes unable to defend the exchange rate any longer.

Originally published in *Journal of Money, Credit, and Banking* 11, 3 (August 1979), pp. 311–325. Copyright © 1979 by Ohio State University Press.

It sometimes happens. however, that the government is able to weather the crisis by calling on some kind or secondary reserve: It draws on its gold tranche or negotiates an emergency loan. At this point there is a dramatic reversal—the capital that has just flowed out returns, and the government's reserves recover. The reprieve may only be temporary, though. Another crisis may occur; it will oblige the government to call on still further reserves. There may be a whole sequence of temporary speculative attacks and recoveries of confidence before the attempt to maintain the exchange rate is finally abandoned.

One might question whether dramatic events of this sort, depending so heavily on the psychology of speculators, can be captured by a formal model. An analogy with another area of economics suggests, however. that sudden crises in the balance of payments may not be so hard to model after all. In the theory of exhaustible resources it has been shown that schemes in which the government uses a stockpile of an exhaustible resource to stabilize its price—an obvious parallel to using foreign reserves to peg an exchange rate—eventually end in a speculative attack in which private investors suddenly acquire the entire remaining government stock.[1] The increase in private stocks is justified, ex post, by the increased yield on holding stocks; when the price stabilization policy breaks down, the price of the resource begins rising, providing a capital gain that makes the holding of stocks more attractive.

In this chapter I show that a similar argument can be used to explain balance-of-payments crises. A speculative attack on a government's reserves can be viewed as a process by which investors change the composition of their portfolios, reducing the proportion of domestic currency and raising the proportion of foreign currency. This change in composition is then justified by a change in relative yields, for when the government is no longer able to defend the exchange rate the currency begins depreciating.

Perhaps more surprising is that the pattern of alternating speculative attacks and revivals of confidence is also a natural event when the market is uncertain about how much of its potential reserves the government is willing to use. The reason is that speculators are faced with a "one-way option"; they do not lose by speculating against the currency even if fears of abandonment of fixed rates prove unjustified.

This chapter, then, develops a theory of crises in the balance of payments. It is organized in six sections. Section 4.1 develops the macroeconomic model within which the analysis is conducted: a simple one-good, two-asset model originally expounded by Kouri (1976). In sections 4.2 and 4.3 the working of the model, and the evolution of the economy over time, are analyzed for flexible and fixed exchange rates, respectively. Section 4.4 contains the central analysis of the chapter, an analysis of the circumstances under which government pegging of the exchange rate suddenly collapses. This basic analysis is extended in section 4.5 to the case where government policy is uncertain, producing the possibility of alternating crises and recoveries of confidence. Finally, section 4.6 discusses the significance and limitations of the analysis.

### 4.1 A Macroeconomic Model

To study balance-of-payments crises, we must have a model with two characteristics: (1) The demand for domestic currency depends on the exchange rate; (2) the exchange rate that clears the domestic money market changes over time. An elegant and tractable model with these characteristics was developed by Kouri (1976), and I will use a slightly modified version of his model to provide the underpinnings for the discussion. The model involves many special assumptions, and no claims are made for its realism. But it should become clear later that the main points of the analysis would go through in a variety of models.

We will assume, then, that we are dealing with a small country producing a single composite tradable good. The price of the good will be set on world markets so that purchasing power parity will hold. That is to say,

$$P = sP^*, \tag{1}$$

where $P$ is the domestic price level, $s$ is the exchange rate of domestic currency for foreign, and $P^*$ is the foreign price level. I will assume $P^*$ fixed, so we can choose units to set $P^* = 1$. We can then identify the exchange rate with the price level.

The economy will be assumed to have fully flexible prices and wages, ensuring that output is always at its full employment level $Y$. The balance of trade, which will also turn out in the model to be the balance of payments on current account, will be determined by the difference between output and spending:

$$B = Y - G - C(Y - T, W), \qquad C_1, C_2 > 0, \tag{2}$$

where $B$ is the real trade balance, $G$ is real government spending, $T$ is real taxation, and $W$ is real private wealth (to be defined).

Turning now to the asset markets, investors are assumed to have available a choice between only two assets: domestic and foreign money. Both currencies bear zero nominal interest.[2] The total real wealth of domestic residents is the sum of the real value of their holdings of domestic money $M$ and their holdings of foreign money $F$:

$$W = \frac{M}{P} + F. \tag{3}$$

As a final simplifying assumption we suppose that foreigners do not hold domestic money. Then $M$ is also the outstanding stock of domestic money and in equilibrium domestic residents must be just willing to hold that stock. Since I assume that the desired holdings of domestic money are proportional to wealth, the condition for portfolio equilibrium is

$$\frac{M}{P} = L(\pi) \cdot W, \qquad L_1 < 0, \tag{4}$$

where $\pi$ is the expected rate of inflation. In this model $\pi$ is also the expected rate of depreciation of the currency. The determination of $\pi$ is of crucial importance for the analysis, but it can more usefully be discussed in the context of a full dynamic analysis. For the moment I will treat $\pi$ as exogenous.

In this chapter two exchange rate regimes will be considered. First will be a freely floating exchange rate, with the government abstaining from either buying or selling foreign money. Second will be a fixed exchange rate: the government holds a reserve of foreign money and stands ready to exchange foreign for domestic money at a fixed price. The short-run behavior of the economy under the two systems can be analyzed using figure 4.1, in which the upward-sloping schedule $LL$ represents the condi-

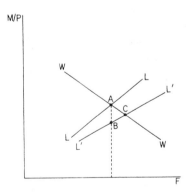

**Figure 4.1**
Effects of a change in $\pi$ with fixed and floating rates

tion for portfolio balance (4); an increase in holdings of foreign money will. be accompanied by an increase in real domestic money for a given $\pi$. The downward-sloping schedule $WW$ represents the wealth constraint (3). To acquire foreign money at any instant, domestic residents must reduce their real holdings of domestic money.[3]

Under a flexible rate regime, since neither the government nor foreigners will trade domestic money for foreign, there is no way for domestic residents to alter the composition of their aggregate portfolio. If they attempt to alter portfolio composition, the effect will be to change the price level (exchange rate) instead. Suppose, for instance, that $\pi$ rises. This will make domestic money less attractive, lowering $LL$ to $L'L'$. Since $F$ cannot change, $P$ rises, moving the equilibrium from $A$ to $B$.

Matters are different if the government has a reserve of foreign money $R$, and stands ready to exchange foreign for domestic money at a fixed price. Domestic residents can now trade freely up and down their wealth constraint, $WW$. An increase in $\pi$ that leads to a downward shift in $LL$ to $L'L'$ now leads to a shift in the portfolio of domestic residents, with the equilibrium moving from $A$ to $C$. There is a compensating change in the government's reserve position as the government supplies the desired foreign money; the changes in asset holdings are related by

$$\Delta R = -\Delta F = \frac{\Delta M}{P}.$$

Thus under flexible rates changes in expectations are reflected in the short run in changes in the exchange rate, whereas under fixed rates they are reflected in changes in the government's reserves. The next step is to examine the determination of expectations. This must be done in the context of an analysis of the economy's dynamics.

## 4.2 Dynamic Behavior with a Flexible Exchange Rate

If the government does not peg the exchange rate, the exchange rate can change for any of three reasons: a change in the quantity of domestic money outstanding, a change in private holdings of foreign assets, or a change in the expected rate of inflation. We will analyze each of these in turn, then combine them to describe the evolution of the economy over time.

I will assume that creation of money is dictated by the needs of government finance. Money will be created only through the government deficit;

conversely, the government deficit will be financed entirely by printing money. Then the growth of money stock will be determined by

$$\frac{\dot{M}}{P} = G - T. \tag{5}$$

A convenient, if somewhat artificial, assumption is that the government adjusts its expenditure so as to keep the deficit a constant fraction of the money supply. If we let $M/P = m$, this means that $G$ is adjusted to make $G - T = gm$, where $g$ is constant. This in turn takes the rate of change of real balances depend only on the rate of inflation, for

$$\dot{m} = \frac{\dot{M}}{P} - \left(\frac{M}{P}\right)\left(\frac{\dot{P}}{P}\right)$$

$$= \left(g - \frac{\dot{P}}{P}\right) m. \tag{6}$$

Turning next to holdings of foreign money, recall that such holdings represent claims on the rest of the world. They can only be increased by exchanging goods in return. So the rate of accumulation of foreign money must equal the current account balance.

$$\dot{F} = B = Y - G - C(Y - T, W). \tag{7}$$

Finally, we arrive at the question of expectations of inflation. This is a subject of considerable dispute. For our purposes it is essential to recognize that speculators are actively attempting to forecast the future in a sophisticated manner. This sort of sophisticated forward-looking behavior is best captured by the assumption of *perfect foresight*,[4]

$$\pi = \frac{\dot{P}}{P}. \tag{8}$$

To analyze the system as a whole, we begin by eliminating $\dot{P}/P$. Recall the portfolio balance condition (4). Combined with perfect foresight, this function implies a relationship between real balances, foreign money holdings, and inflation, of the form

$$\frac{\dot{P}}{P} = \pi\left(\frac{m}{F}\right), \qquad \pi_1 < 0. \tag{9}$$

The partial derivative in (9) follows from the fact that domestic residents will only be willing to increase the proportion of domestic money in their portfolio if they are offered a higher yield in the form of reduced inflation.

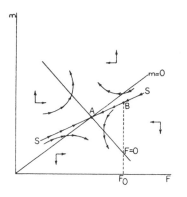

**Figure 4.2**
Dynamic behavior with a floating exchange rate

Substituting back, we get a dynamic system in the state variables $m$, $F$:

$$\dot{m} = \left[ g - \pi\left(\frac{m}{F}\right) \right] m,$$

$$\dot{F} = Y - G - C(Y - T, m + F). \tag{10}$$

This system is shown in figure 4.2, with arrows indicating representative paths.

There are two points that should be noted about the dynamic system. First. even if we know the asset holdings of domestic residents, the exchange rate is indeterminate. For any arbitrary initial price level, given $M$ and $F$ we have an initial position $(m, F)$ and an implied path for the economy. The second point is that the system exhibits knife-edge instability. There is only one path converging to a steady state: If the initial exchange rate is not chosen so as to put the system on that path, the system will diverge ever further from the steady state.

A natural solution to both these difficulties is to assume that investors do not believe in the possibility of endless speculative bubbles and that the initial exchange rate must therefore be one that implies eventual convergence to the steady state. Some theoretical justification for this assumption has been given by Brock (1975). The best argument for the assumption, however, is that it gives economically sensible results.

In figure 4.2 then the economy is assumed to always be on the stable arm $SABS$. If the initial holdings of foreign money are $F_0$, the price level will adjust so as to make the real domestic money supply be $m_0$, with the initial position of the economy being at point $B$. The system then converges gradually to $A$.

Notice that the real money supply depends positively on the stock of foreign money and is independent of the nominal stock of domestic money. Other things equal, then, the price level is proportional to the money supply and negatively related to $F$. We can write

$$P = M \cdot G(F), \qquad G_1 < 0, \tag{11}$$

where (11) is the equation of the stable path $SABS$.

### 4.3 Dynamic Behavior with a Fixed Exchange Rate

Suppose now that the government possesses a stock of foreign money $R$ and uses it to stabilize the exchange rate. This is of course equivalent to stabilizing the price level at some level $\bar{P}$. How does the economy evolve over time?

The easiest way to proceed is by examining the budget constraints of the private sector and the government in turn. The private sector can acquire assets only by spending less than its income. Let us define *private savings* as the excess of private income over spending,

$$S = Y - T - C(Y - T, W). \tag{12}$$

Then from the budget constraint and the fact that the price level is pegged, we immediately know that

$$\dot{W} = \frac{\dot{M}}{\bar{P}} + \dot{F} = S. \tag{13}$$

But private savings is in turn a function of private wealth, with $\partial S/\partial W = -C_2 < 0$. So (13) is a differential equation in $W$, and since $\partial S/\partial W$ is negative it is stable.

How is saving allocated between domestic and foreign money? This is determined by the portfolio balance condition (4). As long as investors believe that the government will continue to peg the price level, $\pi$ will be zero and there will be a stable relationship between wealth and money holdings. Of a change in wealth, a proportion $L$ will be allocated to domestic money and $1 - L$ to foreign money, so we have

$$\frac{\dot{M}}{\bar{P}} = LS,$$

$$\dot{F} = (1 - L)S. \tag{14}$$

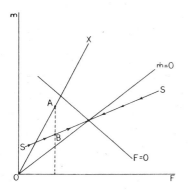

**Figure 4.4**
Windfall capital gains from the transition to a floating rate

exchange rate is allowed to float, real balances jump so as to put the system
on the stable path SS. So the economy moves suddenly from A to B.
Because the nominal money supply is fixed at any instant, this occurs
through a jump in the price level.

The argument I have just made depends on the assumption that when
reserves run out, the economy's position is to the right of the intersection
of the expansion path OX with the stable path SS. Otherwise. the exchange
rate would fall instead of rising when reserves run out. But it is easily shown
that at the moment of exhaustion of reserves private wealth must be large
enough to put the economy in the assumed position.[5] So if there is no
speculation against the currency, the exhaustion of reserves will always
produce a discrete jump in the price level, causing a windfall capital loss.

But investors cannot have expected such a capital loss to happen, because
they would have avoided it. In particular, by exchanging domestic for
foreign money an instant before reserves are exhausted, a speculator could
earn an infinite rate of return. If everyone tried to do this, the government's
reserves would of course be eliminated; the prospect of this would cause
speculators to attempt to get out of domestic money still earlier, and so on.

The upshot of all this is that if investors correctly anticipate events, the
reserves of the government must be eliminated by a speculative attack that
enables all investors to avoid windfall capital losses. Consider what such a
speculative attack involves. From the government's point of view, it represents a liquidation of its reserves. From the point of view of domestic
residents, however. what they are doing is altering the composition of their
portfolio, exchanging domestic for foreign money. If we let $M$, $F$ be the
asset holdings of domestic residents just before the attack, and $M'$, $F'$ be

holdings afterward, we know that

$$\frac{M'}{\bar{P}} = \frac{M}{\bar{P}} - R,$$

$$F' = F + R. \tag{18}$$

Immediately following the attack, the economy is on a flexible rate regime. As discussed in section 4.2, the immediate postcrisis price level $P'$ can be determined from asset holdings:

$$P' = M'G(F') \tag{19}$$

or

$$\frac{P'}{\bar{P}} = \left(\frac{M'}{\bar{P}}\right)G(F')$$

$$= \left(\frac{M}{\bar{P}} - R\right)G(F + R).$$

In order that there be no windfall capital loss, the speculative attack must not lead to a discrete change in the price level—that is, we must have $P' = \bar{P}$ or $P'/\bar{P} = 1$. It is this condition that determines when a balance-of-payments crisis occurs, for both $M/\bar{P}$ and $F$ are, under a fixed rate, functions of private wealth $W$. So the condition $P'/\bar{P} = 1$ can be written as an implicit function in $R$ and $W$,

$$1 = [L(O)W - R]G[W - L(O)W + R]. \tag{20}$$

Equation (20) defines a *threshold* in $W$, $R$ space. Under a pegged exchange rate $W$ and $R$ gradually evolve over time until they cross the threshold. Then there is a sudden balance-of-payments crisis, which eliminates the remaining reserves and forces a transition to a floating exchange rate.

Figure 4.5 shows what happens in the crisis. Just before the speculative attack the economy is on the fixed-rate expansion path $OX$; just after, it is on the flexible-rate stable path $SS$. Suppose that at the moment of the attack, private asset holdings are represented by point $A$. In the attack investors reallocate their portfolio. moving southeast along the line of constant wealth $WW$ to point $B$. The increase in holdings of foreign money is achieved by acquiring the government's reserves $R$.

Suppose that at the time of the crisis, private wealth had been larger—that is, $WW$ had been further to the right. It is then obvious from the diagram that the reserves acquired from the government must also have

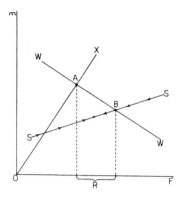

**Figure 4.5**
The elimination of reserves by a speculative attack

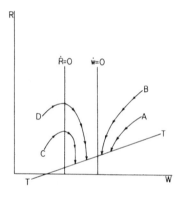

**Figure 4.6**
The approach to a crisis

been larger. This establishes that the threshold at which a crisis occurs is upward sloping in $W$, $R$ space.

The approach to the crisis is illustrated in figure 4.6, where the threshold (20) is represented by $TT$; it is upward sloping and cuts the horizontal axis to the left of $\dot{R} = 0$.[6] We can learn something about the factors determining the timing of a crisis by comparing some representative paths like those leading from $A$, $B$, $C$, and $D$. $B$ differs from $A$, and $D$ from $C$, only in there being a higher initial level of reserves. In each case we can see that when reserves are larger, the absolute value of the change in private wealth before the crisis is larger. Since $\dot{W}$ is independent of $R$, this means that the time until the crisis is longer. Thus we confirm the intuitively plausible result that the length of time for which a government can peg the exchange rate is an increasing function of its initial reserves.

When the government policy is certain, then an economy with a balance-of-payments problem will pass through three stages: a period of gradually declining reserves, a sudden speculative attack. and a postcrisis period during which the currency gradually depreciates. The next step is to examine what happens if government policy is uncertain.

## 4.5 Speculation When Government Policy Is Uncertain: The "One-way Option"

Many different kinds of uncertainty could be introduced into the preceding analysis. I will deal with only one source of uncertainty: incomplete knowledge on the part of investors about how much of its reserves the government is willing to use to defend the exchange rate. This produces the possibility of alternating balance-of-payments crises and recoveries of confidence.

To consider the simplest case, suppose that the government's reserves can be divided into a primary reserve $R_1$, which investors know it will commit to the defense of the exchange rate, and a secondary reserve $R_2$, which it may or may not be willing to use. We may suppose that the market believes that $R_2$ will be used with probability $\alpha < 1$. I also assume that once the government has used any part of $R_2$ to defend the exchange rate, the market can be sure that it will use all of it.

As before, we suppose that there is an initial period during which reserves gradually decline. Eventually there comes a point at which a speculative attack would take place *if $R_1$ were the only reserve*, but at that point there would not yet be a crisis if the market knew that the reserves committed to defending the exchange rate were $R_1 + R_2$. What happens?

The answer is that the speculative attack takes place, as investors acquire the whole of the government's remaining primary reserve $R_1$. If the government then commits its secondary reserve to maintain the value of the currency, investors reverse themselves and exchange foreign for domestic money, producing a recovery of the government's reserves.

To see why this must be so, consider two points. First, in the absence of transaction costs the speculative attack is costless. Investors need only hold a higher proportion of foreign money for an infinitesimally short period until it becomes clear whether or not the secondary reserve will be used. Second, if the capital outflow did not take place, there would be a possibility of a windfall capital loss. Suppose that there were no speculative attack, or that the attack was not large enough to completely eliminate the primary reserve. Then, if the government eventually decided not to commit the secondary reserve, when $R_1$ was exhausted there would be a discrete jump in the exchange rate—a capital loss that an individual wealth owner could have costlessly avoided. So there must be a speculative attack just as if there were no secondary reserve. Once the secondary reserve is committed, the risk of capital loss has of course been eliminated, and the holdings of domestic money return to their previous level.

We can obviously extend this analysis to a whole series of reserves: $R_1, \ldots, R_n$. The effect is to produce a series of balance-of-payments crises, each ended by the government's decision to commit the next reserve.

## 4.6  Summary and Conclusions

This chapter has been concerned with the circumstances in which a balance-of-payments problem—defined as a situation in which a country is gradually losing reserves—becomes a balance-of-payments crisis in which speculators attack the currency. I have shown that balance-of-payments crises are a natural outcome of maximizing behavior by investors. When the government's willingness to use reserves to defend the exchange rate is uncertain, there can be a series of crises in which capital flows out of the country, then returns, before the issue is finally resolved.

The analysis is subject to two major limitations. The first is that it is based on a highly simplified macroeconomic model. This makes it easier to develop the main points of the argument, but it means that the analysis of the factors triggering a balance-of-payments crisis is incomplete. The second limitation is that the assumption that only two assets are available places an unrealistic constraint on the possible actions of the government because the only way it can peg the exchange rate is by selling its reserves. In a more realistic model we would have to allow for the possibility of other policies to stabilize the exchange rate, such as open-market sales of securities or intervention in the forward market. Despite these limitations the analysis is suggestive and does help explain why efforts to defend fixed exchange rates so often lead to crises.

## Appendix: The Determination of the Price Level under Flexible Rates

In section 4.2 I derived a relationship between asset stocks and the price level under flexible rates from the requirement that the economy be on the stable path in figure 4.2. An alternative algebraic derivation is the following:

The dynamic system (10), linearized around the steady-state values $\bar{m}, \bar{F}$, can be written

$$\begin{bmatrix} \dot{m} \\ \dot{F} \end{bmatrix} = \begin{bmatrix} -\dfrac{\pi_1 \bar{m}}{\bar{F}} & \pi_1 \left( \dfrac{\bar{m}}{\bar{F}} \right)^2 \\ -C_2 & -C_2 \end{bmatrix} \begin{bmatrix} m - \bar{m} \\ F - \bar{F} \end{bmatrix}. \tag{A1}$$

This system has the characteristic values

$$\lambda_1 = -\frac{1}{2}\left( C_2 + \frac{\pi_1 \bar{m}}{\bar{F}} \right) - \frac{1}{2}\sqrt{\left( C_2 + \frac{\pi_1 \bar{m}}{\bar{F}} \right)^2 - 4C_2\pi_1\left( \frac{\bar{m}}{\bar{F}} \right)^2} < 0,$$

$$\lambda_2 = -\frac{1}{2}\left( C_2 + \frac{\pi_1 \bar{m}}{\bar{F}} \right) + \frac{1}{2}\sqrt{\left( C_2 + \frac{\pi_2 \bar{m}}{\bar{F}} \right)^2 - 4C_2\pi_1\left( \frac{\bar{m}}{\bar{F}} \right)^2} > 0.$$

A solution must be of the form

$$\begin{bmatrix} m - \bar{m} \\ F - \bar{F} \end{bmatrix} = \begin{bmatrix} a_{11} & a_{12} \\ a_{21} & a_{22} \end{bmatrix} \begin{bmatrix} e^{\lambda_1 t} \\ e^{\lambda_2 t} \end{bmatrix}. \tag{A2}$$

If the system is to converge to a steady state, the initial condition must be such that $a_{12} = a_{22} = 0$, so $m$ and $F$ converge exponentially to $\bar{m}, \bar{F}$. But then we have

$$\dot{m} = \lambda_1(m - \bar{m})$$

$$= \pi_1\left( \frac{\bar{m}}{\bar{F}} \right)(m - \bar{m}) + \pi_1\left( \frac{\bar{m}}{\bar{F}} \right)^2 (F - \bar{F}), \tag{A3}$$

which defines the stable path

$$m - \bar{m} = \frac{\pi_1(\bar{m}/\bar{F})^2}{\pi_1 + \pi_1(\bar{m}/\bar{F})}(F - \bar{F}).$$

The rest of the argument in the text then follows.

# 5  Target Zones and Exchange Rate Dynamics

Wide attention has been given to proposals to establish "target zones" for exchange rates. Indeed, we are already arguably living under a weak target zone regime. The reference zones established under the Louvre Accord, and in subsequent consultations among the major industrial nations, are not publicly announced, nor is it clear how strongly they will be defended, but the principle of setting limits on the range of exchange rate variation has been established.

A target zone differs from a fixed rate regime in allowing a fairly wide range of variation for the exchange rate around some reference rate. Williamson (1985), for example, called for a range of 10 percent on either side of the central rate. The appeal of this idea, as opposed to a more strict pegging, is that a target zone should not need as much maintenance. Some exchange rate flexibility would be allowed, and thus the defense of the exchange rate would become only an occasional problem rather than a continuous preoccupation.

With the widespread attention given to target zones and the apparent drift of actual exchange rate policy toward something that looks increasingly like such zones, one might have supposed that the theory of how a target zone system would work would be fully worked out. In particular, since the whole idea of target zones is that exchange rates will normally be inside the zone, one would expect considerable focus on how the exchange rate will actually behave inside the band. In fact, there is essentially no literature on this question. Even advocates of target zones, such as Williamson and Miller (1987), have not actually modeled the behavior of rates inside the zone; instead, they attempt to approximate a target zone by a continuous monetary policy of leaning against the wind.

Originally published in *Quarterly Journal of Economics* 56, 3 (August 1991), pp. 669–682.

The principal issue in modeling exchange rate dynamics under a target zone regime is the formation of expectations. A naive view would suppose that the exchange rate behaves as if the regime were one of free floating until the rate hits the edge of the band, whereupon the regime switches to a fixed rate. This cannot, however, be right. The existence of a band constrains possible future paths of the exchange rate; exchange markets, knowing this, should behave differently than they would were there no target zone. In other words, the existence of a band should affect exchange rate behavior even when the exchange rate is inside the band and the zone is not actively being defended.

This chapter offers a new approach to the modeling of exchange rate dynamics under a target zone regime. The approach is related to earlier work by Flood and Garber (1983), but the methods employed are different and, as it turns out, much simpler. More surprisingly, the analysis of target zones turns out to have a strong formal similarity to that of problems in option pricing and irreversible investment. This unexpected linkage with other areas may in itself be of some interest to readers who are not directly concerned with target zones.

The model used to exposit the logic of target zones is a minimalist monetary model. Clearly the next step is to move to more sophisticated and realistic underlying models. In work based on earlier versions of this chapter, Miller and Weller (1988) have shown how the same general approach may be applied to a Dornbusch-type model with intrinsic dynamics as well as the "extrinsic" dynamics that arise from a target zone.

The chapter is in five sections. Section 5.1 lays out the basic model and presents some intuition on the results. Section 5.2 derives an explicit solution for exchange rate behavior under a target zone, except for the question of tying down the ends of the S-curve (a concept whose meaning will become clear in context). Section 5.3 then tackles this issue, uncovering a fundamental similarity between target zones and option analysis. Section 5.4 considers the money supply behavior necessary to enforce the target zone. Finally, section 5.5 examines the behavior of an imperfectly credible target zone.

## 5.1 The Basic Model

We consider a minimalist log-linear monetary model of the exchange rate. Expressing all variables in natural logarithms, the exchange rate at any point in time is assumed equal to

$$s = m + v + \frac{\gamma E[ds]}{dt}, \tag{1}$$

where $s$ is the (log of the) spot price of foreign exchange, $m$ the domestic money supply, $v$ a shift term representing velocity shocks, and the last term is the expected rate of depreciation.

There are two "fundamental" variables in (1): the money supply and the velocity shift term. I will assume that monetary policy is passive; that is, $m$ is shifted only in order to maintain a target zone. Specifically, the monetary authority is prepared to reduce $m$ in order to prevent $s$ from exceeding some maximum value $\bar{s}$, and to increase $m$ to prevent $s$ from falling below some minimum value $\underline{s}$. As long as $s$ lies within the band between $\bar{s}$ and $\underline{s}$, the money supply remains unchanged. The actual money supply dynamics implied by this policy are best described in the context of a full solution of the model.

With no loss of generality, and some saving in notation, we can choose units to center the target zone around zero so that $\underline{s} = -\bar{s}$. The velocity term $v$ will be the only exogenous source of exchange rate dynamics. It will be assumed to follow a continuous-time random walk:

$$dv = \sigma\, dz. \tag{2}$$

There is no good economic reason for assuming a random walk on $v$. The assumption is made here for two reasons. First, the random walk assumption allows us to focus entirely on the dynamics caused by the presence of a target zone, as opposed to the effects of predictable future changes in $v$. Second, the random walk assumption gives rise to a simple analytic solution; more realistic target zone models with, say, some inherent auto-regression require the use of numerical methods (see Miller and Weller 1989).

This is the complete model. One might not at first suppose that there could be any interesting exchange rate dynamics arising from so simple a structure, yet it will yield some surprising insights about the functioning of a target zone. Before proceeding to algebraic analysis, it is useful to start with an intuitive approach to the effects of a target zone on exchange rate behavior. Figure 5.1 plots the exchange rate against $v$; the target zone is indicated by the broken lines that define a band that bounds the exchange rate between $-\bar{s}$ and $\bar{s}$. We consider the behavior of the exchange rate when starting with some initial money supply, say, $m = 0$.

Now a naive view would run as follows: Since $m$ is locally held constant and since $v$ follows a random walk, there should be no predictable change in

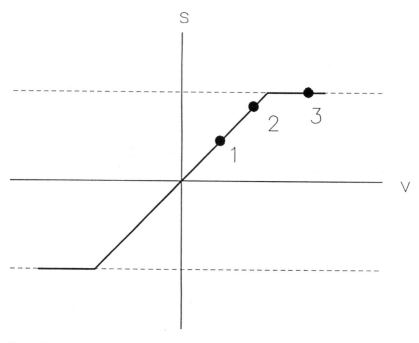

**Figure 5.1**

the exchange rate: $E[ds]/dt = 0$. Thus the exchange rate might be expected simply to equal $m + v$ inside the band, namely, to behave like a freely floating rate inside the target zone. If successive shocks to $v$ push the exchange rate to the edge of the band, then the money supply will be adjusted to prevent $s$ from drifting any further. Thus this naive view would suppose a relationship between $v$ and $s$ that looks like the heavy line in figure 5.1.

Why isn't this right? Suppose that it were the correct description of exchange rate behavior, and consider the situation at an exchange rate that is just inside the band, say, at point 2. Starting at point 2, if $v$ falls a little, the exchange rate would retreat down the 45-degree line to a point such as 1. If $v$ rises a little, however, the exchange rate will not rise by an equal amount because the monetary authority will act to defend the target zone. So the exchange rate will move to a point such as 3.

But this says that when we are near the top of the band, a fall in $v$ will reduce $s$ more than a rise in $v$ will increase $s$. Since $v$ is assumed to follow a random walk, *the expected rate of change of $s$ is negative*. Since expected depreciation enters the basic exchange rate equation (1), this negative rate

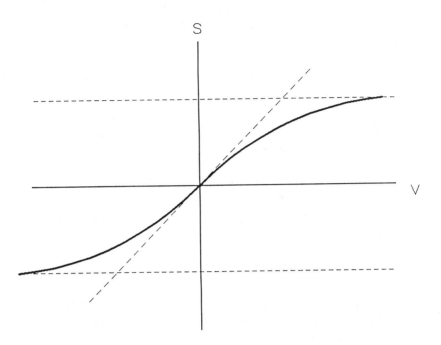

**Figure 5.2**

will affect the exchange rate: The exchange rate would be "dragged" down from 2 to a lower point. The same must be true at the bottom of the band. In effect the relationship between $v$ and $s$ must be bent as it approaches the edges of the target zone.

We cannot stop here, however. Once exchange rate behavior near the edges of the zone lies off the 45-degree line, this relationship will affect exchange rate expectations farther inside the zone as well. It seems intuitively obvious that repeated revisions of exchange rate expectations will lead to a relationship between $v$ and $s$ that looks like the S-shaped curve in figure 5.2, below the 45-degree line in the upper half of the target zone and above it in the lower half.

There are two important points to make about the S-curve in figure 5.2. First is the relationship between geometry and behavior. Note that the exchange rate lies below the 45-degree line in the upper half of the figure, below it in the lower half. By (1) this must mean that the expected rate of change of $s$ is negative in the upper portions and positive below. Yet how is this possible with $m$ constant and $v$ following a random walk? The answer lies in the *curvature* of the S. Since the S is concave in the upper half, even though the expected rate of change in v is zero, the expected rate of change of $s$ is negative, and conversely in the lower half. It is thus the concavity or convexity of the relationship between $v$ and $s$ that drags the relationship off the 45-degree line.

Second, note that the effect of the target zone on exchange rates is stabilizing. With a constant money supply and no target zone, the exchange rate would simply move up and down the 45-degree line. The S-curve in figure 5.2, however, is flatter than the 45-degree line: Shocks to velocity have a smaller effect on exchange rates, and thus the exchange rate itself has less variation than under a free float. This reduction in variation occurs even while the exchange rate is inside the band, and thus no current effort is being made to stabilize it.

This is about as far as we can go using rough intuition and geometry. The next step is to develop an explicit analysis of the S-curve.

## 5.2 Algebraic Analysis

We have implicitly defined equilibrium as a relationship between the fundamental variables $m$ and $v$ and the exchange rate. More formally, we want to determine a relationship

$$s = g(m, v, \bar{s}, \underline{s}) \tag{3}$$

that is consistent with (1) and the assumed monetary behavior. The S-curve in figure 5.2 is a partial relationship between $v$ and $s$ for a given $m$. We will define (3) initially by finding a family of such curves.

Suppose that we hold $m$ constant; that is, we consider a situation where $s$ lies inside the band. Then the only source of expected changes in $s$ lies in the random movement of $v$. By the usual rules of stochastic calculus, we have

$$\frac{E[ds]}{dt} = \left(\frac{\sigma^2}{2}\right) g_{vv}(m, v, \bar{s}, \underline{s}). \tag{4}$$

Substituting (4) into (1), we have

$$g(m, v, \bar{s}, \underline{s}) = m + v + \left(\frac{\gamma\sigma^2}{2}\right) g_{vv}(m, v, \underline{s}, \bar{s}). \tag{5}$$

The general solution of (5) has the form

$$g(m, v, \bar{s}, \underline{s}) = m + v + Ae^{\rho v} + Be^{-\rho v}, \tag{6}$$

where

$$\rho = \left(\frac{2}{\gamma\sigma^2}\right)^{1/2}, \tag{7}$$

and $A$ and $B$ are constants still to be determined.

We can further simplify the problem by appealing to symmetry. Suppose that $m = 0$. Then we would expect the relationship to go through the middle of figure 5.2; we should have $s = 0$ when $v = 0$. This can only be true if $B = -A$, so we simplify (6) to

$$g(m, v, \bar{s}, \underline{s}) = m + v + A[e^{\rho v} - e^{-\rho v}]. \tag{8}$$

To get the S-curve illustrated in figure 5.2, we clearly need to have $A < 0$. This will yield a value of $s$ that falls increasingly below $m + v$ for positive $v$, increasingly above for negative $v$. However, we need something else to determine the precise value of $A$. Equivalently, we may note that the value of $A$ determines where (8) intersects the edges of the band. The problem of determining $A$ is thus equivalently viewed as a problem of tying down the ends of the S.

## 5.3   Tying Down the Ends of the S

The choice of $A$, which determines the S-curve for any given $m$, must be such as to produce the following result: *The curve defined by (8) must be tangent to the edges of the band.* This condition ties down the ends of the S.

To see why this condition must obtain, we consider what would happen if it did not. Figure 5.3 illustrates part of a hypothetical S-curve that crosses the band rather than forming a tangency. For this to be the right S-curve, a point such as 2, which is very close to the edge of the band, must represent an equilibrium value of $s$ given $v$.

Now the construction of the S-curve (8) is such that any curve (a curve corresponding to any value of $A$) is self-validating. If the values of $s$ corresponding to future realizations of $v$ are expected to lie on a curve passing through the current $v$, $s$, then the current $s$ is in fact an equilibrium. Specifically, if a small fall in $v$ will bring us to point 1 while a small increase will bring us to point 3, then point 2 will be an equilibrium.

But if point 2 is right at the edge of the band, then an increase in $v$ will not lead to 3 because $s$ will not be allowed to rise. Instead, it will lead to 3', a point with a lower value of $s$. This in turn means that the expected rate of appreciation of $s$ will be *larger* than that consistent with equilibrium at point 2; the $s$ corresponding to that $v$ would instead be lower, say, at 2'. This means that 2 was not an equilibrium after all. So it is

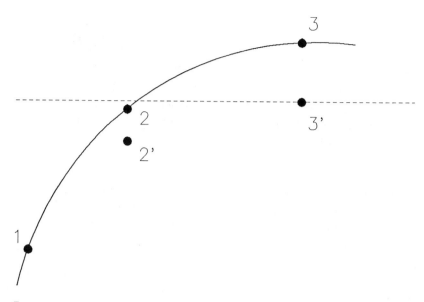

**Figure 5.3**

not possible to approach the edge of the band on an S-curve that actually crosses that edge. The only possible curves are those that are just tangent to the edge.

Evidently what we have here is a result that is closely related to the high-order contact, or smooth pasting, conditions that occur in option theory and in the analysis of irreversible investment. The analogy with option pricing comes as a surprise. However, we can show that there is indeed an option-pricing interpretation of a target zone.

To see this, note that the basic exchange rate equation (1) can be viewed as arising from a more underlying equation

$$s_t = \left(\frac{1}{\gamma}\right) \int_t^\infty (m + v)e^{-(1/\gamma)(\tau - t)}\, d\tau. \tag{9}$$

Differentiating (9) with respect to $t$ yields (1). Thus the current exchange rate may be viewed as a sort of present discounted value of future realizations of $(m + v)$.

Now imagine an asset whose price is the present discounted value of $m + v$, with $m$ held constant at its current level, say, $m_0$. The value of this asset would be

$$\tilde{s}_t = \left(\frac{1}{\gamma}\right) \int_t^\infty (m_0 + v)e^{-(1/\gamma)(\tau - t)}\, d\tau. \tag{10}$$

The actual exchange rate may be viewed as the price of a compound asset. This asset consists of the imaginary asset whose price is determined by (10), plus the right to sell the asset at a price $\underline{s}$, plus the obligation to sell at the price $\bar{s}$ on demand.

The deviation of the S-curve from the 45-degree line may now be viewed as the combined price of the two options. Not surprisingly, the requirement to sell on demand at $\bar{s}$ becomes more important the higher the $\bar{s}$ is, so the price of the compound asset falls below $\bar{s}$ at high $v$. Conversely, the right to sell at $\underline{s}$ supports the value of the asset at low $v$.

The options-pricing analogy could be followed up further, but the basic point is that at a formal level the target zone is essentially the same as a variety of problems involving choice under uncertainty. S-shaped curves tangent to a band at top and bottom have appeared recently in some seemingly unrelated papers on entry and exit under exchange rate fluctuations by Dixit (1989) and Krugman (1988) and in analysis of irreversible investment problems by Dumas (1988).

We may determine $A$ then by the requirement that the curve (8) be tangent to the band at top and bottom. Let $\bar{v}$ be the value of $v$ at which $s$ reaches the top of the band. Then we have

$$\bar{s} = \bar{v} + A[e^{\rho\bar{v}} - e^{\rho\bar{v}}] \tag{11}$$

and

$$0 = 1 + \rho A[e^{\rho\bar{v}} + e^{\rho\bar{v}}] \tag{12}$$

These equations implicitly define $A$ and $\bar{v}$.

### 5.4  Money Supply Behavior

So far the chapter has not been explicit about the monetary behavior implied by the defense of a target zone. However, this is easily derived. Let $\bar{v}$ be the value of $v$ at which a particular S-curve touches the top of the band. This is of course dependent on the money supply: $\bar{v} = \bar{v}(m, \bar{s}, \underline{s})$. If $v$ goes beyond $\bar{v}$, the money supply must be reduced. This will shift the market to a new S-curve displaced to the right; the money supply reduction must always be such as to imply that at the current $v$ the market is at the top of the new S-curve. What we will see then is a family of curves, as illustrated in figure 5.4.

The dynamics of the money supply can perhaps best be illustrated by considering a possible cycle. Suppose that initially the market is at point 1 and that for a while there is a series of positive shocks to $v$. Initially this

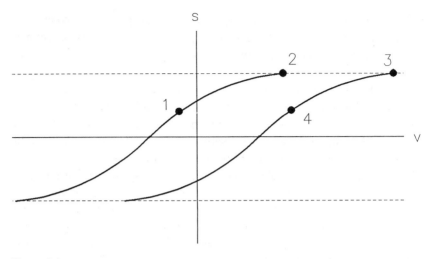

**Figure 5.4**

will move the market along the original curve until point 2 is reached. Any further increase in $v$ will, however, be offset by reductions in $m$, so the exchange rate would remain constant as the market moves from 2 to 3. Next suppose that $v$ starts to have negative shocks. Then the market will not retrace its steps because the monetary authority will not react to shocks that push $s$ into the band. Thus the market will move back down a new S-curve to a point such as 4.

In this family of S-curves the market stays on any one curve as long as $v$ remains within the range where $s$ lies inside the band. The money supply shifts whenever the edge of the band is reached, placing the market on a new curve. The monetary behavior is identical to what would occur under a gold standard with costly shipment of gold: Specie flows out whenever the upper gold point is reached and does not return unless the lower gold point is hit.

We can write a simple expression for the whole family of curves in figure 5.4. Let $A$ be determined so that the curve is tangent for some particular $m$. Then the whole family of curves is defined by

$$g(m, v, \bar{s}, \underline{s}) = m + v + A[e^{\rho(m+v)} - e^{-\rho(m+v)}] \tag{13}$$

with the same $A$. Whenever positive shocks to $v$ push (13) to the edge of the band, $m$ will be reduced to keep $m + v$ constant. Clearly this will keep $s$ at the edge of the band and also preserve the tangency.

It follows that we can draw the whole family of S-curves as a single curve in $(m + v)$, $s$ space, as shown in figure 5.5. The edges of the band now

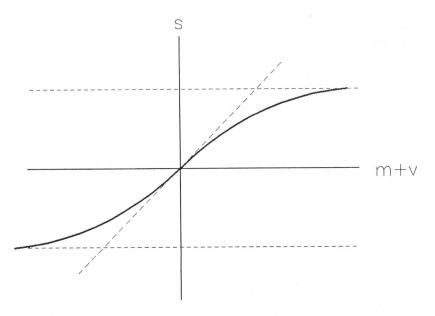

**Figure 5.5**

in effect represent reflecting barriers. Whenever $s$ hits the edge of the band, $m$ adjusts to keep $m + v$ from going any farther. If shocks move $s$ back into the band, $m$ remains unchanged and thus $m + v$ is allowed to change.

## 5.5 Imperfect Credibility

Up to this point we have been assumed that the commitment to defend the target zone is completely credible. One might wonder whether the results are fragile, whether some lack of credibility will completely undermine the description of exchange rate behavior. Indeed, some economists have been concerned that an imperfectly credible target zone could lead to instability, with markets driving the exchange rate to the edge of the band in order to test the authorities' resolve. We can show that this is not the case in this model.

Suppose that the market does not know whether the monetary authority is prepared to alter policy to defend the zone. A value $\phi$ is assigned to the probability that the zone will in fact be defended and $1 - \phi$ to the probability that it will not. The only way to resolve the issue is to see what happens when the edge of the band is reached.

When the exchange rate reaches the end of the band, one of two things will happen. Either the monetary authorities will reveal their willingness to do what is necessary, making the zone fully credible thereafter, or they will not, and the market will discover that it is living under a free float after all. If the zone proves credible, the exchange rate will jump to the full credibility locus derived in section 5.3. If it does not, the exchange rate will jump to its free float value.

What ties this down is the requirement that there not be an infinite rate of expected capital gain when the target zone is challenged. The *expected* jump of the exchange rate must be zero. Let $\tilde{v}$ be the value of $v$ at which the target zone must be defended. Then, if the target zone is proved credible, $s$ jumps to the full credibility value $g(m, \tilde{v}, \bar{s}, \underline{s})$. If the zone proves to be a sham, $s$ jumps to its free floating value $m + \tilde{v}$. The condition of an expected zero jump may therefore be written

$$\bar{s} = \phi g(m, \tilde{v}, \bar{s}, \underline{s}) + (1 - \phi)(m + \tilde{v}), \tag{14}$$

which implicitly defines $\tilde{v}$.

Once $\tilde{v}$ is known, the behavior of the exchange rate inside the band can be determined. Within the band $s$ must still lie on an S-curve of the form (8), with $A$ chosen so that

$$\bar{s} = m + \tilde{v} + A[e^{\rho\tilde{v}} - e^{-\rho\tilde{v}}]. \tag{15}$$

The situation is illustrated in figure 5.6. The full credibility locus is shown along with the tangency point $\tilde{v}$. If there is to be a zero expected jump in

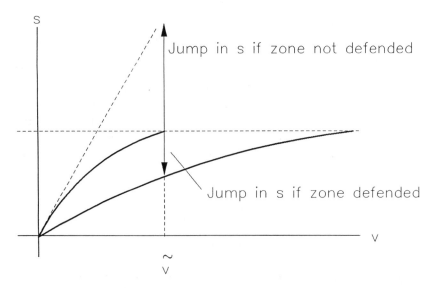

**Figure 5.6**

$s$, then $\tilde{v}$ must lie between $\bar{v}$ and the 45-degree line. The imperfect credibility exchange rate behavior is then seen to be a curve that is steeper than the full credibility locus but still flatter than the 45-degree line. That is, the target zone is less stabilizing if it is imperfectly credible, but it is still stabilizing. Also it is apparent that the extent of stabilization depends on the degree of credibility. As $\phi$ approaches 1, the imperfect credibility locus approaches the full credibility one; as $\phi$ goes to zero, it approaches the 45-degree line.

## Postscript

An early version of this chapter was presented in November 1987; a literature of several dozen papers using related methodology has already emerged. Several of the important extensions to the results should be mentioned.

First, Froot and Obstfeld (1989a) have recast the formalization in a somewhat different way, by positing directly that the central bank places limits on the range of variation of an otherwise stochastic fundamental. This approach allows the use of known results from Harrison (1985), placing the analysis on a more solid formal footing.

Flood and Garber (1989) have examined the case in which the central bank makes discrete interventions to defend the band. This extension is of interest in its own right and provides a rather neat way of deriving the smooth pasting result for infinitesimal interventions.

Miller and Weller (1989) have developed a geometric technique for analyzing cases in which the assumed stochastic process does not lead to a closed-form analytical solution. Their work shows that the intuition derived from the simpler models carries over when more realistic assumptions, such as autoregressive velocity, are made.

Bertola and Caballero (1990) have extended the analysis to the case where drift in the fundamental variables can provoke realignments, the shifting of the band itself.

Finally, in Krugman (1989) a bridge is built between the target zone model and the older literature on speculative attack; smooth pasting is shown to be a limiting case that emerges when reserves are sufficiently large.

# 6    Speculative Attacks on
        Target Zones

There are two extensive theoretical literatures that emphasize the interaction between shifts between fixed and floating exchange rates, on one hand, and expectations, on the other. The speculative attack literature, in which the seminal insight of Salant and Henderson (1978) was applied by Krugman (1979), Flood and Garber (1984), and many others to exchange rates, focused on the collapse of fixed rate systems; the stochastic target zone literature, building on the initial contribution of Krugman (1991), focuses on the behavior of floating rates subject to limits. There are evident affinities between these two literatures, already noted by Flood and Garber (1989). This chapter attempts to build an explicit bridge.

To do this, we consider a model in which the monetary authority uses unsterilized intervention to attempt to keep the exchange rate within a target zone, but has limited reserves. Because these reserves are limited, the target zone may be unsustainable. A potentially unsustainable target zone, not surprisingly, has different implications for exchange rate behavior than a fully credible one.

The chapter is in five sections. Section 6.1 lays out the basic exchange rate model and derives its behavior under a pure exchange rate float. Section 6.2 considers the effect of a one-sided exchange rate target in a situation in which the monetary authority has "small" reserves (in a sense that will become apparent). This analysis turns out not to yield the "smooth pasting" result of the now-standard target zone model but instead to yield a result closer to that found in the earlier speculative attack literature. Section 6.3 then examines how the result changes as the monetary authority's reserves get larger and shows how there is a transition to the smooth pasting equilibrium. Sections 6.4 and 6.5 apply the analysis to the case of

Originally published in Paul Krugman and Marcus Miller (eds.), *Target Zones and Currency Bands*, Oxford: Oxford University Press, 1991.

an occasionally collapsing gold standard, which we show can usefully be regarded as the boundary between two one-side target zones.

## 6.1 The Basic Model

We consider a basic log-linear monetary model of the exchange rate. The exchange rate at any point in time is determined by

$$s = m + v + \frac{\gamma E[ds]}{dt}, \tag{1}$$

where $s$ is the log of the price of foreign exchange, $m$ the log of the money supply, and $v$ a money demand shock term (incorporating shifts in real income, velocity, etc.); the last term captures the effect of expected depreciation.

Money demand is assume to follow a random walk with drift:

$$dv = \mu \, dt + \sigma \, dz. \tag{2}$$

As Miller and Weller (1989) have shown, more complex processes, notably autoregressive ones, can be incorporated into the analysis without changing the qualitative results. We stick with this process for simplicity.

The general solution to the model defined by (1) and (2) for a fixed money supply has by now become familiar (e.g., see Froot and Obstfeld 1989b). It takes the form

$$s = m + v + \gamma\mu + Ae^{\alpha_1 v} + Be^{\alpha_2 v}, \tag{3}$$

where $\alpha_1$, $\alpha_2$ are parameters that will be determined in a moment, and $A$ and $B$ are free parameters that need to be tied down by the economics of the situation.

To determine $\alpha_1$ and $\alpha_2$, we first note that by applying Ito's lemma, we have

$$\frac{E[ds]}{dt} = \mu + \mu[\alpha_1 Ae^{\alpha_1 v} + \alpha_2 Be^{\alpha_2 v}] + \frac{\sigma^2}{2}[\alpha_1^2 Ae^{\alpha_1 v} + \alpha_2^2 Be^{\alpha_2 v}]. \tag{4}$$

Substituting (4) back into (1), and comparing it with (3), we find that the roots are

$$\alpha_1 = \frac{-\gamma\mu + \sqrt{\gamma^2\mu^2 + 2\gamma\sigma^2}}{\gamma\sigma^2} > 0,$$

$$\alpha_2 = \frac{-\gamma\mu - \sqrt{\gamma^2\mu^2 + 2\gamma\sigma^2}}{\gamma\sigma^2} < 0. \tag{5}$$

We can now turn to the economic interpretation of (3). The first three terms in (3) evidently represent a sort of "fundamental" exchange rate: They reflect the combination of money supply, money demand, and the known drift in money demand. The other terms represent a deviation of the exchange rate from this fundamental value.

Suppose that the money supply were expected to remain unchanged at its initial level forever. Notice that $v$ can take on any value. It seems reasonable to exclude solutions for the exchange rate that deviate arbitrarily far from the fundamental level when $v$ takes on large positive or negative values. Thus under a pure float, in which the monetary authority is expected to remain passive whatever the exchange rate may do, we may assume that $A = B = 0$. The exchange rate equation under a pure float is therefore

$$s = m + v + \gamma\mu. \tag{6}$$

### 6.2   An Exchange Rate Target with "Small" Reserves

Now let us suppose that instead of being passive, the monetary authority attempts to place an upper limit on the price of foreign exchange. Specifically the monetary authority is willing to buy foreign exchange in an unsterilized intervention, up to the limit of its reserves, when the exchange rate goes above some level $s_{max}$. If these reserves are small enough (we will calculate the critical size below), this attempt will lead to a speculative attack in which the whole of the reserves are suddenly exhausted when the exchange rate reaches $s_{max}$.

We start by defining the initial money supply as the sum of reserves and domestic credit:

$$m = \ln(D + R). \tag{7}$$

Following the speculative attack, the money supply will fall to

$$m' = \ln(D). \tag{8}$$

Figure 6.1 illustrates the equilibrium before and after the speculative attack. After the attack the exchange rate will be freely floating, with money supply $m'$, so the postattack exchange rate equation is

$$s = m' + v + \gamma\mu, \tag{9}$$

shown in figure 6.1 as the locus $F'F'$.

The attack will occur when $v$ reaches the level at which the reduction in the money supply that results from the attack validates itself, by leading to the exchange rate $s_{max}$. This is shown in figure 6.1 as point $C$ and corre-

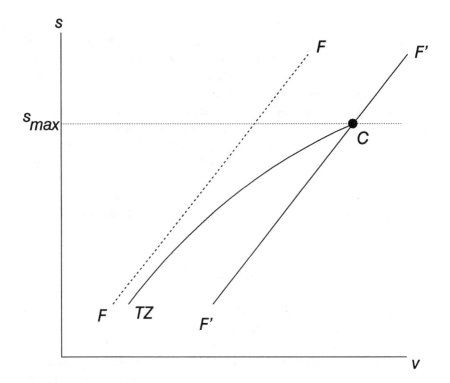

**Figure 6.1**

sponds to the level of $v$, $v'$ such that

$$s_{max} = m' + v' + \gamma\mu. \tag{10}$$

What about the exchange rate before the speculative attack? First, we note that since a regime change will be triggered if $v$ goes above a certain level, we can no longer use a no-bubbles argument to require $A = 0$ in equation (3). (Since this exchange rate target is one-sided, there is no lower limit on $v$, so we still must have $B = 0$). The pre-attack exchange rate equation is therefore

$$s = m + v + \gamma\mu + Ae^{\alpha_1 v}. \tag{11}$$

To tie down $A$, we use the standard speculative attack argument: Given that there must be no foreseeable jump in the exchange rate, we must choose $A$ so that $s = s_{max}$ when $v = v'$. It is apparent from figure 6.1 that this requires that $A < 0$. In other words, until the attack, the knowledge that the monetary authority will attempt to defend the currency will tend to hold down the price of foreign exchange. This may be seen in figure 6.1 from the fact that the relationship between $v$ and $s$ before the attack lies everywhere below the free float relationship $FF$ corresponding to the initial money supply $m$.

When reserves are small, then, the monetary authority fails in its effort to enforce an exchange rate target. The knowledge that it will try supports the currency, but eventually the target is overrun by a speculative attack. Notice that smooth pasting nowhere makes its appearance in this analysis. Indeed the pre-attack schedule in figure 6.1 is not tangent to the exchange rate target.

Our next step is to enlarge the monetary authority's reserves and to show that if these reserves are sufficiently large, a smooth pasting solution emerges.

### 6.3  A Target Zone with Large Reserves

A variety of alternative potential speculative attack scenarios can be generated by varying the parameter $A$ in equation (11). In figure 6.2 we show the curves traced out by increasingly negative values of $A$. A small absolute value of $A$ corresponds to a speculative attack at $C_1$. A larger absolute value of $A$ would produce an attack somewhere to the right of $C_1$, and this attack would consume more reserves because the implied fall in the money supply—measured as the horizontal distance from the attack point to the free float locus—would be larger.

It is immediately apparent, however, that one cannot in this way generate arbitrarily large speculative attacks. The reason is that the family of curves corresponding to different (negative) values of $A$ all turn downward at some point, and for a sufficiently negative $A$ the maximum of the curve lies below $s_{max}$. But it is not possible for the exchange rate pre-attack to lie on a locus that passes above $s_{max}$ before the attack takes place, since that would trigger the central bank's intervention.

The upshot is that the analysis of the previous section is valid only if the size of reserves is not too large, specifically if the free float locus corresponding to the money supply that would follow elimination of all reserves does not lie to the right of the point $C_2$ in figure 6.2.

If reserves are larger than this level, what must happen is that the pre-attack exchange rate equation is precisely that which leads to $C_2$. That is, $A$ must be chosen so that the exchange rate locus is tangent to the target. Smooth pasting therefore emerges, not as the general solution of this model but as its solution when the central bank's reserves are sufficiently large.

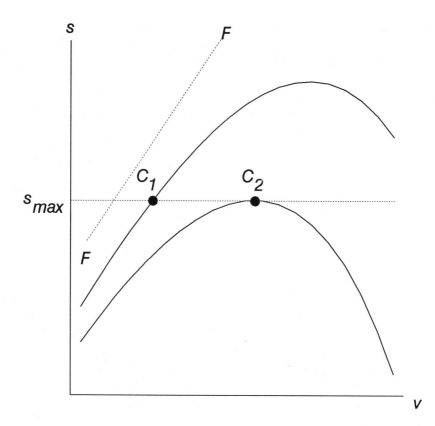

**Figure 6.2**

We can derive the critical level of reserves as follows. First, the exchange rate locus must be flat at $v'$:

$$\frac{ds}{dv} = 1 + \alpha_1 A e^{\alpha_1 v'} = 0. \tag{12}$$

It must also be true that the actual exchange rate at $v'$ is precisely the target rate $s_{max}$:

$$s_{max} = m + v' + \gamma\mu + A e^{\alpha_1 v'}. \tag{13}$$

Substituting (12) into (13), we find that

$$s_{max} = m + v' + \gamma\mu - \frac{1}{\alpha_1}. \tag{14}$$

But now notice that immediately following a speculative attack, the exchange rate must also be $s_{max}$:

$$s_{max} = m' + v' + \gamma\mu. \tag{15}$$

From (14) and (15) we can therefore determine the change in the money supply that occurs at the maximum size speculative attack:

$$m' - m = -\frac{1}{\alpha_1}. \tag{16}$$

But the change in the money supply in a speculative attack depends on the ratio of reserves to domestic credit.

$$m' - m = -\ln\left(\frac{D + R}{D}\right) = -\ln\left(1 + \frac{R}{D}\right), \tag{17}$$

so the nature of the equilibrium changes from speculative attack to smooth pasting when

$$\frac{R}{D} > e^{1/\alpha_1} - 1. \tag{18}$$

When this criterion is met, the central bank is able to hold the line at $s_{max}$ with an infinitesimal intervention that slightly reduces the money supply, shifting the relationship between $v$ and $s$ down. If $v$ then falls again, the exchange rate retreats down this new schedule; if $v$ rises, another intervention must take place. These successive interventions would gradually shift the exchange rate schedule to the right. As long as the reserves remain sufficiently large, $s_{max}$ will act as a reflecting barrier for the exchange rate, which will sometimes rise to $s_{max}$ and sometimes fall below it.

It is immediately apparent, however, that this process cannot go on indefinitely. When $v$ is high, the monetary authority loses reserves; when it falls again, it does not regain them. So there is a gradual loss of reserves, which will gradually shift the exchange rate schedule to the right. Eventually the level of reserves will fall to the critical level where a speculative attack becomes possible. At that point the next time that the exchange rate drifts up to the level $s_{max}$ there will be a full-scale speculative attack that eliminates all remaining reserves. In other words, a country that starts with large reserves will go through a smooth pasting phase where small interventions succeed in holding the line on the exchange rate, but there will be a gradual (albeit intermittent) drain on reserves and, as in conventional speculative attack models, eventually a crisis when reserves drop to a critical level.

This is not a very complicated analysis. Nonetheless, it makes several points that have been obscured in some of the recent literature on the subject.

First, it is clear from this model that looking at the case of bounded fundamentals is not equivalent to looking at the case of an exchange rate target. If we were to use the bounded fundamentals technique on this model, we would replace the idea of a target on $s$ with that of an upper limit on $m + v$. This would correctly capture the notion of what happens as long as reserves are sufficiently large to achieve the smooth pasting solution, but it would miss both the case where initial reserves are small and the logic of eventual crisis.

Second, in a related point, smooth pasting is not a general result of this model, the way it appears to be in the bounded fundamentals formulation. On the contrary, it is a special case that obtains when reserves are sufficiently large. Otherwise, the logic is that of speculative attack: The exchange rate is tied down by the requirement that there be no foreseeable jumps in the exchange rate.

Third, this model helps settle a controversy about the justification for the smooth pasting result. Some economists approaching the problem from the perspective of optimization models have questioned the use of the smooth pasting condition in ad hoc monetary models of this kind, arguing that a condition that arises from optimization is hard to justify when optimizing behavior is at best implicit. Those of us doing the ad hoc models have argued on the contrary that the condition can equally be seen as being implied by arbitrage.[1] In this model we see smooth pasting emerge as the limit of the "no foreseeable jumps" condition of a speculative attack model—essentially an arbitrage condition—when reserves are sufficiently large.

## 6.4   A Gold Standard Model

In the remainder of this chapter we make use of the type of analysis developed in earlier sections to attack a particular problem that has been the subject of several recent papers, that of the role of speculative attacks under a gold standard system.

Several papers, notably Buiter (1989) and Grilli (1989), have analyzed the problem of speculative attack in a gold standard model. Grilli implements the model empirically as well. However, as we will show shortly, straightforward application of the standard speculative attack model to the problem of a gold standard runs into serious problems. The standard model, in its simplest version, seems to suggest that there will be no speculative attacks on a gold standard, that such a regime will end with a whimper rather than a bang. This runs counter to both intuition and experience. Worse yet, with a little elaboration one runs into a a serious conceptual paradox that undermines the logic of the analysis. In this section we show how an economically reasonable model of speculative attacks on a gold standard can be created by treating such a standard as a boundary between two imperfectly sustainable target zones.

The basic gold standard model may be presented as a two-country version of the model at the beginning of this chapter. The exchange rate depends on the ratio of two countries' money supplies, a demand shock term, and the expected rate of depreciation:

$$s = m - m^* + v + \gamma \frac{E[ds]}{dt}. \tag{19}$$

Each country's money supply consists of domestic credit plus reserves:

$$m = \ln(D + R),$$
$$m^* = \ln(D^* + R^*). \tag{20}$$

Reserves, however, are now taken to consist of gold, which is in fixed world supply:

$$R + R^* = G. \tag{21}$$

As before, we need to specify a process for the money demand term. We will initially suppose that it is a simple random walk without drift—that is, $\mu = 0$. The implications of more complex stochastic processes are discussed below.

We suppose that the monetary authorities of the two countries stand ready to buy or sell gold to maintain fixed prices of their currencies in terms of gold, and hence in terms of each other. The implied exchange rate is $s_{par}$. This regime will continue until one country or the other runs out of gold.

The seemingly obvious assumptions are that as long as the regime is in effect, there will be no expected change in exchange rates, and that when the regime collapses, the exchange rate reverts to a free float. It turns out, however, that this combination of assumptions yields the economically implausible result that there are no speculative attacks.

To see why, first ask how reserves would appear to evolve if we assume that $E[ds]/dt = 0$. Then when $v$ rises, gold will flow from the first country to the second; when it falls, it will flow in the other direction. Ignoring the possibility of speculative attack, this process could continue until the ratio of money supplies reaches either a maximum or minimum value. The maximum value of $m - m^*$ occurs when all gold has flowed out of the first country. At that point we have

$$m = \ln(D) \tag{22}$$

and

$$m^* = \ln(D + G). \tag{23}$$

Similarly $m - m^*$ reaches a minimum when all the gold has flowed to the first country, so

$$m = \ln(D + G) \tag{24}$$

and

$$m^* = \ln(D). \tag{25}$$

In the conventional speculative attack literature we show the necessity of a speculative attack by noticing that if agents were naive and did not anticipate the possibility of regime collapse, there would be a foreseeable capital gain or loss at the moment of transition. Suppose then that agents were naive and did not realize that a regime change was in prospect. Would they be missing a profit opportunity? Under the assumption of naïveté, the gold standard would last until reserves of one country or another run out. Let's suppose that it is the first country that runs out of gold. It would run out at a level of $v$, $v_1$, determined by the condition

$$s_{\text{par}} = m - m^* + v_1. \tag{26}$$

If the exhaustion of the country's gold is followed by a transition to pure floating, the exchange rate following the transition would be determined by

$$s = m - m^* + v. \tag{27}$$

But by comparing (26) and (27), we find that

$$s = s_{\text{par}}. \tag{28}$$

That is, there is no jump in the exchange rate. This implies that there need not be any speculative attack.

This is an economically implausible conclusion. Matters become even worse if the process determining $v$ is not a simple random walk—if it has drift or autoregression. In that case one arrives not simply at an implausible result but at a paradox: Under some conditions a country may run out of reserves under a fixed rate *before* it meets the usual criterion for a speculative attack. This "gold standard paradox" has been the subject of several recent papers (Krugman and Rotemberg 1990; Buiter and Grilli 1990). However, in this chapter we focus only on the case of a random walk in which there is not strictly speaking a paradox, simply an implausible result.

What we show next is that a much more satisfactory result emerges if we view a gold standard not as a one-time regime that is gone once it has collapsed but instead as a regime that is reinstated when feasible. In this case, as we will see, the gold parity becomes a boundary between two target zones.

## 6.5    Gold Parity as a Boundary[2]

The analysis of speculative attacks on a gold standard can be made much more plausible if we make one assumption that is slightly different from the usual speculative attack setup. The necessary assumption is the following: *Central banks do not give up when they run out of gold.* Instead, they remain willing to buy gold at the par value and thus to reinstate a gold standard if the opportunity arises.

An example may convey the essence of this assumption. Suppose that our two countries are America and Britain and that they have established par values of gold of $35 and £7 per ounce. If both countries have positive gold reserves, this will peg the dollar-pound exchange rate at 5. Suppose, however, that America has run out of gold. Then the exchange rate may float above this level, say, at $7 per pound. The price of gold will be set by the willingness of the British central bank to sell it, at £7 per ounce.

We will assume that even though America has run out of gold, its central bank still remains willing to buy gold if the price falls to $35. (It would be willing to sell gold at that price also, but it doesn't have any to sell.) With an exchange rate of 7 the price of gold of course is $49, so there will be no current sales; if the exchange rate falls (the dollar appreciates) to 5, gold purchases will commence.

Conversely, if Britain has run out of gold, the exchange rate will float at a level below 5, but if it rises to 5, Britain's central bank will again buy gold. Consider what this implies. If the exchange rate is above 5, then everyone knows that when it falls to 5, America will buy gold and Britain sell it—which means that America will increase its money supply and Britain reduce its money supply. This means that when America is out of gold, and the exchange rate is floating, the float is *not* free. Instead, there is in effect a one-sided target zone in which there is a de facto commitment to support the pound with sterilized intervention if the dollar strengthens too much.

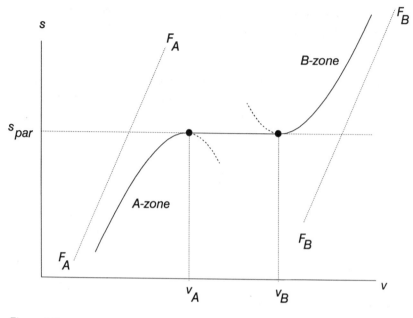

**Figure 6.3**

The reverse is also true: When Britain has run out of gold, the float is in effect a target zone with a commitment to support the dollar with sterilized intervention if the pound strengthens to its par value. This tells us that the par value implied by the prices at which each currency is pegged to gold may be regarded as a boundary between two one-sided target zones. In the lower zone, where America has all the gold—which we will call the A-zone—the dollar-pound exchange rate is held below its free-float locus by the prospect of U.S. gold sales and British gold purchases if the pound rises too much. In the B-zone, where Britain has all the gold, the rate is correspondingly held above its free-float locus.

If the world's gold stock is large enough, the picture looks like figure 6.3, which plots the exchange rate against $v$. (We will describe the case with insufficient gold backing for the world's currencies below.) The 45-degree lines represent the free-float loci—that is, the 45-degree line on the left represents how $s$ would vary with $v$ if America had all the gold and there was no prospect of future intervention, and the 45-degree line on the right the corresponding case with all gold in British hands. The actual relationship in the A-zone, however, is a curve that lies below the free-float locus and is tangent to the par value line at some value $v_A$, as which we have already seen for a one-sided target zone with large reserves. Similarly in the B-zone the relationship between $v$ and $s$ lies above the free-float locus and is tangent to the par value line at $v_B$.

The relationship between $v$ and $s$ is therefore indicated by the curve on the left up to $v_A$, the par value is sustained between $v_A$ and $v_B$, and $s$ follows the curve on the right for $v$ greater than $v_B$. Outside the range where the par value is sustained, the prospect of a return to the gold standard either supports or depresses the exchange rate.

What happens if $v$ starts within the range where the par value can be sustained and then drifts out of that range, say, to $v_B$? The answer is that as long as we are on the "flat," there will be a gradual American loss of gold. When $v_B$ is reached, however, there will be a speculative attack that leads to a discrete American loss of its remaining gold. The reason is that the postattack $v - s$ relationship is convex, so the variance term makes $E[ds]/dt$ positive. That is, when the gold standard collapses, the expected rate of dollar depreciation immediately goes from zero to some positive number, reducing relative American money demand—even if $v$ is expected to fall. Similarly, if $v$ drops to the bottom of the range, there will be a speculative attack that leads to a discrete British loss of its remaining gold.

The reason why the currency of the country that runs out of gold is expected to depreciate immediately following the gold exhaustion is somewhat ironic: It is the result of the expectation that the country will try to buy gold if its currency should subsequently appreciate to the par value, which therefore depresses its value under the float. What happens if America has no gold and $v$ drifts back into the range in which the par value is enforced? The answer is that there is a speculative run *into* the dollar, leading to a discrete gain in reserves at British expense.

It may be useful to illustrate this model of the gold standard more explicitly, retaining the assumption that $v$ follows a random walk (although figure 6.3 remains valid even when $v$ follows more complex processes; see Krugman and Rotemberg 1990). We begin by noting that when $v$ follows a random walk with no drift, the two roots in the solution sum to zero. Thus the basic exchange rate equation may be written

$$s = m - m^* + v + Ae^{\alpha v} + Be^{-\alpha v}, \tag{29}$$

where $\alpha$ may be calculated using the methods of section 6.1.

There are now two de facto target zones: the A-zone in which America has all the gold and the B-zone in which Britain has all the gold. The relative money supplies in these zones are therefore as follows: In the A-zone,

$$m - m^* = \ln\left(\frac{D + G}{D^*}\right), \tag{30}$$

while, in the B-zone,

$$m - m^* = \ln\left(\frac{D}{D^* + G}\right). \tag{31}$$

To calculate $v_A$, we first note that since in the A-zone $v$ is unbounded below, we must have $B = 0$ and must choose a value of $A$ such that the exchange rate reaches its par value at $v_A$:

$$s_{par} = \ln\left(\frac{D + G}{D^*}\right) + v_A + Ae^{\alpha v_A}. \tag{32}$$

Also the curve must be flat at $v_A$:

$$\frac{ds}{dv} = 1 + \alpha Ae^{\alpha v_A} = 0. \tag{33}$$

Putting these together, we find that

$$v_A = s_{par} - \ln\left(\frac{D + G}{D^*}\right) + \frac{1}{\alpha}. \tag{34}$$

A similar calculation shows that

$$v_B = s_{par} - \ln\left(\frac{D}{D^* + G}\right) - \frac{1}{\alpha}. \tag{35}$$

What is the significance of the term $1/\alpha$? It is the horizontal distance from each end of the gold standard range to the corresponding free-float locus. It therefore measures the extent to which the target zone aspect of the exchange regime, when one country has run out of gold, leads to a collapse of the gold standard before the gold would have run out under a perfectly credible system. And $1/\alpha$ also measures the change in the log of the ratio of national money supplies that occurs when there is a speculative attack.

This example illustrates how a gold standard with limited gold reserves may be modeled as a boundary between two target zones. However, the example also reveals a problem. As drawn in figure 6.3, we show that $v_B > v_A$, so there is a range in which the par value can be maintained. But there is no guarantee that this is true. We note that

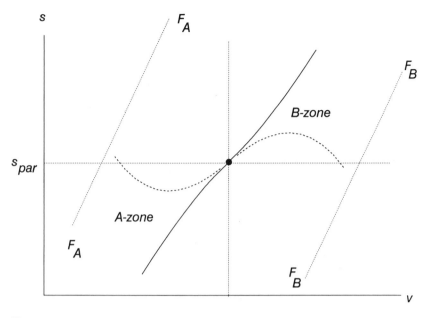

**Figure 6.4**

$$v_B - v_A = \ln\left(\frac{D^* + G}{D}\right) + \ln\left(\frac{D + G}{D^*}\right) - \frac{2}{\alpha}. \tag{36}$$

This will be positive only if gold reserves G are large enough relative to the world money supply. When gold reserves are sufficient, we get the story illustrated in figure 6.4. But what if they aren't sufficient?

On reflection, the story is apparent: It is illustrated In figure 6.4. The par exchange rate $s_{par}$ still represents the boundary between two target zone regimes, but the loci in each regime no longer "smooth paste" to the par value. Instead, they smooth paste *to each other* at some critical value of $v$. Whenever $v$ crosses that value, there is a speculative attack that transfers all of the gold from America to Britain, and vice versa. The central banks are trying to enforce a gold parity, but one or the other is always failing.

## 6.6  Conclusions

The literature on deterministic speculative attacks and the more recent literature on target zones share the insight that to understand how an exchange regime works, one must also understand how it ends. Capital flows under fixed rates depend critically on expectations of abandonment of parities. Exchange rates under floating may depend equally critically on expectations of future efforts to peg. These literatures therefore are closely related in spirit, and one would like to tie them together.

This chapter offers one way to link the two views. Speculative attacks on target zones emerge in much the same way as speculative attacks on fixed rates, but the stochastic aspect of the model makes the analysis richer and, one hopes, adds insight. In particular, a target zone approach allows a much more satisfying analysis of speculation under a gold standard than is possible using the previous standard models.

# III

## The Debt Crisis and Its Aftermath

# 7 Financing versus Forgiving a Debt Overhang

Discussion of new approaches to the developing country debt problem is more intense now than at any time since 1983. Some proposals, such as the Baker initiative, involve revitalization and continuation of the 1983 strategy of financing without either debt forgiveness or change in the nature of claims. Other proposals, such as the Bradley Plan, call for major debt forgiveness in an effort to clear the books and restore normal conditions. In between are a variety of proposals for changing the character of the relations between debtors and creditors, including interest capitalization, lending or debt relief contingent on world prices, conversion of debt into equity or equitylike claims, and so on.

Somewhat surprisingly, this practical discussion is taking place with little parallel analytical discussion among economists. While there is a fairly substantial theoretical literature on the problem of sovereign risk (surveyed by Eaton et al. 1986), the bulk of this literature has focused either on the case of creditor rationing of a country that is borrowing with no existing debt or on the choice by a country to repay or default. The position in the real world, however, is one of both repayment and new borrowing; countries have arrived in the current situation with a stock of "inherited" debt, which they cannot fully service without new borrowing. If the countries' future repayment were not in doubt, they would have no difficulty in borrowing to service existing debt. But for a group of large debtors, doubt about future repayment is sufficient that only through extraordinary measures have creditors been induced to provide new money.

Now there does exist a small theoretical literature that bears on the actual debt problem fairly closely. This is the literature on the problems posed by a debt *overhang*. By a debt overhang I mean the presence of an existing,

Originally published in *Journal of Development Economics* 29 (1988), pp. 253–268. Copyright © 1988 by Elsevier Science Publishers B.V. (North-Holland).

inherited debt sufficiently large that creditors do not expect with confidence to be fully repaid. The effects of such a debt overhang have been analyzed in only a few papers, including Sachs (1984, 1986) and Krugman (1985b, d). These papers have shown that the presence of a debt overhang may give creditors an incentive to lend at an expected loss to protect their existing claims (Sachs 1984; Krugman 1985b, d). They also show that there may be a conflict between creditors' individual and collective interest and that free-rider problems may compromise the ability to achieve desirable new lending. On the other hand, the incentives of a debtor may be distorted by the presence of a debt overhang, and the distortion will be reduced if creditors provide immediate debt forgiveness rather than providing new money and hoping for more favorable future conditions (Sachs 1986). The debt overhang approach is highly suggestive of the desirability of innovative approaches to the provision of funds, and perhaps of changes in the nature of bank claims on developing countries.

This chapter provides a synthetic presentation of the debt overhang analysis that, though abstract, may help clarify ideas for practical discussion. Section 7.1 sketches out three examples that are intended to convey some of the key issues. Section 7.2 presents a more formal model that focuses on the trade-off between new lending and debt forgiveness as ways of coping with a debt overhang. Section 7.3 then examines how changing the nature of claims might help resolution of a debt overhang.

### 7.1   The Debt Overhang Problem: Some Illustrative Examples

A debtor country is something like a debtor firm, although the parallel is not exact. At any given time the creditors of a firm view that firm as having a probability distribution over streams of future earnings, out of which debt service can be paid. If the present value of the stream of earnings is expected to be less than the firm's debt, then creditors will not expect to be fully repaid—although they may prefer to wait and see rather than force the firm immediately into bankruptcy proceedings.

A country, like a firm, has an expected stream of earnings, but not all of this stream is potentially available to service debt. Instead, some fraction of national income represents the maximum resource transfer that the country can be induced to make. We can loosely think of the expected stream of potential resource transfers a country to its creditors as analogous to the expected stream of earnings of a firm.

Now the analogy is less than exact because the potential resource transfer from a country to its creditors is not really a fixed number. Instead, the maximum level of resource transfer is determined ultimately by the country's willingness to pay, which in turn reflects both rational calculations of the cost of default and internal political considerations. There is a bargaining problem between creditors, who would like to get the most possible out of a country, and the country, which would like to minimize resource transfer. Some progress has been made on the bargaining issue, for example, by Bulow and Rogoff (1986). However, it is useful for analytical purposes to put this bargaining issue aside and imagine that the rate of resource transfer that is possible at any point in time is a well-defined number (although perhaps uncertain ex ante).

If we grant ourselves the enormous simplification of taking maximum resource transfer as given, we are left with a straightforward definition of the problem of debt overhang. *A country has a debt overhang problem when the expected present value of potential future resource transfers is less than its debt.*

To illustrate the implications of debt overhang, I will consider three highly stylized examples of the problems that such overhang can cause. The three examples share a common structure, in which the action takes two periods. In the first period a country starts with an inherited debt, all of which (for simplicity) is due during that period. The country attempts to pay that debt with resource transfer plus new borrowing. The new borrowing in turn must be repaid with resource transfer in the second period.

What happens if a country is unable to repay fully at the end? For the moment I will ignore the problem of costs of default and assume that creditors simply share the maximum resource transfer the country can make. Thus, if the country is unable to repay fully in the second period, the result is effectively that part of the debt is forgiven. This shifts the emphasis to the first period. The key question is whether the country will experience a liquidity crisis. Will the country be able to attract new borrowing in order to service its inherited debt? This depends on the behavior of lenders. I will assume that lenders are risk neutral and face a given opportunity cost of funds on world markets. An important question is whether creditors are purely competitive or can operate collusively in their joint interest. We will consider both cases.

Debt Overhang without Uncertainty

Consider first the situation where there is no uncertainty, where the potential resource transfers in periods 1 and 2 are known from the beginning. We assume that all of the debt comes due in period 1, with required debt repayment $D$; the resource transfer possible in each period is $x_1$, $x_2$. We let $i$ be the opportunity cost of funds to lenders.

Does this country have a liquidity problem? The country can make repayment of debt equal to $x_1$ out of current resources. If current debt service exceeds this amount, it must engage in new borrowing equal to $D - x_1$. Lenders will supply this voluntarily at their opportunity cost $i$ if they believe that they will be fully repaid, as indeed they will provided that $(1 + i)(D - x_1) < x_2$, or equivalently that $x_1 + x_2/(1 + i) > D$. Not surprisingly, there will be no problem of liquidity if the present value of potential resource transfer exceeds the inherited debt.

Suppose, on the other hand, that $x_1 + x_2/(1 + i) < D$. Then the country will not be able to meet its debt service. It certainly cannot borrow the needed resources $D - x_1$ at the safe rate, since it will be seen to be unable to repay its loans in full. Nor can it attract additional lending by offering an interest rate above the safe rate. The total resources available for debt repayment in period 2 are $x_2$, with a present value of $x_2/(1 + i)$. Regardless of the interest rate on period 1 loans, that is what creditors will get, and it is less than the value of the necessary loans.

Thus the best that the initial creditors can do is reach a settlement with the country that immediately reduces the country's obligations. The mechanics of the settlement are, at this level of abstraction, arbitrary. Any combination of rescheduling, forgiveness of principal, forgiveness of interest, and new lending at concessional rates will do as long as it brings the actual resource transfer in line with what is possible.

In the absence of uncertainty, then, the problem of what to do about debt overhang would be straightforward. If the country can pay, there will be no liquidity problem. If it cannot, the debt must be written down at the outset.

Debt Overhang with Uncertainty

Now consider a country that similarly has inherited a debt $D$ but faces an uncertain future. Either because the world economic environment is uncertain, or because the country's own economic performance cannot be predicted, the potential resource transfer in period 2 is a random variable. To keep things simple, we suppose that first-period resource transfer is a known value $x_1$, while in the second period the maximum transfer will take on only one of two values, $x_G$ (good case) or $x_B$ (bad case). In the bad case the present value of potential resource transfer will be less than the initial debt, while in the good case it may be possible that the debt can be repaid.

Is this country solvent? This is not a well-defined question. Unless the present value of resource transfer is less than the debt in both states, it is simply unknown whether the country can earn enough to repay its debt.

However, we can ask whether the country will have a liquidity problem, and here there is a straightforward answer: It will be able to borrow to service its debt if and only if the *expected* present value of the resource transfer is at least as great as the debt.

To see this, let $p$ be the probability of a good outcome and $1 - p$ be the probability of a bad outcome. What we want to ask is whether there is an interest rate that the country can offer that will induce lenders to supply the resources $L = D - x_1$ that are necessary to allow debt service. Suppose that the country offers an interest rate $r$ on its new borrowing such that $L(1 + r) = x_G$. This is the highest interest rate that makes sense, since the country cannot even in the best case pay more than this. Then lenders will receive all of the potential resource transfer in either state. The expected present value of their receipts will be $[px_G + (1 - p)x_B]/(1 + i)$. They will be induced to lend if this exceeds the necessary lending $D - x_1$. But the condition $[px_G + (1 - p)x_B]/(1 + i) > D - x_1$ is simply the condition that the expected present value of resource transfer exceed the value of the inherited debt.

As long as this criterion is satisfied, the country will be able to borrow enough to service its debt simply by paying a sufficiently high interest premium. If it is not satisfied, the country will not be able to attract voluntary borrowing and will thus be unable to service its debt.

Now if that were that, we would simply see a default whenever financial markets view a country as having less future ability to pay than its existing debt. However, it is in the interest of existing creditors to prevent this. Even without any explicit modeling of how a liquidity crisis is played out, it seems obvious that the creditors are not likely to collect the full potential resource transfer from the country if there is a disorderly default. Let $Z$ be the present value of what creditors expect to be able to collect from a country if there is a liquidity crisis in period 1; it seems safe to assume that $Z < x_1 + [px_G + (1 - p)x_B]/(1 + i) < D$. Yet it is not necessary that creditors accept the certainty of loss. Suppose that they are able to relend enough to the debtor to avert default in period 1 and postpone the reckoning until period 2. Then, if they are lucky, they may receive full repayment after all; if they are unlucky, they will still be better off than if they had allowed a default to take place immediately.

We can easily construct a strategy that will achieve this aim. Let the existing creditors relend the country $L = D - x_1$ at an interest rate such that $L(1 + r) = x_G$. Then the creditors will receive all of the potential second-period resource transfer in either state. Viewed in isolation, this will still be a losing proposition: the expected present value of their receipts will be $[px_G + (1 - p)x_B]/(1 + i) < L$. Thus no lender would voluntarily enter the package if she had no stake in the repayment of the original debt. From the point of view of the initial creditors, however, a lending package insures that they receive the full present value of the country's potential resource transfer, which is more than they would get without the lending. Thus lending that would be unprofitable viewed in isolation is worth doing as a way of defending the value of existing debt.

There are several points worth noting about this kind of defensive lending scenario, since even this simple an example is enough to show that several commonly held beliefs about debt problems are incorrect.

First, much discussion about the debt problem tries to make a clear distinction between liquidity and solvency, with the argument being that new lending to cover debt service is appropriate for liquidity but not for solvency problems. Even this simple schematic approach makes clear, however, that the distinction is not useful. If we knew that the country could repay the full present value of its debt—or even if the expected value of potential payments were large enough—the country could attract voluntary lending by offering a sufficiently high interest premium. The inability to attract funds comes because the expected ability to pay is too low; a liquidity crisis must occur because of doubts about solvency. As we have just seen, however, the expectation of insolvency does not prevent new lending from being in the interest of existing creditors.

Second, some commentators have pointed to the large discounts at which developing country debt sells on secondary markets as evidence that further lending is inappropriate. Clearly in this model new lending to the debtor would immediately sell at a discount, since it has an expected present value less than the value of the lending. The discount is just another aspect of the fact that the new lending is unprofitable viewed in isolation. The point is, however, that it is still worth doing because it does not take place in isolation; it is essential to the repayment of existing debt.

Third, we have seen that it is in the interests of existing creditors to relend enough to avoid an immediate default on the part of the country. However, it is only in their *collective* interest. Any *individual* creditor would be better off if it could opt out of the new lending and let other creditors carry the burden. Thus we have the free-rider problem emphasized by Cline (1983) and many others. This free-rider problem could lead to a liquidity crisis even though this is not in anyone's interest.

Fourth, we often ask whether or not the new lending that takes place to debtors is at concessionary terms or not. The standard usually used is a comparison with market interest rates. However, the example makes it clear that the market rate comparison is essentially irrelevant. From the point of view of the lenders, the loans yield an expected return less than the market rate, whatever the face interest rate; thus they will view this as lending at concessional terms. Whether the interest rate on the loan is more or less than their opportunity cost of funds depends on how favorable the good state is. The interest they charge is defined by the relationship $L(1 + r) = x_G$. The rate $r$ will exceed $i$ if $x_G/(1 + i) > D - x_1$, be less than $i$ if $x_G/(1 + i) < D - x_1$, that is, on whether even in the good state the present value of resource transfer exceeds the opportunity cost of funds.

This last observation raises a puzzle. The example suggests that if there is *any* state in which the present value of resource transfer exceeds the value of existing debt, the interest rate charged by creditors on new lending should exceed their opportunity cost of funds. Presumably for most debtors there is at least the possibility of such a favorable state; even Bolivia might discover a valuable, unsuspected natural resource. Yet this description of creditor behavior seems both wrong in practice and disturbing: Isn't there any circumstance under which new lending (or rescheduling of existing debt) will take place at concessional rates? To develop a motivation for debt forgiveness, we need to have an example in which creditors have to be concerned about the incentives they give the debtor.

## Incentive Effects

In the last example creditors have an incentive to lend to the debtor, even at an expected loss, as a way to defend the value of their existing claims. However, their incentive is to lend at the highest interest rate that could be paid, even in the most favorable state of nature. Only in this way can they ensure that they collect the maximum resource transfer from the country. In effect, while the creditors are taking an expected loss, they will have an incentive to provide financial relief to the country entirely through new money rather than through interest rate reduction. Indeed, as long as there is any state of nature in which the present value of resource transfer exceeds the value of inherited debt, the creditors will charge an interest rate that is higher than their opportunity cost of funds.

To soften this result, we need to take into consideration the effect of the debt burden on the incentives facing the debtor. In the real world there are a variety of actions that debtors can take that affect their future ability to make resource transfers: exchange rate adjustment, investment, budget policies, and so on. Let us summarize these policies under the vague heading of "adjustment effort." Then creditors will want a country to make as much adjustment effort as possible, certainly more than the country would like to undertake. Now suppose that the debt burden on a country is as large as the maximum that the country could possibly pay, even with maximum adjustment effort. Then there is in fact no reason for the country to make the adjustment effort, since the reward goes only to its creditors. It makes sense therefore for the creditors to demand less than this maximum, in order to provide the creditor with some incentive to adjust.

For our third example we consider the extreme case where the potential resource transfer depends only on the action of the debtor, and not at all on the state of nature (this is the case considered by Sachs 1986). In period 1, as always, there is a debt service requirement $D$ and a known maximum resource transfer $x_1$. Creditors thus must lend $D - x_1$ to prevent a liquidity crisis. In the second period, however, the potential resource transfer depends on the adjustment effort. If the adjustment effort is high, maximum resource transfer is $x_H$; if it is low, $x_L$. Other things equal, the debtor would prefer to make the lower adjustment effort.

The maximum interest rate that could conceivably be paid is defined by $L(1 + r) = x_H$. If the creditors charge this interest rate, however, the debtor will have no incentive to make the high adjustment effort. It may thus be in the interest of creditors to charge an interest rate sufficiently low that the debtor make the higher adjustment effort. If there is a liquidity problem, and no uncertainty, the optimal interest rate in the absence of uncertainty must be one that is below the market rate $i$.

Several observations follow from this example. First, we note that charging an interest rate that is below the maximum resource transfer and below the market rate is actually in the interest of the creditors. If we compare the value of their claims with the optimal interest rate with the value with a higher interest rate, we will find that reducing the face value of loans actually raises their market value.

Second, this example suggests both the motivation for conditionality and the problems of enforcing it. The creditors would like to impose a requirement for high adjustment as a condition for the loan—in which case the interest rate could be higher. On the other hand, the threat not to lend if the country fails to act correctly may be hard to establish credibly, since it remains in the interest of the creditors to avoid provoking a liquidity crisis.

Third, while debt forgiveness may be desirable from the point of view of creditors as a way of creating incentives, it is clearly a blunt instrument for this purpose. The example immediately suggests that loans are the wrong form of claim; some form of contingent claim would be preferable.

(The specification of the optimal claim is left to the more elaborate discussion below.)

We have now gone about as far as we can with simple examples. In order to integrate the insights from these examples, we now turn to a formal model.

## 7.2 A Formal Model of Debt Overhang

As in the simplified examples we consider a country that has inherited a stock of debt $D$, all of it due in the first of two periods. In period 1 the country can make a known maximum resource transfer $x_1$. In period 2 the country's resource transfer potential is unknown, so

$$x_2 = s + z, \tag{1}$$

where $s$ is a random variable that ranges from $\underline{s}$ to $\bar{s}$ and $z$ is a choice variable capturing the concept of "adjustment effort" by the debtor country.

The country is assumed to care about two things: the level of resources left to it in the second period, and the size of the adjustment effort it is required to make. Let $C_2$ be the difference between the country's potential resource transfer $x_2$ and the actual payment it must make to creditors:

$$C_2 = x_2 - P. \tag{2}$$

For simplicity, and to avoid mixing insurance issues into our analysis, the country's objective function will be assumed linear in $C$:

$$U = C_2 - v(z), \qquad v' > 0, v'' > 0, \tag{3}$$

where the function $v(z)$ captures the dislike of the country for making adjustments that enlarge its future ability to pay creditors.

Suppose that the creditors are able to overcome the free-rider problems we mentioned in the previous section and lend enough to avert default in the first period. Then it follows that first-period lending will be equal to the difference between maximum potential debt service and the value of the debt,

$$L = D - x_1. \tag{4}$$

Suppose that the creditors have charged an interest rate $r$ on their new lending. If potential resource transfer exceeds $L(1 + r)$, the loan will be repaid in full. If it does not, we assume that the creditors will receive the maximum possible, so that

$$P = x_2 \qquad \text{if } x_2 < L(1 + r),$$

$$= L(1 + r) \qquad \text{if } x_2 > L(1 + r). \tag{5}$$

We can now think of this as a game in which the creditors first choose the interest rate, then the debtor chooses the level of adjustment effort. To solve this game, we first solve the debtor's problem conditional on the interest rate. From (3) and (5) we derive the expected utility of the country:

$$EU = \int_{L(1+r)-z}^{\bar{s}} [(s + z) - L(1 + r)] f(s) \, ds - v(z). \tag{6}$$

An increase in the adjustment effort $z$ raises the resources of the country in favorable states when it does not have to pay all of its potential resource transfer to the creditors but is costly in and of itself:

$$\frac{\partial EU}{\partial z} = \int_{L(1+r)-z}^{\bar{s}} f(s) \, ds - v'(z). \tag{7}$$

If the effort level has an interior maximum, we must have $\partial EU/\partial z = 0$ and $\partial^2 EU/\partial z^2 < 0$, where

$$\frac{\partial^2 EU}{\partial z^2} = f[L(1 + r) - z] - v''(z). \tag{8}$$

We now want to calculate the response of adjustment effort to the interest rate charged by creditors. To do this, we first calculate the cross-derivative

$$\frac{\partial^2 EU}{\partial z \partial r} = -L[L(1 + r) - z] < 0. \tag{9}$$

Then we use the implicit function theorem to derive the response

$$\frac{dz}{dr} = \frac{Lf[L(1 + r) - z]}{\partial^2 EU/\partial z^2} < 0. \tag{10}$$

Thus the higher the interest rate, the lower the country's adjustment effort.

The objective of the creditors is to maximize the expected value of their new lending. From (5)

$$ER = \int_{\underline{s}}^{L(1+r)-z} (s + z) f(s) \, ds + L(1 + r) \int_{L(1+r)-z}^{\bar{s}} f(s) \, ds. \tag{11}$$

The creditors' first-order condition is therefore

$$\frac{\partial ER}{\partial r} = L \int_{L(1+r)-z}^{\bar{s}} f(s)\, ds + \left(\frac{dz}{dr}\right) \int_{\underline{s}}^{L(1+r)-z} f(s)\, ds = 0. \tag{12}$$

This condition clearly indicates the two motives facing the creditors. The first term, which is always positive, is the "new-money" bias imparted by the presence of uncertainty. Since something may always turn up that allows the debtor to pay more than you expected, creditors have an incentive to roll over debt at as high an interest rate as possible in order to be able to benefit from good news. The second term, which is always negative, represents the "debt forgiveness" bias imparted by the problem of incentives for the debtor. Creditors do not want to make the country's situation too hopeless, or it will have no incentive to improve its ability to repay.

If the situation were dominated only by one or the other consideration, the choice between new money and debt forgiveness would be clear. If uncertainty were the only issue, it would always be best for creditors to finance but not forgive, so as to preserve the option of cashing in on unexpected good fortune. If incentives were the only issue, it would on the contrary be best for creditors to take their loss up front so that it does not act as a prohibitive tax on debtors' effort. Unfortunately, in reality both issues are present, so the choice of the right strategy is not an easy one.

The dilemma presented by this trade-off, however, is not inescapable. It is due to the fact that both new money and debt forgiveness are rather blunt instruments for dealing with the problem of debt overhang. Can an innovative repayment scheme, one that effectively changes the nature of claims, do better? In principle, at least, it can.

## 7.3   Changing the Nature of Claims

A number of proposals have been advanced for converting debt into some other kind of claim. The proposals range from piecemeal debt-equity conversions, to Bailey's ( 1982) proposal to convert debt to proportional claims on exports, to proposals that either interest rates or new lending be indexed automatically to prices of exports. The approach taken in this chapter cannot do justice to the details of such schemes, since it treats the real economy as a black box out of which resources are somehow extracted. Nonetheless, it is possible to capture some of the spirit of innovative proposals by considering schemes in which the required repayment depends on the size of the potential resource transfer.

We may divide proposals to change the nature of claims into two broad classes. First are schemes that link repayment to some general measure of ability to repay. The best-known examples are proposals that debt repayment be proportional to export revenues. The key point about these schemes is that they make no distinction between favorable results due to national effort and those due to factors outside the nation's control. On the other side are proposals to link repayment to some measure of the shocks experienced by a country, such as the level of world interest rates or the price of the country's principal export good. These two kinds of proposal are quite different at least in principle.

There is a further distinction within these proposals between debt postponement and debt forgiveness. Most proposals that link repayment either to ability to pay or to the state of nature do not, at least on paper, reduce the *eventual* obligation of a country to pay: The obligation is simply rescheduled, at market interest rates, into the future. However, it will be easier analytically to imagine that what is at stake is immediate debt forgiveness. We can then ask whether debt postponement is similar in its implications.

## Repayment Linked to Ability to Repay

Suppose that we have a country exactly like that described in the previous section but that its creditors take an innovative approach to its problem. Instead of lending it the money needed to service its debt, they establish a claim that varies with the ability to repay. We can approximate such a scheme by supposing that repayment is a function of second-period potential resource transfer:

$$P = A + Bx_2, \qquad 0 < B < 1. \tag{13}$$

Does such a scheme resolve creditors' conflict between taking advantage of good news and providing debtors with an incentive to adjust? Unfortunately, it does not. Consider the first-order condition of the debtor. Given the repayment schedule, the difference between potential and actual resource transfer will be

$$C_2 = -A + (1 - B)x_2. \tag{14}$$

Thus the debtor will maximize

$$EU = \int_{\underline{s}}^{\bar{s}} [-A + (1 - B)(s + z)]f(s)\,ds - v(z) \tag{15}$$

with the first-order condition

$$\frac{\partial EU}{\partial z} = (1 - B) - v'(z) = 0. \tag{16}$$

This condition may be interpreted as follows: The country receives only a fraction $(1 - B)$ of the benefit from any improvement in its resource transfer capacity. There is a trade-off in substituting a claim contingent on ability to repay for a simple loan: It is no longer the case that in bad states of nature extra adjustment effort provides no benefit to the debtor, but the benefit it receives in good states is diluted. It is unclear without a detailed model of the economy which will distort incentives more.

This analysis shows that proposals to link repayment to exports or other measures of capacity to repay do not eliminate the problem of incentives and therefore do not eliminate the trade-off between new money and debt forgiveness. Notice, however, that while this is the only issue that can be addressed in the stylized framework presented here, in practice exchange participation notes or other schemes might still be valuable for other reasons, for example, as a way to allow debt service to rise over time in line with economic growth and inflation.

Payment Linked to the State of Nature

The alternative class of proposal would link repayment to some measure of the state of nature. An ideal measure would separate perfectly between the consequences of the country's effort and events outside its control; it is easiest to concentrate our formal analysis on this case and then discuss how the imperfection of real measures affects the argument.

In the context of our formal model, the form of an optimal scheme is obvious: It would appropriate all of the gains that result from the state of nature $s$ but none of the consequences of the effort level $z$:

$$P = A + s. \tag{17}$$

The resulting first-order condition will be

$$\frac{\partial EU}{\partial z} = 1 - v'(z) = 0. \tag{18}$$

Thus the distortion in the country's incentive to adjust is completely eliminated.

For the creditors, the degree of freedom in the scheme would be in setting the constant term $A$. At first glance, it might seem that the creditors could set $A$ equal to the optimal $z$, so they would provide the debtor with a marginal incentive to adjust, yet in the end capture all of the debtor's potential resource transfer by the debtor. This may look too clever to be real, and it is. In addition to satisfying the *marginal* condition (18), the debtor's choice of adjustment effort must be *globally* optimal. If there is no gain from adjusting, the debtor will be better off choosing its own preferred level of effort and simply defaulting on the payment scheme (17). Thus the expected resource transfer that can be extracted from the country will be limited by the need to provide enough incentive for the country to participate in the debt initiative. This constraint is not, however, unique to state-contingent schemes. The only unique feature is that a perfect state-contingent scheme would extract from the country less than its maximum resource transfer in *all* states of nature, even the least favorable.

It is clear from the analysis that an ideal state-contingent scheme should be able to do better than either a simple loan that will probably not be repaid in full or a claim linked to broad ability to repay. In reality of course a scheme will be less than ideal, if only because the state of nature cannot be fully specified. For example, repayment might be linked to the price of the country's principal export, but shocks arising from weather fluctuations might not be included. What this imperfection will do is to blur the effectiveness of the state contingency in eliminating incentive problems. There will be some states of nature in which the country will be unable to meet its obligations, even though these will in principle be indexed to the state of nature. At the margin an improvement in the country's ability to pay will in these states of nature benefit only the creditors, not the country; thus the country's incentive to adjust will be diluted. Clearly, however, the dilution will be less if the obligations at least somewhat reflect the state of nature than if they do not. So an imperfect state-contingent claim is still better than a claim that is not state contingent at all.

Debt Postponement

So far we have discussed only schemes that link debt forgiveness to either ability to pay or the state of nature. However, the more immediate issue is one of proposals to link new money to export revenues or export prices. Is this something completely different, or is the analysis similar?

The essential point here is that once we are in a situation of defensive lending by existing creditors, the creditors do not expect to be fully repaid; nor do the debtors expect to pay fully. Thus new money contains a concessional element, even if it does not do so on paper. As a result, the same considerations that apply to eventual forgiveness also apply to new money.

Consider an extension of our basic model to *three* periods. In period 1 the country makes a decision about adjustment effort that affects maximum resource transfer in period 2; ability to repay in period 3 is also uncertain. Then any relief from the burden of resource transfer in period 2 will not be fully offset by an increase in the expected burden in period 3. It follows that the incentive to adjust initially will depend on the conditions attached to new money in period 2. If creditors will demand the maximum possible resource transfer regardless of the state of nature, there will be no incentive to adjust. If, on the contrary, new lending is linked to the state of nature so that adjustment effort at the margin benefits the country rather than the creditors, the incentive to adjust will be greater.

Although the analysis is highly abstract, we seem to be left with a clear conclusion: Linking either eventual repayment or new money to measures of the state of nature is a good idea.

## 7.4   Concluding Remarks

This chapter has presented a highly abstract analysis of the issues involved in dealing with the developing country debt problem. I have argued that the best way to think about that problem is as one of *debt overhang*: The inherited debt of some countries is larger than the present value of the resource transfer that their creditors expect them to make in the future.

Much popular discussion seems to presume that the appropriate handling of a debt problem is simply contingent on the distinction between liquidity and solvency. If it is a liquidity problem, financing should be provided until the country has worked its way out; if it is a solvency problem, some kind of bankruptcy procedure is called for. What even a highly abstract analysis of the debt overhang problem shows is that this is a misleading way to view the issue. There is no such thing as a pure liquidity problem; it must arise because of doubts about solvency. Even if there is a significant possibility that debt will not be repaid in full, it may still be in creditors' interest to provide enough financing to avert an immediate default. As is fairly widely appreciated, however, there is a conflict between the collective interest of creditors in providing financing and the individual interest of each creditor in getting out.

The choice between financing and debt forgiveness should not, according to the analysis presented here, hinge on some attempt to settle the liquidity versus solvency question. Instead, it represents a trade-off between the option value of a large nominal debt and the incentive effects of a debt that is unlikely to be repaid. Since good news is always possible, creditors would like to keep their claims high so that, if by some chance a country should turn out to be able to repay, they will not turn out to have forgiven debt unnecessarily. On the other hand, if a country is not going to be able to repay except in exceptional circumstances, it will have little incentive to try to adjust. Thus creditors may wish to forgive part of a country's debt to increase the likelihood that it will repay what remains. It is because of the tension between these two objectives that the issue of how much to rely on debt forgiveness and how much to rely on financing is a difficult one.

There seems to be a compelling case that the trade-off between forgiveness and financing can be improved by indexing repayment to the state of nature. If payment is linked to some measure of conditions outside the country's control, the probability for any given expected payment that adjustment effort will at the margin benefit the country, not its creditors, will be increased. Thus the analysis in this chapter, abstract though it is, does suggest that linking new money and possibly debt relief to measures of economic conditions could be to the mutual benefit of debtors and their creditors.

# 8            Market-Based Debt Reduction Schemes

In the early years of the Third World debt problem, there was widespread consensus among creditors, international organizations, and the debtor countries themselves about the kind of solution that was needed. The basic post-1982 strategy was one of financing the debt overhang—that is, creditors were expected not only to reschedule debt but to engage in concerted, "involuntary" lending. This lending was intended to reduce the burden of outward resource transfer on debtor nations to levels compatible with economic recovery, while growth and inflation were expected to make a growing nominal debt consistent with declining indebtedness as measured by the ratio of debt to GNP or exports. The emergence of this strategy represented a remarkable turnabout from the market-oriented policies that the United States had been urging on the International Monetary Fund only months before the debt crisis broke. Suddenly the market mechanism for credit was discarded. Although the effort was intended to protect the property rights of existing creditors, new lending was expected to be provided as part of a collective decision process, and in an environment in which individual lenders acting independently would not have been willing to extend credit. Thus there was, as Carlos Díaz-Alejandro put it, an abrupt socialization of the international capital market.

More recently the consensus in favor of financing the debt overhang has begun to erode. One challenge has come from advocates of debt forgiveness who argue that, instead of reducing current resource transfer burdens by providing new money, creditors should offer a once-for-all reduction in the future obligations of countries. This view is held not only by those who favor the interests of debtor countries over those of their creditors but also by many who argue that such forgiveness would actually be in the credi-

Originally published in Jacob Frenkel, Michael P. Dooley, and Peter Wickhan (eds.), *Analytical Issues in Debt*, Washington: International Monetary Fund, 1989, pp. 258–278. Copyright © 1989 by International Monetary Fund.

tors' interest, reducing debt to levels that are more realistic and thus more likely to be serviced. While the debt forgivers offer a very different prescription from those advocating the established strategy, both parties agree in their advocacy of collective action as opposed to laissez-faire.

A different kind of challenge, however, has come from the advocates of market-based solutions to the debt problem. A variety of schemes—debt buy-backs, securitization, debt-equity swaps—have emerged in the last few years in an effort to find a way out of the debt problem through voluntary actions on the part of creditors. The advocates of these schemes claim that through a "menu approach" of new financial arrangements, the exposure of banks and the liabilities of countries can be reduced without the need for collectively bargained new money or debt forgiveness. That is, market solutions are being offered as an alternative to the concerted-action strategy that has dominated the handling of the debt problem until now.

Can the market solve the debt problem? Despite the popularity of the new market-based schemes, there has been surprisingly little sensible discussion of their pros and cons. This chapter provides a framework for thinking about market-based schemes for dealing with debt and compares these schemes with more orthodox strategies of financing and forgiveness.

The chapter is in six sections. Section 8.1 reviews the rationale for the original strategy of rescheduling and concerted lending. Section 8.2 considers the alternative case for debt forgiveness, with emphasis on the conditions under which forgiveness is in the interests of creditors as well as debtors (conditions that turn out to be crucial for the evaluation of market-based schemes). It then considers three kinds of market-based debt scheme: buy-backs, securitization, and debt-equity swaps. Section 8.3 offers some tentative evaluations.

## 8.1 Rationale for Concerted Lending

The defining feature of a problem debtor is its inability to attract voluntary lending—its lack of normal access to international capital markets. The essence of the concerted-lending strategy followed since 1982 has been to substitute nonmarket for normal sources of finance: to use a combination of official lending and involuntary lending from existing creditors to supply debtor nations with sufficient foreign exchange to service their debts. To many observers this strategy seems absurd. After all, what sense does it make to lend still more to countries that already owe more than they can repay? It is important as a starting point to understand the rationale for new lending to problem debtors.

This rationale is often stated in terms of the distinction between liquidity and solvency: A country is asserted to be worth lending to if it is solvent (is expected to be able to repay its debt eventually) but not liquid (lacks the cash to service its debt on a current basis). This distinction is, however, a misleading one for the debt crisis. If it is *known* to be solvent, a country can find voluntary lending, and there is no liquidity problem. The liquidity problem arises precisely because there is a possibility that the country will not be able fully to repay its debt—specifically because nonpayment is sufficiently possible that the expected present value of repayment is less than the debt already outstanding (see Krugman 1988 [chapter 7 in this book]).

Why then should creditors lend still more to such a country? Because while incomplete payment is possible, it is not certain. Suppose that a country might be able eventually to make payments equal in present value to its outstanding debt but that the risk of nonpayment is sufficiently large that it cannot find voluntary lenders. In the absence of concerted action by its creditors, the country will either have to meet its obligations out of current resources or, if this is impossible, default immediately. The latter will guarantee that creditors do not get all that they are owed, foreclosing the possibility of benefiting from any later good fortune on the part of the country. It may therefore be in creditors' interest to postpone at least part of a country's obligations, avoiding a current default and preserving at least the possibility of a favorable outcome later on.

A country's obligations to amortize debt can be postponed by a rescheduling of principal. which is a standard procedure. For heavily indebted countries this is not enough, however, since even the interest payments on debt exceed what they can reasonably be expected to pay out of current resources. Thus there is a need to postpone interest obligations as well. Such a postponement could be achieved directly through interest capitalization, but this has so far been strongly opposed by creditors because it makes the process excessively automatic (and perhaps also excessively transparent). Instead, the method has been to round up existing creditors and require them to provide new loans that cover a fraction of interest payments, effectively deferring interest obligations. This is the process of "involuntary" or "concerted" lending.

The potential gains from concerted lending were argued strongly in the well-known study by Cline (1983) and have been demonstrated in formal models (see Sachs 1984; Krugman 1985b). The point may be seen informally if considered in terms of the subjective discount on debt—the percentage by which existing creditors expect the present value of actual repayments on debt to fall short of a country's legal obligations. Suppose that creditors believe that if no concerted lending is undertaken, a country will be forced into a disorderly default in which creditors will receive only a fraction $(1 - d)$ of the nominal value of their claims. Suppose also that they believe that a sufficiently large program of concerted lending—say, lending $L$ dollars—will reduce the expected loss from $d$ to $d^*$. Then it is straightforward to see how such a program can produce a net gain. Each additional dollar lent as part of the concerted lending program is lent at an expected loss of $d^*$; however, the program increases the value of existing debt by $(d - d^*)D$, where $D$ is the initial stock of debt outstanding. Thus the benefits of the program to creditors exceed its cost as long as $d^*L < (d - d^*)D$, or as long as $L/D < (d - d^*)/d^*$.

To take an example, suppose that absent a program of concerted lending, the subjective discount would be 0.5—creditors would expect to get only half what they are owed—but that with a program avoiding immediate default the discount falls to 0.25. Then it is in the interest of creditors to pursue such a program as long as $L/D < 1$—that is, as long as the increase in their exposure is less than 100 percent.

This example clearly shows the fallacy of some common arguments against lending to problem debtors. It is not true, for example, that the existence of a secondary market discount on debt (presumably more or less equal to the subjective probability of nonpayment $d$) means that new money should not be put in. It only means that such new money will not be provided voluntarily, but that is by definition true of a problem debtor. It is also therefore not true that unwillingness of lenders other than the existing creditors to provide funds, or for that matter export of capital by domestic residents, are arguments against provision of new money by the creditors.

While thinking of the problem in this way makes the potential benefits of concerted lending clear, it also makes clear one of its problems. The gains from concerted lending are collective. They arise because, by lending enough to avoid immediate default, creditors raise the value of the claims they already have. Looked at in isolation, however, each new loan is made at a loss. Thus nobody who is not already a creditor of the problem country will be willing to lend, and even existing creditors will lack an individual incentive to lend. We therefore have the now-familiar free-rider problem, in which lending may be in everyone's collective interest but fails to take place because no individual finds it in his or her interest. The process of concerted lending—with creditors negotiating collectively, with pressure from creditor central banks and international agencies, and with the not-too-implicit threat by countries to declare moratorium if new money is not provided—is designed to overcome this free-rider problem. In practice, the problem remains serious, not just because it has been difficult to get agreements to provide new money but because of capital flight that in effect rides free on the provision of new money by banks and official agencies.

Even aside from the free-rider problem, however, there are important objections to the strategy of concerted lending. The crude complaint against such a strategy is that it simply puts heavily indebted countries deeper into debt. Clearly this is not right. As many have emphasized, in a world in which countries can grow and there is still some inflation, it is possible for nominal debt to grow yet for a country to become more creditworthy over time (Feldstein 1986). In fact, problem debtor nations have grown much more slowly since the onset of the debt crisis than before, and partly as a result, their debt indicators have improved little if at all. To at least some extent the slow growth can be attributed to the debt burden itself. This at least raises the possibility that the insistence of creditors on maintaining the full extent of their claims on debtor nations may be self-defeating, reducing their expected repayment below what might be achieved through a settlement that reduces countries' debt burden.

The possibility that less may be more—that a reduction in the debt burden of highly indebted countries, rather than financing that simply postpones debt repayment, might be to everyone's advantage—underlies the case for a replacement of the strategy of financing debt with forgiving it.

### 8.2 Analytics of Debt Forgiveness

Why should creditors ever forgive debt rather than postpone repayment? If the stream of payments from the debtor were unaffected by the burden of the debt, it would always be preferable to maintain the nominal value of creditors' claims. After all, even the most seemingly hopeless debtor might conceivably discover a valuable mineral resource or experience an unexpected surge of economic growth, and it makes sense for the creditors to preserve the option of benefiting from such good fortune if it arises. If they reduce the obligations of a country, they have sacrificed this option.

Nevertheless, potential repayment by a country is not independent of its debt burden. When a country's obligations exceed the amount it is likely to be able to pay, these obligations act like a high marginal tax rate on the country: If it succeeds in doing better than expected, the main benefits will accrue not to the country but to its creditors. This discourages the country from doing well at two levels. First, the government of a country will be less willing to take painful or politically unpalatable measures to improve economic performance if the benefits are likely to go to foreign creditors in any case. Second, the burden of the national debt will fall on domestic residents through taxation, and importantly through taxation of capital, so the overhang of debt acts as a deterrent to investment.

Over and above these costs to potential repayment is the fact that no clean Chapter XI proceeding exists for sovereign debtors, and a confrontational and disorderly default may reduce the actual receipts to a creditor below what could have been obtained if debt had earlier been reduced to a level that could have been paid.

The upshot of these negative effects is that the higher is the external debt of a country, the larger the probability of nonpayment and thus the greater the subjective discount on that debt. If debt is high enough, further increases in the level of debt may actually lead to a smaller expected value of payments.[1]

A useful way to think about the relationship between debt and expected repayment is in terms of the curve $CD$ illustrated in figure 8.1. On the horizontal axis is the nominal value of a country's debt; on the vertical axis the actual expected payments. At low levels of debt nominal claims may be expected to be fully repaid, so the outcome lies along the 45-degree line. At higher levels of debt, however, the possibility of nonpayment grows, so the expected payment traces out a curve that falls increasingly below the 45-degree line. At a point such as $L$ the ratio of expected payment to nominal debt may be measured by the slope of a ray from the origin; ignoring risk and transaction costs, we may regard this as approximating the secondary-market price of debt.

Although increased levels of debt above point $C$ will be associated with lower secondary-market prices, at first the total value of debt will still rise. At high enough debt levels, however, the disincentive effects discussed above may be large enough so that the curve actually turns down.

We may now ask: Under what conditions will a reduction in nominal claim—that is, debt forgiveness—actually leave the creditors better off? Many authors have suggested that when debt sells at a discount on the secondary market creditors should "recognize reality" and reduce their claims on the country correspondingly. However, it is clear from figure 8.1 that this is not necessarily right. At point $L$ there is a secondary discount, but a reduction in the claims of creditors would still reduce what they expect to receive overall. The reason is implicit in the discussion of the previous section. Given the uncertainty about the future, a reduction in claims deprives creditors of the option value of sharing in good fortune.

Value

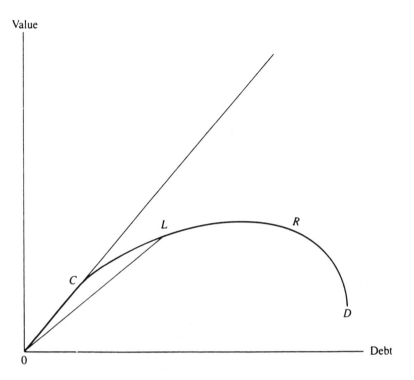

**Figure 8.1**
The debt relief Laffer curve

Only if this option value is outweighed by the improved incentives offered by a debt reduction do the creditors gain by passing on part of the secondary discount to the debtor. This is going to happen only if the debt burden is very large, so that these incentive effects predominate, at a point such as $R$.

The curve $DRLC$ should by now be a familiar sort of object. It is the *debt relief Laffer curve*. That is, just as governments may sometimes actually increase tax revenue by reducing tax rates, creditors may sometimes increase expected payment by forgiving part of a country's debt. In both cases the proposition that less is more depends on an initial extreme situation, whether of taxes that provide extreme disincentives or of a debt burden that is crippling in its effect on economic growth. Arguments that debt relief is in everyone's interest are, in effect, arguments that countries are on the wrong side of the debt relief Laffer curve.

Of course in practice it is very difficult to ascertain which side of the curve a highly indebted country is on. A consensus holds that hugely indebted countries with weak governments, such as Bolivia, are on the wrong side, and this has led to granting of debt relief with few arguments. But for the major debtors the question is anybody's guess.

Despite the difficulty of applying the concept of the *DRLC* in practice, it remains useful as a way of organizing our thinking. For one thing, it is worth knowing what we don't know—figure 8.1 makes it clear that both the confidence that secondary discounts can be freely passed on to debtors and the hard-line view that debt should never be forgiven are wrong in principle. Equally important, the *DRLC* is useful as a way to think about the market-based schemes for debt reduction that have recently gained so much prominence. For it turns out that the prospects for success of these schemes are intimately tied to where on the debt relief Laffer curve we are.

The reason should be apparent. Although market-based debt-reduction schemes are sometimes aimed at producing other benefits, they are in large part intended to "harness" the discount in the secondary market to the mutual benefit of debtors and creditors. As we have just seen, however. when concerted debt relief is considered, a secondary discount offers the possibility of mutual gain only when the debt is large enough to put the country on the wrong side of the curve. Can a market-based scheme harness the discount where collective action cannot? As we will see, it cannot— mutually beneficial debt reduction through market-based schemes is possible only under the same circumstances as mutually beneficial debt relief.

## 8.3 Debt Buy-backs

Some of the problem debtors have accumulated substantial foreign exchange reserves, and others could possibly choose to run large enough trade surpluses to do the same. At the same time the debts of these countries continue to trade at substantial discounts, reflecting doubts about the willingness or ability of the countries to continue to achieve such favorable trade performance. This raises an obvious possibility for reducing countries' debt through voluntary action rather than concerted debt for- giveness. Simply let them buy back their own debt on the secondary market, and the effect will be to reduce debt even net of foreign exchange reserves because of the discount at which the debt sells. Is there anything wrong with this?[2]

Legally debtors are normally prohibited from repurchasing their own debt at a discount. The reason is twofold. First, there is the issue of seniority. Use of reserves to repurchase debt may impair the debtor's ability to repay the remaining debt, and existing creditors are entitled to first claim

**Table 8.1**
Effects of a buy-back

|                                        | Bad state | Good state |
| -------------------------------------- | --------- | ---------- |
| **Foreign exchange generated**[a]      | 20        | 110        |
| **No buy-back**                        |           |            |
| Payments to creditors                  | 25        | 100        |
| Residual benefit to country            | 0         | 15         |
| **Reserves used for buy-back**         |           |            |
| Payments to creditors who sell out     | 5         | 5          |
| Payments to other creditors            | 20        | 90         |
| Total payments                         | 25        | 95         |
| Residual benefit to country            | 0         | 20         |

a. Country is assumed initially to have five in reserves.

on whatever repayment the debtor is in fact able to make. In addition there is a moral hazard problem: Allowing debtors to buy back their debt at a discount rewards the least reliable, who therefore have the lowest secondary prices.

If it is decided that buy-backs are in the interest of both debtors and creditors, the moral hazard argument may be something that can be dealt with. For one thing, conditionality could be applied to the granting of permission for buy-backs. There are no doubt practical problems with this, but these may be left aside to focus instead on the question of whether it is in the interest of creditors to allow buy-backs.

To get some insight into this, it is useful to consider a simple numerical example, illustrated in table 8.1. Here we imagine a hypothetical country that owes its creditors $100 billion and that has uncertain prospects of repayment. Ignoring the question of when the country can make payments, we simply assume that there are two possibilities: a bad state in which the country can generate only $20 billion of foreign exchange and a good state in which it can generate something more than $100 billion, say, $110 billion. We also assume that the country starts with foreign exchange reserves of $5 billion. The probability of the bad state is $\frac{2}{3}$, that of the good state $\frac{1}{3}$.

Consider first what happens if there is no buy-back. In the bad state the creditors collect 25—the foreign exchange the country is able to earn plus the reserves it has available. In the good state the country pays the 100 it owes. Thus the expected payments to creditors are $25^*(\frac{2}{3}) + 100^*(\frac{1}{3}) = 50$. Ignoring risk, the secondary market price on the country's debt will be 0.5.

Now suppose that the country uses its foreign exchange reserves to buy back part of its debt. Let us also initially suppose that the buy-back has no impact on the probability of a good outcome—which, as we will see, is crucial. At a secondary-market price of 0.5, the foreign exchange reserves can be used to buy back $10 billion of debt, reducing the outstanding debt to $90 billion.[3] Those creditors who sold out will receive $5 billion, whatever happens. Those who did not will receive $20 billion in the bad state (because the foreign exchange reserves are now gone) and $90 billion in the good state. Has the change hurt or helped the creditors?

The answer is that it has hurt them. The expected payments to the creditors are 5 in either state (the value of debt sold off in the secondary market) plus 20 in the bad state, plus 90 in the good state, implying expected payments of

$$5 + 20^*(\tfrac{2}{3}) + 90^*(\tfrac{1}{3}) = 48\tfrac{1}{3}.$$

That is, the buy-back reduces the expected total payment to the creditors. The effect of a buy-back in this case should be to lower the price of debt on the secondary market and make the creditors worse off.

The reason for this result is that the buy-back reduces the net contribution of the country in the good state, when it could repay its whole debt but now gets to pay less, while it has no effect in the bad state, when the country in any case pays all that it can. So the country gains at creditors' expense. It should be clear that this is a fairly general result. If a country's ability to pay is not affected by a buy-back, then the buy-back reduces the net payments by a country when it can pay and produces no gains for creditors when it cannot.

The only way that this result could be reversed is if the buy-back improves the country's ability to pay by a sufficient amount to offset this negative effect. The incentive effects indeed work in that direction. Consider the benefits to the country of having the good state occur. In the bad state the creditors take whatever the country can give. In the good state the country gets to keep any excess above its nominal debt. We have assumed that the country's foreign exchange earnings are 110 and its reserves 5 while its debt is only 100, so in the absence of a buy-back it gets to keep 15 in the good state. After a buy-back its reserves are gone, but its debt is reduced to 90, so in the good state it gets to keep 20. This greater gain in the good state should provide a greater incentive for the country to pursue adjustment policies, to invest, to do all those things that we think the country can do to increase its future ability to pay.

The creditors can then benefit from a buy-back but only if the increased probability of the good state is enough to outweigh the loss of their rights to share in the good fortune if it comes. But this is exactly the condition that we saw was necessary for creditors to benefit from debt forgiveness. So in fact it is only in the interest of creditors to allow buy-backs of debt on the secondary market when the debtor country is on the wrong side of the debt relief Laffer curve.

We can see the equivalence precisely in the context of our numerical example. Suppose that instead of allowing the country to buy back part of its debt, the creditors had simply reduced the face value of outstanding claims from 100 to 95. Then the aggregate payments to creditors would be the same as in the buy-back case: 25 in the bad state and 95 in the good. Also in the good state the country would have the same amount of foreign exchange left over: earnings of 110, less debt of 95, plus reserves of 5 = 20. Thus the incentive to increase the probability of the good state would be the same. It follows then that allowing buy-backs on the secondary market will benefit creditors if and only if debt forgiveness would do the same.

This suggests that creditors will not readily agree to buy-backs unless they are convinced that debt forgiveness is definitely desirable—this therefore also implies that debt buy-backs are not going to be in any meaningful sense an alternative to the collective-action strategies that were discussed in the first two sections of this chapter.

## 8.4  Securitization

Debt buy-backs are limited in their possible extent by the quantity of foreign exchange reserves available. Recently, however, investment bankers have proposed a way in which this limitation might be overcome. The idea of securitization is that a country issues new debt in the form of bonds that either are sold for cash that can then be used to repurchase debt on the secondary market or are directly exchanged for debt (as in the recent Morgan-Mexico deal). If the new bonds sell at a smaller discount than existing debt, the effect will be to reduce the debt outstanding without any expenditure of foreign exchange reserves by the debtor.

What should be immediately clear—though it has been obscure in most practical discussions—is that such schemes will work only if the new debt is somehow made senior to the existing debt. If the new debt is not senior, it will face the same probability of nonpayment as the existing debt and should therefore sell at the same discount. This will mean that there will be no prospect for a reduction in net debt. Suppose, for example, that a country's existing debt sells at a 50 percent discount and that the country attempts to reduce its debt through a securitization scheme involving the issue of $10 billion in face value of new bonds. If these are not senior to the existing debt, we can suppose that they will sell for only $5 billion. This will allow retirement of $10 billion of old debt, but the country will still end up exactly where it started. (This also confirms that the discount should not have changed.) So securitization depends on making the new debt senior to the old, with some perceived first claim on payments.

Such seniority is difficult to achieve. A sovereign debtor cannot make a truly credible commitment to service some of its debt more reliably than others, since any default puts it outside international law anyway. Nonetheless, it may be possible in some cases to establish de facto seniority. In the Morgan-Mexico plan the de facto seniority was supposed to come from the fact that the new debt took the form of bonds rather than bank loans. Since 1982 Mexican bonds have not been subject to reschedulings and new-money requests, essentially because of their relatively minor importance and the difficulty of achieving collective action from bondholders. So the Mexican government claimed that the new bonds should be regarded as effectively senior to the existing bank debt. In practice they were only marginally successful in this: A few bonds were sold at a discount somewhat smaller than that on bank debt, but most of the offering went untaken.

Suppose, however, that it were indeed possible to establish the principle that new securities issued to retire part of existing debt are senior to the old debt remaining. Would such a securitization plan be in the mutual interest of debtors and creditors? We can show that the problem is exactly

**Table 8.2**
Effects of securitization

|                                         | Bad state | Good state |
|-----------------------------------------|-----------|------------|
| **Foreign exchange generated**          | 25        | 115        |
| **No securitization**                   |           |            |
| Payments to creditors                   | 25        | 100        |
| Residual benefit to country             | 0         | 15         |
| **Senior bonds exchanged for part of debt** |       |            |
| Payments to new creditors               | 5         | 5          |
| Payments to other creditors             | 20        | 90         |
| Total payments                          | 25        | 95         |
| Residual benefit to country             | 0         | 20         |

analogous to that of debt buy-backs, and that the answer once again depends on which side of the debt relief Laffer curve the debtor is on.

Table 8.2 shows an example that is designed to stress the parallel with the example we used to examine debt buy-backs. We consider a country that has an initial debt of $100 billion. In the bad state it can pay 25; in the good state it generates resources of 115. The probabilities of the two states are again $\frac{2}{3}$ and $\frac{1}{3}$, respectively, so in the absence of a securitization plan the expected repayment is 50.

Now suppose that the country issues $5 billion of new bonds that are somehow guaranteed to be senior to the existing debt. These bonds will be fully repaid even in the bad state, so they will sell at full face value and can be used to buy back $10 billion of old debt.[4] The country's net debt will be reduced to 95.

The parallel with the case of a buy-back should now be apparent. In the bad state the new creditors receive 5, the old creditors 20, for a total payment of 25. In the good state the new creditors also receive 5, the old creditors 90, for a total payment of 95. Thus, if the probability of a good state has not been increased by the package, the total expected payments to creditors have been reduced to

$$(\tfrac{2}{3})^*25 + (\tfrac{1}{3})^*95 = 48\tfrac{1}{3}.$$

To make creditors better off, the probability of the good state must rise enough to compensate for creditors' loss of the option of benefiting as much from that state. The incentive for the country to increase the probability of the good state rises, just as in the buy-back case: Before the debt reduction the country gets to keep $115 - 100 = 15$ in that state; after the debt reduction it gets to keep $115 - 95 = 20$. Thus, just as in the buy-back case, a debt reduction can benefit the creditors, but only if the debtor is on the wrong side of the debt relief Laffer curve.

It is also apparent that a straightforward debt forgiveness, reducing debt from 100 to 95, will have precisely the same effects as the securitization scheme.

## 8.5  Debt-Equity Swaps

The most publicized market-based scheme for debt reduction is the use of deals in which creditors sell debt at some discount in return for local currency that must be invested in equity. In some of the more enthusiastic descriptions of such swaps, the impression has been given that they solve all problems at once: that they could simultaneously provide a source of capital inflow and cancel countries' external obligations,

In fact a debt-equity swap neither provides a capital inflow nor cancels a country's obligations. The foreign investor does not bring foreign exchange to the country since it is the country's own debt that is presented to the central bank. Thus there is no capital inflow. The country's obligations are not canceled; the foreigners acquire an equity claim on the country to replace their previous claim. What has really happened is essentially the same as what happens in securitization. The country has exchanged a new kind of liability for some of its existing liabilities.

Now a first question about this exchange is whether it can lead to a net reduction in the country's external obligations by harnessing the discount in the secondary market. The answer should be immediately clear when we realize that a debt-equity swap is a kind of securitization: The country can capture the secondary-market discount to the extent that the new claims are regarded as senior to the old. In the current political and economic climate, it is widely expected that direct foreign investors will be allowed to repatriate earnings or use their profits as they wish within the debtor nations even if these countries are failing to repay debts fully. This has allowed debt-equity swaps to capture part of the discount, though by no means all. Once one realizes, however, that the ability to reduce net obligations through debt-equity swaps depends on seniority of equity (which is itself a fairly weird idea), the limitations become apparent.

While debt-equity swaps are, at a fundamental level, a kind of securitization, the fact that the assets involved are so different introduces three other considerations that do not arise in securitization schemes involving issue of bonds. These are the effects of the swaps on the timing of payment, the possibility of "round-tripping" or other diversions of capital inflows, and the fiscal impacts.

In principle, exchanging a debt for equity should have a favorable effect on a country's timing of obligations. Where even a rescheduled debt requires a country to make a stream of payments that is flat in nominal terms, an equity claim on a country will normally provide a stream of repatriated earnings that rises over time with both growth and world inflation, and that is therefore lower at the beginning, higher later. Thus converting debt to equity can serve the same purpose that concerted lending is supposed to serve, of postponing payment to a time when the country is presumed likely to be more able to afford it. An ideal debt-equity swap would clearly loosen the short-run liquidity constraint on a problem debtor.

In practice debt-equity swaps will not always be ideal, and it is unfortunately easy for them to worsen the immediate foreign exchange position of countries that allow them. The most extreme case is that of round-tripping: After swapping debt for equity, an investor sells the equity and withdraws the proceeds from the country. In this case the debt-equity swap ends up being in effect a use of foreign exchange reserves to buy back debt on the secondary market, probably at less than the full discount. (Of course, if investors know they can get away with round-tripping, they will be prepared to pay the full discount for the right to carry out the transaction.)

Even if round-tripping does not occur, debt-equity swaps can still consume foreign exchange on net. Suppose that a foreign firm uses a debt-equity swap to carry out an investment that it would have undertaken anyway. Had it carried out the investment without a swap, it would have brought foreign exchange to the central bank to exchange for local currency with which to make the investment. If it does the swap instead, this foreign exchange inflow fails to occur. So in effect the central bank has used some of its own foreign exchange reserves to make a purchase of debt on the secondary market.

The net impact on foreign exchange reserves from a debt-equity swap is not, as many people continue to think, a trade-off between the capital inflow aspect and the diversion through round-tripping and substitution for alternative financing. At best, in the case of an ideal swap that represents 100 percent "additionality," there is a zero capital inflow; any round-tripping or substitution turns this into a net capital outflow. Since in practice there is bound to be some leakage, debt-equity swaps are realistically a mixture of securitization and buy-back.

In its fiscal effects, however, the securitization involved in debt-equity swaps is very different from straight securitization. In straight securitization the debtor government offers a new asset in exchange for old debt; in a debt-equity swap it offers assets belonging to the private sector. To make this offer, the government must provide the local currency with which to buy these assets; this currency issue will be inflationary unless offset by domestic borrowing. In the latter case the counterpart of the foreign investor's swap of debt for equity is a debtor swap of foreign for domestic debt.

So far so good, but many debtor governments have a domestic debt problem as wall as a foreign debt problem. They have large budget deficits, so anything that aggravates the budget deficit has a real cost, and, crucially, they pay much higher real interest rates on their internal debt than they do on their external debt—say, 20 percent versus 5 percent. So even if a debt-equity swap does not have a large negative effect on foreign exchange reserves, it is virtually certain to aggravate a debtor country's fiscal problems.

As this discussion shows, debt-equity swaps are quite complex in their effects and difficult to evaluate even after the fact. They are in principle a kind of securitization that has the additional advantage of tilting the stream of payments away from the present and toward the future, but they are in practice likely to involve buy-back of debt at a higher effective price than the secondary price and will typically aggravate debtor fiscal problems .

Will creditors benefit from debt-equity swaps? To the extent that these swaps are a combination of buy-back and securitization, the answer depends as usual on the debtor's position on the debt relief Laffer curve. The financing aspect may improve the debtor's prospects as well, while the fiscal consequences will tend to reduce creditworthiness. There is also an important, though not too laudable, possibility for gain: The countries may mishandle the swaps in such a way as to allow those who get the chance to make swaps to make substantial rents.

### 8.6   Summary and Conclusions

The main conclusion of this chapter can be stated bluntly: There is no magic in market-based schemes for debt reduction. The secondary-market discount on developing country debt does not automatically constitute a resource that can be harnessed to provide free debt relief; in many circumstances repurchase of debt on the secondary market, whether through reserve-financed buy-backs or through creation of new, senior securities, will hurt existing creditors. There is a mutual benefit from such repurchases only when a reduced debt burden strongly increases a country's likely ability to repay—the same situation in which unilateral debt forgiveness is in the interests of creditors in any case.

The most heavily advertised scheme for market-based debt reductions is the use of debt-equity swaps. This chapter has argued that such swaps are in principle a kind of securitization, that round-tripping and other leakages tend to make them degenerate into buy-backs financed by reserves, and that they are likely both to be disappointing in terms of their ability to capture the secondary-market discount and costly in their effects on countries' fiscal positions. While there are potential advantages as well, the claims made for debt-equity swaps by their sponsors are clearly exaggerated.

Clearly then market-based debt reduction cannot serve as an alternative to the orthodox strategy of rescheduling and concerted lending. Schemes that benefit the debtor at the expense of the creditor—such as buy-backs and securitization for countries not on the wrong side of the debt relief Laffer curve—will be opposed by existing creditors when they become more than marginal. Schemes that benefit the creditors at the expense of the debtor—such as debt-equity swaps that fail to capture the secondary discount, while allowing firms to make investments they would have made in any case—will be opposed by the debtors as their effects become clear. Mutual agreement on schemes will come only when, as in the recent Bolivian case, there is more or less universal agreement that the debtor is so heavily indebted that a reduction in claims actually increases expected repayment.

## Appendix:   A Formal Model of Forgiveness, Buy-backs, and Securitization

A key point in the text was that the condition under which it is in creditors interest to allow buy-backs, whether financed out of foreign exchange reserves or by the issue of new senior securities, is the same as that under which it is in their collective interest to reduce a country's debt obligations—namely, when the country is on the wrong side of the debt relief Laffer curve so that a reduction in the country's nominal obligations actually increases its expected repayment. This point was suggested both in the text and with numerical examples; here I make the point with a simple formal model. The model is closely based on an earlier model of mine (Krugman 1988) but is even further simplified to allow market-based debt-reduction schemes to be introduced with a minimum of complication.

Consider then a country that may not be able to repay all its external debt. We assume for simplicity that there are only two possible states of the world: a bad state in which the country definitely cannot repay all its debt and a good state in which the country definitely can. The maximum trade surplus that the country can run in each state is $F_B$, $F_G$. The actual payment made in each state is $T_B$, $T_G$.

Creditors are assumed to be able to make the country pay all that it can, up to the level of its debt obligations. In the bad state this implies that

$$T_B = F_B + R, \tag{1}$$

where $R$ is the country's foreign exchange reserves. In the good state the country simply pays what it owes:

$$T_G = D, \tag{2}$$

where $D$ is the country's debt.

Let $S$ be what the country has left over after paying its creditors—that is, the sum of feasible trade surplus and foreign exchange reserves less actual payment. We have

$$S = F + R - T \tag{3}$$

in each state.

Now a key element of any case for debt forgiveness must be an incentive effect from debt on a country's ability to repay. We introduce this by assuming that the probability of the good state depends on how hard the country tries, as measured by a variable we can call adjustment effort $A$:

$$p_G = h(A). \tag{4}$$

The country is assumed to dislike making an adjustment effort but to like receiving a surplus $S$; in particular, the country's objective function may be written[5]

$$U = S - V(A). \tag{5}$$

Since the country must make an adjustment effort before it knows whether the state will be good or bad and since there is something left over for the country only if the state is good, we have an expected value of the country's objective function

$$EU = h(A)(F_G + R - D) - V(A), \tag{6}$$

where the term in brackets is what is left over to the country in the good state. Since the country will maximize this with respect to $A$ and since the country's choice of $A$ determines the probability of a good state, we may write the outcome of the country's maximization as

$$p_G = p_G(F_G + R - D), \tag{7}$$

with $p_G' > 0$.

Next consider the expected receipts of the country's creditors. We can write the expected value of repayments as

$$ET = p_G D + (1 - p_G)(R + F_B). \tag{8}$$

And we can now ask: Does a reduction of nominal debt raise or lower the expected repayment? Clearly

$$\frac{\partial ET}{\partial D} = p_G - p_G'(D - R - F_B). \tag{9}$$

A reduction in debt will therefore increase expected repayment—that is, we are on the wrong side of the debt relief Laffer curve—whenever

$$p_G - p'_G(D - R - F_B) < 0.$$

The interpretation of this condition is that the positive incentive effects of the debt relief must outweigh the cost to creditors of the fact that they get paid less in the good state.

Now we consider what happens if a country is allowed to use part of its foreign exchange reserves to buy back debt on the secondary market. We assume that the secondary-market price of a dollar of debt is simply the expected payments on that debt so that

$$\sigma = \frac{ET}{D}, \tag{10}$$

where $\sigma$ is the secondary-market price.

Suppose that a small quantity of reserves $-dR$ is used to repurchase debt on the secondary market. These reserves will buy back a larger nominal value of debt so that

$$dD = \sigma^{-1} dR. \tag{11}$$

The fact that debt falls by more than reserves means that the country will have more left over in the good state, so it will have an incentive to do more adjustment, raising the probability of that state occurring:

$$dp_G = p'_G(dD - dR) = p'_G(\sigma^{-1} - 1) dR. \tag{12}$$

The change in the secondary-market price reflects both any change in the expected payments and the fact of a smaller remaining debt:

$$d\sigma = D^{-1}(dET - \sigma dD) = D^{-1}(dET - dR). \tag{13}$$

But the change in expected repayment is

$$dET = (1 - p_G) dR + p_G dD + (D - R - F_B) dp_G$$

$$= dR + p_G(\sigma^{-1} - 1) dR - p'_G(D - R - F)(\sigma^{-1} - 1) dR. \tag{14}$$

Substituting back into (13), we find that

$$d\sigma = D^{-1}(\sigma^{-1} - 1)[p_G - p'_G(D - R - F_B)] dR. \tag{15}$$

A buy-back that uses part of reserves $(dR < 0)$ will therefore produce a rise in the secondary price, benefiting creditors, if and only if $p_G - p'_G(D - R - F_B) < 0$. This is precisely the condition for a reduction in debt to raise expected payment. Thus allowing a buy-back will benefit creditors only if the country is on the wrong side of the debt relief Laffer curve.

Next suppose that the debtor country is able to issue new debt in exchange for old and that this new debt is somehow made effectively senior to the old so that it receives first claim on available resources in the bad state. We will suppose that a small quantity of new debt $dN$ is issued. Since the new debt is senior, it will trade at par, and it can be used to retire old debt at the secondary-market price:

$$dD = \sigma^{-1} dN. \tag{16}$$

In the bad state the new debt gets served first, and old debt receives only what is left:

$$T_B = F_B + R - N. \tag{17}$$

As before, the incentive for a country adjustment effort depends on what is left over after paying both new and old debt; thus we can write

$$p_G = p_G(F_G + R - D - N). \tag{18}$$

Now consider the effect of issuing some new debt on the expected payments to the remaining creditors:

$$dET = -(1 - p_G) dN - p_G \sigma^{-1} dN + p_G'(D - F_B - R)(\sigma^{-1} - 1) dN$$

$$= -dN + [p_G - p_G'(D - F_B - R)](\sigma^{-1} - 1)(-dN). \tag{19}$$

Substituting back into (13) gives us the change in the secondary-market price:

$$d\sigma = D^{-1}(\sigma^{-1} - 1)[p_G - p_G'(D - F_B - R)](-dN). \tag{20}$$

As in the case of a buy-back using reserves, the value of the remaining debt increases if and only if $p_G - p_G'(D - R - F_B) < 0$—that is, if the country is on the wrong side of the debt relief Laffer curve.

# 9          Reducing Developing Country Debt

In the spring of 1989 Nicholas Brady, the U.S. treasury secretary, announced what at first appeared to be a major about-face in the creditor nation strategy toward the debt of developing countries. In place of the earlier U.S. insistence that problem debtors should grow out of their debt rather than receive debt forgiveness, Brady announced support for a program of debt reduction backed by the resources of the creditor nations and of multilateral agencies. Many of the players in the debt game took Brady's speech as the signal that a process of widespread writedowns and forgiveness of debt was about to begin.

At least so far, however, that has not happened. While arrearages are widespread, and many banks have provisioned extensively against their developing country debt, only Mexico has negotiated a large-scale debt reduction package. There is widespread dispute about whether the Mexican example can be generalized, about what the Brady Plan really means, and about what to do next. In general, the results of the seemingly dramatic turnabout in policy have come to look increasingly disappointing.

There are many reasons for the failure of the Brady Plan to take off, but a least one of them is lack of clear thinking. There is still widespread confusion about the costs and benefits of reductions in developing country debt and about the usefulness of alternative mechanisms for achieving this debt reduction. Debtor countries want banks to pass secondary-market discounts on in the form of debt forgiveness, banks want debt reduced through buy-backs, and the U.S. government does not seem to understand that these are not the same thing. The result is an impasse.

This chapter offers a sort of primer on the economics of debt reduction for developing countries. For the most part it is a discussion of the analytics

Originally published in *Revista de Análisis Económico* 4, 2 (November 1989), pp. 3–18. Revista de Análisis Económico special invited lecture delivered at the 9th Latin American Meeting of the Econometric Society, Santiago, Chile, August 1–4 1989.

rather than the facts, although some facts and empirical results will be alluded to in passing. The main point is, however, to clarify thinking and offer a framework for assessing alternative debt reduction schemes.

The chapter begins with the simplest case, that of unilateral debt forgiveness. Following this is an analysis of a variety of schemes for "voluntary" debt reduction, including buy-backs, debt swaps, and debt-equity swaps. A concluding section compares the prospects for market-based debt reduction with that for a concerted, negotiated debt reduction.

## 9.1   Unilateral Debt Reduction

By definition, a problem debtor is a nation that is perceived as likely to pay its creditors considerably less than it owes. Many economists have argued that when such a situation arises, it is in the interest of all concerned to "recognize reality" and reduce the country's obligation to what it can pay. Unfortunately, matters are not that simple. While debt reduction may sometimes be in everyone's interest, often it is not. The reason is *uncertainty*: The amount that a country can (or at any rate will) pay is not a known quantity; it is a variable that depends on uncertain future events. Thus Mexico's eventual ability to pay its debts depends on oil prices, on its drive to develop a manufacturing export base, on the success of its internal economic reforms, and so on. It is perfectly conceivable, though not likely, that by the end of the century a booming Mexican economy will be able to pay its entire debt with little difficulty; it is equally conceivable that the weak government of a shaky Mexico will be unable to pay any debt service at all.

To illustrate the effects of debt reduction in the face of uncertainty, it is useful to work with a simple numerical example. While obviously highly stylized, this example can be used to exposit the main principles, and I will use variants of this example throughout the chapter.

Consider then table 9.1. It illustrates the situation of a country that owes $100 billion. There is some possibility that the country can actually pay the full amount. Specifically, we assume that there is a "good state" in which the country pays in full This good state, however, has a probability of only $\frac{1}{3}$. More likely is the "bad state" in which the country pays only $25 billion.

The country's expected payments are therefore $(\frac{1}{3}) \times 100 + (\frac{2}{3}) \times 25 =$ $50 billion. If there is a secondary market in the country's debt, we would expect the debt to sell at 50 percent of par.

A naïve view would be that in this situation the creditors should "recognize reality" and pass the secondary discount on to the country. In this

**Table 9.1**
Hypothetical debt repayments

|                       | Good state | Bad state |
| --------------------- | ---------- | --------- |
| **Probability**       | $\frac{1}{3}$ | $\frac{2}{3}$ |
| **Receipts of creditors** | 100    | 25        |
| Expected receipts = 50 |           |           |
| Secondary price = 0.5 |            |           |

**Table 9.2**
Hypothetical debt repayments after debt reduction to 50

|                       | Good state | Bad state |
| --------------------- | ---------- | --------- |
| **Probability**       | $\frac{1}{3}$ | $\frac{2}{3}$ |
| **Receipts of creditors** | 50     | 25        |
| Expected receipts = $33\frac{1}{3}$ |  |        |
| Secondary price = 0.67 |           |           |

example that would mean reducing the debt to $50 billion. The results of doing this and the reason why it is not necessarily in the creditors' interest are presented in table 9.2. The debt forgiveness reduces payments in the good state to 50, while leaving payments in the bad state unaffected. If the probability of the good state is unaffected by the debt reduction, the expected payments fall to $(\frac{1}{3}) \times 50 + (\frac{2}{3}) \times 25 = 33\frac{1}{3}$. In other words, by reducing their claims to what the debt was originally worth on the market, the creditors further lower its value (albeit by much less than the debt reduction). The reason is that what the debtor is *expected* to pay is not the same as what it *might* pay. The debt reduction deprives creditors of an option value—the possibility of sharing in the country's good fortune if it gets lucky. So even if debt sells at a large discount, debt reduction may not be in the creditors' interests.

Taken at face value, this example seems to suggest that debt reduction should never be offered as long as there is any possibility that a country will pay its debt in full. Since even the most hopeless debtors could suddenly discover huge reserves of valuable minerals, this would seem to rule out debt reduction as a mutually beneficial action. However, table 9.2 was based on a key assumption that may not be realistic: that the ability of a debtor to pay is unaffected by the size of its obligations.

In reality there are several reasons why a large nominal debt burden may impair a country's ultimate ability to repay debt. First, a debt that is so large that the country is unlikely to be able to repay in full acts like a high marginal tax rate on efforts to expand the country's foreign exchange earnings: The bulk of any improvement will go to benefit creditors rather than the country. Second, the debt burden may ultimately appear as a tax on domestic capital and thus acts as a disincentive for domestic investment. Third, to the extent that an inability to pay debt leads to a confrontational and/or disorderly default, the end result may be to reduce eventual payment to less than the country might have paid had a reduced debt been agreed on in advance.

For all these reasons a reduction in creditors' nominal claims on a country will normally be offset at least in part by an increase in the probability that the country will pay the remaining claims. (In terms of the numerical example we have been using, a lower debt level will be offset in part by a higher probability of the good state occurring.) At very high levels of debt, the "incentive effect" may be so strong that a reduction in debt will actually increase the debtor's expected payment.

It is helpful to think about this in terms of a diagram (figure 9.1). On the horizontal axis we show the present value of a country's debt obligations; on the vertical axis the expected present value of its future debt service. If the country had a low initial level of debt, it would be expected to repay

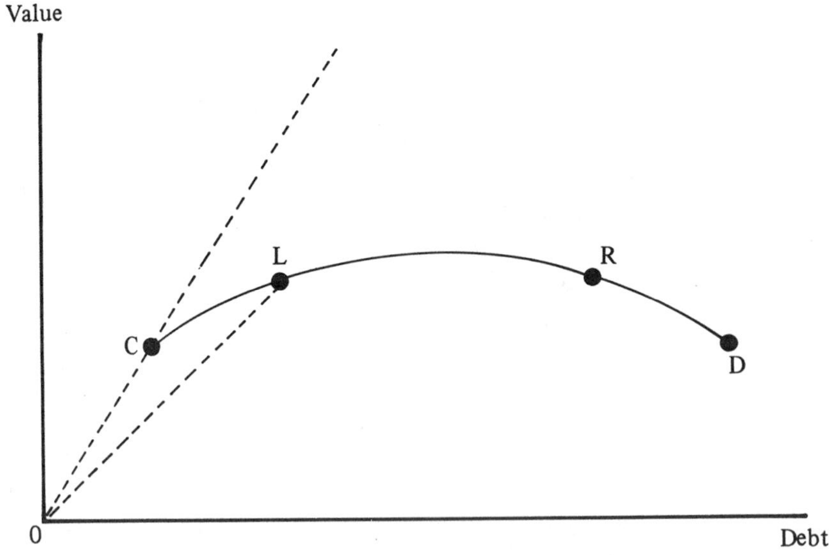

Figure 9.1

that debt in full; thus the expected value would lie along the 45-degree line. At higher levels of debt, however, there would be an increasing probability of default, and thus expected payments would lie along a curve like CD, falling increasingly below the 45-degree line. At sufficiently high levels of debt, a higher level of indebtedness would actually be associated with lower levels of expected repayment. This curve presents an obvious analogy to the Laffer curve in tax analysis, and can be described as the "debt Laffer curve."

The point is now the following: If a country is so hopelessly in debt that a reduction in that debt will actually increase its expected payments—that is, if it is on the wrong side of the debt Laffer curve—it is in the collective interest of creditors to offer unilateral debt forgiveness. The reason is that in this case the improvement in the country's prospects outweighs the cost to creditors of having their claims reduced.

Table 9.3 presents a borderline case in which debt forgiveness can be offered at no cost to existing creditors. In the table it is assumed that a reduction in our hypothetical country's debt from 100 to 75 is enough to raise the probability of a good state from $\frac{1}{3}$ to $\frac{1}{2}$. Thus such a debt reduction would leave expected payments unchanged at $(\frac{1}{2}) \times 25 + (\frac{1}{2}) \times 75 = 50$. Obviously if the incentive effects of a debt reduction were even larger, a debt reduction would make everyone better off.

Two important points need to be made about the debt Laffer curve analysis. First is that the analysis has nothing to do with the question of whether a debt reduction is advantageous to the *debtor*. Debt forgiveness is always beneficial to the debtor, if it can be arranged. The question is instead whether it is possible to devise a scheme that benefits both the debtor and the creditor, other than through contributions from a third party.

Second, the mere existence of a secondary discount does not guarantee that debt can be reduced without harming the creditors. At point L in figure 9.1 there is a secondary market discount (with the price of the debt

**Table 9.3**
A debt reduction to 75 with incentive effects

|  | Good state | Bad state |
|---|---|---|
| **Probability** | $\frac{1}{2}$ | $\frac{1}{2}$ |
| **Receipts of creditors** | 75 | 25 |
| Expected receipts = 50 |  |  |
| Secondary price = 0.67 |  |  |

measured by the slope of *OL*), but debt reduction will hurt the creditors. Only if the debt is so large that it puts the country on the wrong side of the curve, as at point *R*, is there potential for mutual gain.

This means that the question of where countries really are on the curve is a controversial one. There are now a number of studies that attempt to estimate the debt Laffer curve using cross-sectional data. While initial estimates seemed to suggest that only a few countries were on the wrong side, more recent estimates put a number of countries on the wrong side and suggest that the "typical" problem debtor is at or near the top of the curve.

A sample recent estimate is that of Claessens et al. (1989). We fit the following function to cross-sectional data:

$$\ln\left(\frac{P}{1-P}\right) = 7.88 - 1.41 \ln\left(\frac{D}{X}\right),$$

where *P* is the secondary-market price of a country's debt, *D* the face value of that debt, and *X* its exports of goods and services. The implied debt Laffer curve is shown in figure 9.2. The curve reaches a maximum at a debt-export ratio of 5.0, compared with an average debt-export ratio for the IMF's group of 15 highly indebted countries of 3.2.

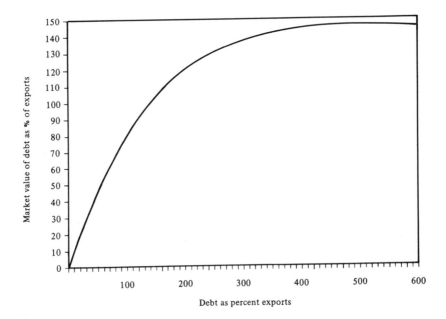

**Figure 9.2**

It is not possible to say with any great confidence which, if any, countries are on the wrong side of the debt Laffer curve. What is fairly clear, however, is that in the relevant range for many problem debtors the curve is, if not actually downward sloping, quite flat. As I will argue below, this observation has a crucial bearing on the comparison between negotiated and market-based approaches to debt reduction.

## 9.2 Externally Financed Debt Buy-backs

Unilateral debt forgiveness by a country's creditors is difficult to arrange. There is no consensus about whether countries are really on the wrong side of the debt Laffer curve. Even if it were agreed that a country is on the downward-sloping segment, there is a severe free-rider problem. Each creditor would like some other creditor to offer the debt forgiveness; the result may therefore be an insistence by all creditors on maintaining the face value of their claims even if there is no realistic chance of collecting.

The upshot of this is that unilateral debt forgiveness must be concerted debt forgiveness. At this point, however, both banks and governments are tired of trying to achieve concerted action; they would like an easier way. The visceral response, given the current ideological climate, is to search for a market solution—essentially to buy back debt on the secondary market.

The key question for buy-backs is where the money comes from. The simplest case is where the funds are supplied by some third party. As I will show, this is not likely to be a route through which large-scale debt reduction will take place. It is, however, a useful case to consider in order to establish some basic principles.

Consider then the effects of a debt buy-back financed by cash donated from some third party. We return to the numerical example introduced in table 9.1, and we temporarily leave aside the incentive effects that might give rise to a downward-sloping debt Laffer curve. To bring out the points most clearly, we first imagine that this third party—call it the World Bank—commits itself to reducing the debt to a level that the country will be able to pay with certainty, namely, $25 billion, which means that it must buy off $75 billion of debt. The effects of a more realistic, smaller buy-back will be considered below.

The effects of the buy-back are shown in table 9.4. We ask, in sequence, the following questions: What is the effect of the buy-back on the secondary-market price of debt? What is the cost of the buy-back to the World Bank? What is the effect on the welfare of the country? What is the effect on the private creditors?

**Table 9.4**
Payments after buy-back of 75

|  | Good state | Bad state |
|---|---|---|
| **Receipts of remaining creditors** | 25 | 25 |
| **Receipts by seller of debt** | 75 | 75 |
| Expected total receipts = 100 | | |
| Secondary Price = 1.0 | | |
| Cost of buy-back = 75 | | |
| Gain to initial creditors = 50 | | |
| Reduction in expected payments by debtor = 25 | | |

1. *The effect on the secondary price.* An externally financed buy-back leaves the country with a smaller debt but with an unchanged ability to pay; thus the secondary market price of the remaining debt will rise. In the extreme example considered here the buy-back is so large that the remaining debt is certain to be fully repaid; thus the secondary price rises to 100 percent of par.

2. *The cost of the buy-back.* Marginal sellers of debt must be indifferent between holding on to the debt and selling it. Since everyone knows that the secondary price will rise to 100 percent, the repurchase must take place at par—the buy-back costs $75 billion.

3. *The benefit to the country.* In the absence of a buy-back, the country would expect to pay $50 billion. With our large buy-back these payments are reduced to $25 billion in both states; thus the country's expected payments are reduced by $25 billion. (This ignores the possibility that there may be an additional gain to the country resulting from the elimination of the necessity of default. I will return to this issue below.)

4. *The benefit to the creditors.* Absent our large buy-back the creditors would expect to receive only $50 billion. With a large buy-back they will instead receive the full value of the debt—some because they sell out to the World Bank, others because the reduced debt can now be repaid in full. Thus the expected payment rises from 50 to 100—a $50 billion gain.

Simple as this example is, it illustrates two important points about attempts to provide debt relief by buying back and canceling Third World debt. First, such relief is typically very expensive because the more debt relief that is expected, the higher the price is that the creditors will demand for their claims. Second, much of the benefit of the buy-back goes to the creditors rather than the debtor—a point that has been forcefully argued by

Bulow and Rogoff (1988), among others. In this particular example, two-thirds of the World Bank's outlay effectively goes to the creditors rather than to the debtor.

The result that much, perhaps most of any externally financed buy-back goes to benefit creditors rather than debtors seems to be a strong argument against this use of the resources of the international community. Is there any counterargument that can be made? The main one seems to be the following: Suppose that there are additional costs to debtor countries if they must default that are not captured by their external payments. These might include disruption of their trade and closure of future access to international capital markets. Then to the extent that debt buy-backs reduce the probability of outright default (which they will almost always do if we recognize that realistically there are more than two possible states of nature), the benefits to the debtor would be larger than are suggested here.

Nonetheless, it remains apparent from our discussion that buy-backs that use externally supplied cash look uncomfortably like relief for the private creditors rather than the debtor, making this a dubious use of public resources. In practice, schemes for debt relief—including what can thus far be discerned of the Brady Plan—generally attempt to supply the externally provided funds as part of a package intended to shift the benefits more fully to the debtor. The key to these packages is that the external funds are used to provide guarantees to the issue of new debt in exchange for old. We will consider such mixed schemes later. First, however, we turn to the pure case of a repurchase of debt financed entirely by the issue of new debt.

## 9.3 Debt Swaps

In a debt swap a country issues new debt and either exchanges this new debt directly for the existing debt or sells it and uses the proceeds to repurchase debt on the secondary market. In either case the effect is to substitute new debt for old.

While debt swap schemes, usually taking the form of offering creditors "exit bonds," have attracted considerable attention, there remains a widespread failure to appreciate the key precondition for such swaps to work. This is that the new debt must somehow be made *senior* to existing debt in the sense that it has a prior claim on the country's payments. To see why this is necessary, consider what would happen if the new debt were expected to be treated in the same way as existing debt, so in effect it would be thrown into the same risk pool. Then the new debt would immediately sell at the same discount as old debt, preventing any net reduction in debt.

Suppose, for example, that debt sells at a discount of 50 percent. An issue of $10 billion (in present value) in new debt would sell for $5 billion; this money could be used to repurchase $10 billion of old debt, but the overall debt burden would not be reduced.

In order for new debt to sell at closer to par then old debt, purchasers must somehow be assured that they will receive priority in the disbursement of available funds. In the attempted Mexican debt swap of early 1988, the selling point was that the new debt would take the form of bonds, which in Mexico have thus far been exempt from the rescheduling and new money calls that have been placed on bank debt. In other exit bond schemes there is a promise that the new bonds will be exempt from new money calls. In some proposals for debt relief, such as that of Williamson (1988), partial World Bank guarantees are expected to confer seniority on the guaranteed debt, on the grounds that countries will be less willing to default on international agencies than on private creditors.

In practice the attempt to confer seniority on new debt is problematic, and difficulties in doing so may constitute a central obstacle to attempts to provide market-based debt relief. For now, however, let us suppose that it is possible to assure purchasers of new debt that they will receive first call on repayment, and examine the implications of a debt buy-back financed by issue of new senior debt.

Consider again the numerical example introduced in table 9.1. A debtor country can pay its full debt of 100 with probability $\frac{1}{3}$ but will pay only 25 with probability $\frac{2}{3}$. As in the buy-back example, the country sets out to repurchase $75 billion of its original debt; however, it now does so by issuing new debt that receives first claim on available resources.

The results are shown in table 9.5. In order to buy back the 75 in old debt, the country needs to issue $25 billion in new debt; its net debt falls to $50 billion. To show why this is the size of the required swap, we need to show what happens to the secondary price. Since the new debt will be paid first, it will be fully repaid in either state, so there will be no discount on the new debt. In the bad state, however, the new debt will receive all of the repayment, leaving nothing for the old debt; since holders of the old debt will be repaid only with a one-third probability, the secondary price of old debt falls from $\frac{1}{2}$ to $\frac{1}{3}$. It follows that $25 billion of new debt can be swapped for $75 billion of old.

The welfare effects of this transaction are quite different from those of an externally financed buyback. The expected payment by the country falls from $50 billion to $33\frac{1}{3}$ billion. This gain comes at the expense of the

**Table 9.5**
Effects of pure debt swap, new debt senior to old

| 1. Before debt swap | Good state | Bad state |
|---|---|---|
| Receipts of creditors | 100 | 25 |
| Expected receipts = 50 | | |
| Secondary price = 0.5 | | |
| **2. After debt swap of 25 new debt for 75 old debt** | Good state | Bad state |
| Receipts of holders of new debt | 25 | 25 |
| Receipts of holders of old debt | 25 | 0 |
| Expected receipts of new creditors = 25 | | |
| Expected receipts of old creditors = 8.33 | | |
| Secondary price of new debt = 1.0 | | |
| Secondary price of old debt = 0.33 | | |
| Change in expected payments by debtor = − 16.67 | | |

original creditors, who see the expected value of their claims fall by the same amount.

A buy-back financed by the issue of new senior debt appears then to benefit the debtor at the expense of its creditors. Thus one might think that creditors should always be opposed to allowing the establishment of the seniority of new debt that makes such swaps possible. However, the conclusion that the creditors lose depends on a key assumption that now needs to be relaxed: that the country's ability and/or willingness to repay is independent of the size of the outstanding debt. As in the case of unilateral debt forgiveness, the creditors as well as the debtor will gain if the country is on the wrong side of its debt Laffer curve, so reducing the face value of debt actually raises expected payments.

## 9.4 Domestically Financed Buy-backs

Externally financed buy-backs are possible only when a third party is prepared to contribute resources; debt swaps work only if seniority can be established. Thus far only Bolivia has managed to assemble external donors to repurchase its debt, and nobody has managed to credibly establish the seniority of new debt over old. There remains, however, the option of self-financed debt reduction, in which a country simply buys back its own debt on the secondary market.

Even this debt reduction method is not automatically available. The sharing provisions under loan agreements, by requiring that payment be made on bank debt equally, prevent direct purchase on the secondary market. However, creditors have been willing to acquiesce in a variety of indirect buybacks, notably those that (as we will see) often result from debt-equity swaps and from the use of reserves to collateralize new debt.

Cutting through these disguises, consider the effects of a direct use of cash generated by a country itself to repurchase some of its debt at a discount. This cash may come from existing foreign exchange reserves, or it may be generated through trade surpluses. In a certain sense even cash supplied by third parties to finance a buy-back can be considered domestically generated, since the cash *could* have been given directly to the country; thus the use of that cash to buy back debt represents a choice not to spend it on something else.

At this point a new issue arises. This is the issue of "appropriability": How much of a dollar that is used to buy back debt would have gone to the creditors if not spent in this way (i.e., how much of a marginal change in a country's resources can be appropriated by the creditors)? At one extreme there is the view that debt service payments by debtors are pretty much independent of their resources, that there is near-zero appropriability. In this view a dollar spent on reducing debt will reduce payments to creditors only in those favorable states of nature when the country would have been able to service its debt in full in any case. This view has been starkly stated by Bulow and Rogoff (1988). At the other extreme there is the view that creditors essentially take as much from a country as it can manage to pay, and that this includes foreign exchange reserves. In this view, with near-complete appropriability, a dollar spent on debt reduction is a dollar that creditors cannot seize in adverse states of nature, and the debt repurchase therefore reduces payments in bad as well as good outcomes.

The effects of a self-financed debt repurchase depend crucially on the degree of appropriability. With near-zero appropriability the repurchase acts just like an externally financed repurchase, which as we have seen typically conveys most of the benefit to the creditors rather than the debtor. In this case, however, the cost of the buy-back falls on the debtor itself. The result is therefore to reduce the debtor's welfare.

Suppose that we were to run once again the thought experiment shown in table 9.3, with a buy-back reducing the debt from $100 billion to $25 billion. As we have seen, the cost of this buy-back is $75 billion, even though the expected payments from the debtor fall by only $25 billion. Now suppose, however, that the debt repurchase is financed by the country itself. Then the country will have expended $75 billion in order to reduce its expected payments by $25 billion, experiencing a net expected loss of $50 billion. Clearly, if appropriability is really very close to zero, self-financed debt repurchases are a very questionable policy.

On the other hand, suppose that the resources that are used to re-purchase debt are in effect taken away from what might have been paid to creditors in unfavorable states of nature. For example, suppose that by using up its foreign exchange reserves through repurchase, a country puts itself in a position where its creditors have to forgive debt in the event of an unfavorable movement in export prices, whereas the country would have been forced to cover the shortfall out of its reserves otherwise. In a case of near-complete appropriability, a self-financed debt repurchase is similar in its effects to debt repurchase financed with issue of senior debt. (In corpo-rate finance, where creditors can seize the assets of bankrupt firms, near-complete appropriability is the rule. This is why repurchase of debt at a discount is normally prohibited.)

The case of debt buy-back financed from domestic resources has created a great deal of dispute—understandably so, since it is simultaneously the easiest kind of debt reduction scheme to implement in practice and the most ambiguous in its results, being potentially either beneficial to the creditors at the expense of the debtors or to the debtor at the expense of the creditors, or beneficial to both. However, the case of domestically financed buy-backs should not be overemphasized. By its nature it cannot be a major contributor to the solution of the debt problem. Almost by definition, problem debtors are short of cash. Thus they cannot be expected to finance large-scale debt relief out of their own resources. Nor are large donations from third parties, which could have been given as direct aid, likely to be forthcoming. If there is going to be a large-scale attempt at voluntary debt reduction, it will for the most part have to take the form of an asset exchange rather than an outright cash purchase.

## 9.5   Debt-Equity Swaps

The most significant mechanism for market-based debt reduction actually in use is the debt-equity swap. Debt-equity swaps remain very popular among bankers, and indeed an extension of such programs is often a key demand of bankers in return for acquiesence to other debt-reduction schemes. Yet debt-equity swaps are complex transactions, whose virtues are much more elusive than their backers would like to claim.

The first point to make is that under no circumstances does a debt-equity swap constitute a net capital inflow. The country simply exchanges one kind of external liability for another. The exchange may be desirable, as we will discuss in a moment, but it does not add to the supply of domestic savings or, what is equivalent, contribute resources toward debt service and thus diminish the trade surplus that the country needs to run to service a given debt.

The second point is that reducing debt is not the same as reducing external obligations. When equity is substituted for debt, foreigners relinquish their claim on a future stream of debt service in return for a claim on a future stream of repatriated earnings. The present value of this latter stream may or may not be smaller than that of the former; again, we will discuss in a moment the factors that determine this.

Before getting to the question of the effects of a reduction in debt offset by an increase in foreign equity holdings, however, it is necessary to address a prior issue. It is unfortunately not always the case that allowing equity purchases to be paid for with debt actually leads to a net increase on foreign equity holdings. This is the issue of "additionality": how much of the equity investment that takes place through debt-equity swaps is actually an increase over the investment that would otherwise have taken place?

The most obvious case in which debt-equity swaps fail to produce additional equity investment is when the foreign investor resells the equity to a domestic investor and takes his cash out of the country again. Such "round tripping" is not unknown, but it is well understood. Actual debt-equity schemes at least attempt to police such abuse.

The more important problem case is where a debt-equity swap is used to finance an investment that would have taken place anyway. Perhaps the most notorious example is that of the Nissan plant in Mexico, which by all accounts would have been built even if no swap program had been available. Given the opportunity to finance the project via a swap, however, the firm naturally took advantage of the lower price, paying for its investment with debt acquired at a discount rather than cash.

What happens when a debt-equity swap fails to generate additional equity investment? The answer is that the swap degenerates into a repurchase of debt using domestically generated resources. Nissan's use of a debt swap meant that the money that it would otherwise have supplied to the central bank did not arrive, requiring the central bank to spend more of its foreign exchange reserves to pay for imports than it otherwise would have.

We should also note that at best a debt-equity swap represents zero net capital inflow if additionality is 100 percent. To the extent the swap has than 100 percent additionality, the result is de facto a capital *outflow*.

Thus a high degree of additionality is necessary if debt-equity swaps are going to constitute a real exchange of assets. Otherwise, they degenerate into a disguised cash buy-back of debt, typically at less favorable terms for the debtor than could have been realized through an explicit buy-back.

Suppose, however, that a debt swap program can be devised so as to ensure a high degree of additionality. The next question is whether the program actually reduces a country's external liabilities in the sense that it reduces the present value of payments to foreigners. The answer is not necessarily: It depends on the size of the premium that foreigners are willing to pay in order their debt to equity. Although the size of the premium depends on a number of factors, it must in turn depend crucially on the same consideration that determines the feasibility of debt reduction through issue of new debt. That is, investors must form a judgment on the seniority of equity as opposed to debt.

This sounds like a strange issue, since in ordinary corporate finance debt is always senior to equity. If this were the case for countries, then a debt-equity swap would typically *increase* the present value of a country's liabilities to foreigners. The current argument, however, is that debt is a source of controversy and bitterness that equity is not, that Latin American nations might default on their debt while still honoring the property rights of direct investors. This is possible, although it is only a decade since multinational firms rather than banks were the chief targets of radical rhetoric in the Third World.

If equity can be made credibly senior to debt, then debt-equity swaps will have the same qualitative effects as debt-for-debt swaps in which the new debt is senior. Even if a debt-equity swap fails to reduce a country's obligations, it may still have some other advantages. The repatriation of profits will ordinarily come later than the debt service it replaces, so a successful swap will improve a country's liquidity position. Also debt-equity swaps can serve other purposes, such as encouraging foreign direct investment that is expected to yield side economic benefits. Against this must be put the risk that the net effect of such swaps will be a net capital outflow, as well as the typically adverse budgetary implications.

My own guess is that in practice a sufficiently high fraction of debt-equity swaps will degenerate into cash buy-backs on unfavorable terms that they will do the debtors more harm than good. Even if one disagrees with this assessment, the potential for debt-equity swaps is clearly limited.

## 9.6 Concerted versus Market-Based Debt Reduction

Up to this point we have discussed a variety of mechanisms for reducing developing country debt. The time has now come to provide an assessment of the alternatives.

Suppose that creditor country governments have decided that it is necessary to engineer a reduction in developing country debt and that they are prepared to throw in some resources to facilitate the process. What kind of debt-reduction scheme should they encourage? Should it be a concerted, negotiated scheme along the lines of the recent Mexican deal, or should it be a market-based scheme?

The instinctive reaction of both the private creditors and the U.S. government is to prefer a voluntary market-based scheme. This preference results primarily from a general presumption that market mechanisms, which maximize freedom of choice, are more efficient than less flexible methods. The preference for voluntarism also arises from the impatience of the banks with concerted action and the fear of the creditor governments that a concerted solution may not be enforceable.

Yet the presumption in favor of the market is somewhat out of place in the debt situation. By definition, a problem debtor is unlikely to meet its legal obligations—that is, the normal market mechanism has broken down. The situation that results is rife with externalities among the creditors—capital flight, free-riding on other banks' lending, and so on, are widely understood to be in the interest of individual banks but destructive if everyone engages in them. So there is no presumption that greater freedom of choice is a good thing. And the emphasis on the virtues of voluntarism obscures a point that would otherwise be very clear: that a given commitment of resources from creditor governments can reduce debt much more through concerted action than through the market.

The point is straightforward. What is the cost to the creditors as a group of reducing their claims on problem debtors by some small amount, say, $10 billion? The answer is very little. Even if the debt Laffer curve is not actually downward sloping at current debt levels, it is certainly very flat; reducing the nominal value of debt by $10 billion would reduce the expected payments to creditors by a very small amount, probably by less than $500 million. It should therefore be possible to negotiate a concerted debt reduction in which the nominal value of debt is reduced substantially in return for small "enhancements" from the creditor governments or multilateral agencies.

On the other hand, suppose that the same debt reduction were to be attempted through a market buy-back. The market price of debt reflects, not the *marginal* contribution of debt to expected payments but the expected *average* payment per unit of debt, which is much higher. The market price of $10 billion of debt is therefore something over $3 billion. Unless it is possible to create new senior debt instruments that subordinate existing debt (which we have seen is very difficult), it will cost more than $3 billion to finance the same debt reduction that a few hundred million dollars in enhancements would have made possible in a concerted reduction.

We may make the point graphically. In figure 9.3 we imagine that the debt Laffer curve is upward sloping in the relevant range but that a third party is prepared to finance a reduction of debt from $D_2$ to $D_1$. A concerted debt-reduction program would need to be supplemented by enough enhancements to compensate the creditors for the reduction in expected value from $V_2$ to $V_1$, but given the flatness of the debt Laffer curve in the relevant range, this cost should be modest. A debt buy-back would have to pay the market price of the debt, indicated by the broken line; the cost to the creditor governments would be $V_3$ minus $V_1$, a much larger sum.

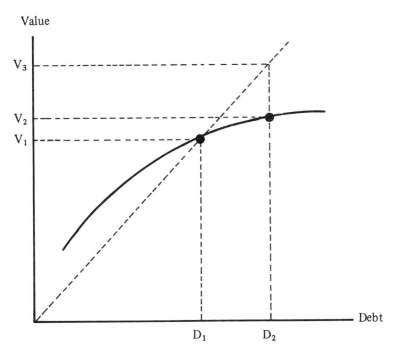

**Figure 9.3**

Suppose that we use the estimated debt Laffer curve from Claessens et al. (1989), described earlier in this chapter. How much would a reduction of the debt of the 15 highly indebted countries by $100 billion cost? The answer is that a concerted debt reduction should require enhancements of $13.0 billion, while a buy-back of the same size would cost $53.2 billion.

Clearly this estimate is contingent on the particular estimate of the debt Laffer curve, in which no great confidence can be placed. It also ignores a number of realistic complications. Creditors are not all alike; a market-based approach might have some advantages in allowing those most eager to get out to sell. Concerted debt reduction is not so easy to negotiate, and more enhancements than the minimum might be necessary to grease the wheels.

Nonetheless, it is difficult to escape the conclusion that substantial debt reduction could be achieved at a modest cost to creditor country governments if it is done through concerted action, while an equal size reduction would be prohibitively expensive through market-based buy-backs.

# IV

# The International Monetary System

# 10

# The International Role of the Dollar: Theory and Prospect

What do people use as money? In studying national economies, we usually do not worry about this question very much; we assume that governments are able to create fiat monies and enforce their acceptance. There are some problems such as the roles of inside and near monies and the case of "dollarization" (as in Israel) where the national currency is partly supplanted by some other currency. But these problems are the exception rather than the rule, and theorists are generally comfortable with the idea of assuming a demand for M/P without having to explain why it is these pieces of paper, rather than something else, that appear in the numerator.

When we study the international economy, however, we can no longer avoid the question. International economic activity, like domestic activity, requires the use of money, and the same forces that lead to convergence on a single domestic money lead the world to converge on a limited number of international monies. Before World War I the pound sterling was the international currency, in the interwar period the dollar and the pound shared the role, in the Bretton Woods era the dollar was dominant. But there is no world government to enforce the role of international monies. The preeminence of sterling and its displacement by the dollar were largely the result of "invisible hand" processes, ratified more than guided by international agreements. The future of the United States monetary system is largely a political question; the future international role of the dollar is largely an economic one.

Yet though central to international monetary discussion in the 1960s and still a major policy issue, the question of the international role of the dollar has virtually disappeared from the research agenda. The reason for this

Originally published in John F. O. Bilson and Richard C. Marston (eds.), *Exchange Rate Theory and Practice*. Copyright © 1984 by The National Bureau of Economic Research. Published by the University of Chicago Press.

neglect lies in the change in the field of international monetary economics. Traditionally dominated by a historical and institutional approach, international monetary economics in the 1970s essentially became a branch of macroeconomics. This meant a drastic change in style. Formal models replaced well-written essays; brief journal articles replaced books. Adjustment, Confidence, Liquidity, became $\dot{p}/p = \lambda(y - \bar{y})$, $i = i^* + \pi$, $\Delta R = \Delta M - \Delta D$. And the change in style meant a change in substance. What we know how to model formally are frictionless markets, where transactions are costless and agents make full use of the information available. The microeconomics of money, however, whether domestic or international, is fundamentally about frictions. Thus the explosion of theory in international economics in the 1970s was concerned with macroeconomic issues and ignored the traditional issues regarding the role of the dollar.

The problem is that the fact that an issue is hard to model rigorously is no guarantee that the issue is unimportant. Fortunately, even a less than fully worked out model can be useful, if one does not demand too much of it. Over the years a number of economists, especially Swoboda (1969), Cohen (1971), McKinnon (1979), and Kindleberger (1981), have developed what amounts to a theory of international money. This theory is not embedded in formal models in the way that, say, the monetary approach to the balance of payments is, but it is tight enough to be informative. This chapter provides a unified exposition of this theory and applies it to the history and the future of the role of the dollar.

The basic concepts of this theory are drawn from the (equally informal) theory of money in a closed economy. Frictions—costs of transacting, costs of calculation—cause agents to use national monies as international media of exchange, units of account, stores of value; economies of scale lead them to concentrate on only a few (often only one) currency for these purposes. The differences between the theory of international money and the ordinary theory of money arise from two facts. First, we are not dealing with a choice among commodities but with a choice among monies, demanded not for their intrinsic usefulness but because of their privileged role in domestic transactions. Second, part of the international role of the dollar reflects choices made by official bodies, the central banks, rather than private agents. A crucial question is, How closely linked are the official and private roles? Would replacing the dollar with some other reserve asset reduce its role in private transactions? Conversely, can central banks be induced to hold a reserve asset which is not a "live" international money?

This chapter is in five sections. Section 10.1 reviews the basic roles of international money and provides an overview of the argument. Section

10.2 examines the role of the dollar as a medium of exchange; it presents a simple model of convergence on a limited number of international media of exchange and discusses the ways in which transitions from one vehicle currency to another might happen. Section 10.3 turns to the unit-of-account role. It tries to combine arguments by several authors to provide a stylized account of the choice of invoice currency in private transactions. Section 10.4 then reviews the store-of-value role, presenting evidence on and an interpretation of recent trends toward diversification in the currency denominations of reserve holdings, Eurocurrency holdings, and international lending. The final section takes a tentative look forward. It reviews the forces leading to a reduction in the dominance of the dollar; a comparison is made between the position of the dollar today and the position of sterling in the 1910s and 1920s. I argue that a "collapse" of the dollar's role is possible, though it is by no means necessary, and I discuss briefly what such a collapse might involve.

## 10.1   The Six Roles of the Dollar

Money, the classical economists argued, serves three functions: It is a medium of exchange, a unit of account, and a store of value. International money does the same: It is used to settle international payments, it is used to fix prices, and it is held as a liquid asset for international transactions. An added dimension is provided by the distinction between private behavior and the decisions of central banks (although the central banks of small countries may behave more like private agents than like Group of Ten monetary authorities). Thus there are six roles of the dollar, presented schematically in table 10.1. (closely based on Cohen 1971). The dollar is used as a medium of exchange in private transactions, or "vehicle," and is also bought and sold by central banks, thus making it an "intervention" currency. Trade contracts are sometimes denominated in dollars, making it an "invoice" currency, and the par values for exchange rates are sometimes

**Table 10.1**
Roles of an international currency

|                    | Private   | Official     |
|--------------------|-----------|--------------|
| Medium of exchange | Vehicle   | Intervention |
| Unit of account    | Invoice   | Peg          |
| Store of value     | Banking   | Reserve      |

stated in terms of the dollar, which makes it serve as a "peg." Finally, private agents hold liquid dollar-denominated assets—the "banking" role—and central banks hold the dollar as a reserve.[1]

In principle, and to some extent in practice, these roles are separable. The separation of roles can be either horizontal or vertical. Thus under the gold standard the official roles were filled by gold, yet sterling played the private roles. In the European snake in the mid-1970s the currencies were pegged to one another, yet the dollar was used as a reserve and intervention currency. One can even separate medium of exchange and unit of account —the famous example is those small Persian Gulf nations which until 1974 set their oil prices in dollars but required payment in sterling. But the roles are not independent. The more the dollar is used in one role, the more incentive there is to use it in the others.

Let us briefly review the actual extent to which the dollar plays the different roles:

1. *Vehicle.* It is important to distinguish three types of transactions here. First is settlement between nonbank firms, which is closely tied to invoicing; as discussed below, the dollar plays a special but not exclusive role here. Second is the "retail" foreign exchange market in which firms deal with banks. Here the dollar plays no special role: A Swedish bank will sell, say, kronor for pesetas, and vice versa. Finally, there is the interbank market: here the dollar is *the* medium of exchange. "Virtually all interbank transactions, by market participants here and abroad, involve a purchase or sale of dollars for a foreign currency. This is true even if a bank's aim is to buy German marks for sterling" (Kubarych 1978, 18).

2. *Intervention.* Central banks usually intervene in the existing private interbank market; thus the dollar is the intervention currency. This is true even for some of the interventions which maintain parities within the European Monetary System.

3. *Invoice.* Data on this are not as good as we might like, but a few generalizations seem possible. In manufactured goods trade between any two countries, there is a preference for invoicing in exporter's currency but also a preference for invoicing in the currency of the larger country. This in itself gives the United States, as the world's largest economy, a disproportionate share of the invoicing. In addition much raw materials trade, even if it does not involve the United States, is also invoiced in dollars. In financial transactions the dollar is the dominant currency for international borrowing and lending, though this dominance is not complete.

4. *Peg.* This is the best-known aspect of the story. In 1970 most of the world was pegged to the dollar; now only a limited number of smaller countries still are. This does not, however, represent the rise of a rival currency but the abandonment of fixed rates altogether.

5. *Banking.* Dollars in New York and Eurodollars in London constitute the main liquid international asset, although there has been some diversification into other currencies, especially Deutsche marks.

6. *Reserve.* The dollar accounts for the bulk of nongold reserves, with some accounting complications introduced recently by the EMS. As will be discussed further below, there is again some trend toward diversification.

It is clear from this brief description that the dollar is an international money, though its moneyness is less than it might be, less than it was eleven years ago, and less than that of sterling in 1913. The natural questions are how this position is likely to change and what difference it makes. To answer these—as best we can, for the answers will be based on loose theory and casual empirics—we need to examine the forces that make the dollar an international money.

## 10.2   The Dollar as an International Medium of Exchange

Economies of Scale and Indirect Exchange

The role of the dollar as a vehicle currency can be attributed to economies of scale in foreign exchange markets, which in turn arise from the lumpiness of transactions. "Since the dollar is the main currency for international trade and investment the dollar market for each currency is much more active than between any pair of foreign currencies. By going through the dollar, large amounts can be traded more easily" (Kubarych 1978, 18).

The nature of the economies of scale can be illustrated if we ignore the distinction between retail and interbank markets and simply think of firms offering to buy and sell foreign exchange. Suppose that at the going exchange rate the total demand and supply for foreign exchange in some market are equal over the course of a year, but that offers to exchange currencies in either direction are of finite size and arrive at random times. Then a firm offering to exchange currencies may find a complementary offer waiting for it in the marketplace, but it may have to wait for one to arrive and may have to wait until earlier offers are consummated. Thus there will on average be some delay before a transaction can be completed. Now suppose the flow through the market were to double. It is obvious that the average waiting time would fall. It is easier to find a match in a thick market than a thin one.[2]

Adding market-making banks, who hold currency stocks, will not much alter this picture. Firms may no longer have to wait, but the law of large numbers will imply that the trade-off between the size of currency stocks and the probability of a stockout will improve as the market gets larger. So bid-ask spreads will be lower in larger markets.

To go from economies of scale in the exchange markets to the emergence of a vehicle currency, it is useful to make a distinction between what I have called (Krugman 1980) the *structure of payments* and *the structure of exchange*. By the structure of payments we will mean the matrix of final demands for foreign exchange for the purposes of trade and investment. By the structure of exchange I mean the matrix of actual foreign exchange transactions. The distinction between these may be illustrated by considering, say, trade and investment flows between Ecuador and the Netherlands. These will appear as positive entries in the Ecuador–Netherlands and Netherland–Ecuador boxes of the structure of payments, but there will be a zero in the guilder-sucre box of the structure of exchange because the actual transactions will take place in the dollar-guilder and dollar-sucre markets. To a first approximation, we can regard the structure of payments as independent of the choice of medium of exchange, determined by "fundamental" trade and investment motives. The question then becomes one of determining the structure of exchange given these fundamentals.

Consider first a world of three countries $A$, $B$, and $C$. They have national currencies, the $\alpha$, the $\beta$, and the $\gamma$. In figure 10.1a is illustrated the structure of payments in this world: $P_{AB}$, $P_{BC}$, and $P_{CA}$ are the final demands for foreign exchange flows, measured in the same (arbitrary) units; they are assumed to be bilaterally balanced.[3]

How will these payments be carried out? One possibility, illustrated in figure 10.1b, is that payments will take place directly, with all three pairs of currencies actively traded. If so, the volume of exchange transactions in each market will equal the final payments. But suppose that $A$ is much more important a trading and investment partner of $B$ and $C$ than either is of the other; that is. $P_{AB}$, $P_{CA} \gg P_{BC}$. Then it will be cheaper to trade $\beta$'s and $\gamma$'s indirectly through the vehicle of the $\alpha$, and the structure of exchange will collapse to that illustrated in figure 10.1c, where there is no active $\beta\gamma$ market. An important point to note is that this channeling of transactions between $B$ and $C$ through $A$'s currency itself swells the markets in that currency, reinforcing its advantage.[4]

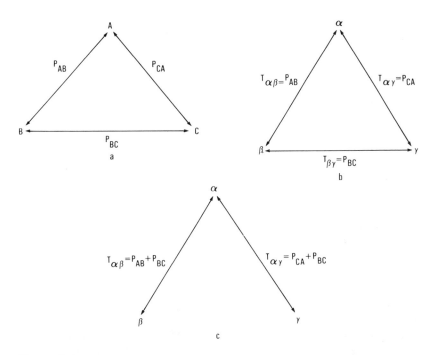

**Figure 10.1**
(a) The structure of payments; (b) the structure of direct exchange; (c) the structure of indirect exchange

## N-Country Complications

When we go beyond three countries, the picture becomes somewhat more complicated, though the principles don't change. Two new possibilities emerge: first, that the currency of a country that is not very dominant in world payments will emerge as vehicle through a process of "snowballing"; second, that there may emerge a multipolar world with several vehicle currencies.

Snowballing may be illustrated by the following example: Suppose that the world consists of several large countries, one only slightly larger than the others, and a number of small countries. Simple trilateral comparisons would lead us to expect payments between large countries to take place through direct exchange; yet the presence of the smaller countries can lead to a complete "supermonetization" of world payments. The process would work as follows: Payments between small countries will take place indirectly, through the medium of the largest country's currency. This will swell these markets, creating an incentive for other large countries to carry

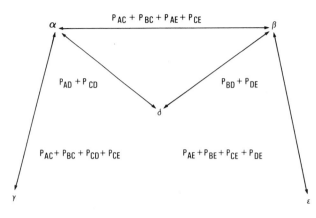

$P_{AC} + P_{BC} + P_{AE} + P_{CE}$

$\alpha$ _____ $\beta$

$P_{AD} + P_{CD}$             $P_{BD} + P_{DE}$

$\delta$

$P_{AC} + P_{BC} + P_{CD} + P_{CE}$      $P_{AE} + P_{BE} + P_{CE} + P_{DE}$

$\gamma$                                            $\varepsilon$

**Figure 10.2**
A bipolar structure of exchange

out their exchanges with the small countries via the same medium, and will swell all of the markets in the largest country's currency, perhaps enough to eliminate all direct bilateral markets. It may not be too far-fetched to suggest that this process explains the rise of sterling to an extraordinary position of dominance at a time when Britain, though the economic leader, was far from having the sort of preeminence that, say, the United States had in 1950.

On the other hand, a many-country world can support several vehicle currencies. Figure 10.2 illustrates a possible structure of exchange among five countries—$A$, $B$, $C$, $D$, $E$—whose currencies are the $\alpha$, $\beta$, $\gamma$, $\delta$, $\varepsilon$, respectively. Payments between the countries are $P_{AB}$, $P_{BC}$, etc.; transactions on the markets are $T_{\alpha\beta}$, $T_{\beta\gamma}$, etc. The illustrated pattern is one in which $A$ and $B$ are both vehicle currency countries. There is an "alpha area" ($A$ and $C$) in which all payments go through $\alpha$'s, and a "beta area" ($B$ and $E$) in which payments go through the $\beta$. One country, $D$, is a part of neither area, so there is both an active $\alpha\delta$ and an active $\beta\delta$ market. A bipolar structure of exchange of this type existed in the dollar-sterling system of the interwar period and is a possible future.

Multiple Equilibria and Changes in the Vehicle

The model of vehicle currencies we have sketched out contains an obvious possibility for multiple equilibria. If the choice of a currency as a vehicle is a response to the relative size of the markets in it, and if a currency's becoming a vehicle itself swells those markets, then the choice of vehicle may be self-justifying. This in turn suggests that once a country's currency gets established as the international medium of exchange, it will continue in that role, even if the country loses the position in the structure of payments that originally gave it that position. Thus sterling remained a vehicle currency long after Britain had ceased to be number 1.

It might be objected that a structure of exchange that does not minimize worldwide transaction costs offers a profit opportunity. A bank could act as market maker and reap the gains. I would offer a guess here: Market making probably involves a one-time fixed cost in getting market partici-pants informed and inducing them to change their behavior. In existing markets this is a sunk cost, which need not be expended again. To change, the structure of exchange requires a new expenditure. The result is that the structure of exchange will change only if it is very far from what the structure of payments would suggest, so the choice of a medium of ex-change exhibits a good deal of inertia. On the other hand, a temporary disruption of the foreign exchange markets can shift the structure of ex-change from one equilibrium to another and thus have lasting effects. The choice of a vehicle currency reflects both history and hysteresis.

The actual decline of sterling as a medium of exchange, and its replace-ment by the dollar, appears to have taken place in a sharp slump, a long slow slide, and a final crash. World War I exchange restrictions disrupted the sterling system and led to the emergence of the dollar, and also the French franc, as rivals, and the dollar slowly gained ground for fifty years. (Remarkably, sterling remained the more important medium of exchange during the interwar period and may even still have been more important than the dollar in the late 1940s.) Finally, sterling vanished from the map in the late 1960s and the early 1970s. The impressive fact here is surely the inertia; sterling remained the first-ranked currency for half a century after Britain had ceased to be the first-ranked economic power.[5]

Relationships to Other Roles of Money

The discussion in this section has concentrated on the medium-of-exchange role of international money in isolation. In fact there is some interdepen-dence among roles. The links that seem clear are these: If the dollar is a good store of value, the costs of making markets against the dollar are lower, thus encouraging the vehicle role. Conversely, the medium-of-exchange role encourages both invoicing in dollars and holding dollars, as I will discuss below.

## 10.3   The Dollar as an International Unit of Account

Most of the analytical work on the use of currencies as international units of account has focused on the official role: on the decision on whether to peg to another currency, and on the choice of peg. I will not attempt to add to this extensive literature; in any case hardly anyone still pegs to the dollar. Instead, I will focus on the private use of currencies as units of account. A good place to start, because there are relatively abundant data, is the invoicing decision.

Even in the 1960s trade contracts were by no means exclusively written in dollars. In an influential work Grassman (1973) showed that most Swedish trade was invoiced in exporting country currency. It seems to be generally true that trade between industrial countries is invoiced in either the exporter's or the importer's currency, with no major role for the dollar in trade between third parties.

Table 10.2 presents some comparative numbers on the share of exports and imports invoiced in a country's currency and on the share of exports to the United States invoiced in dollars. The countries are ranked in order of the value of their 1978 exports. An impressionistic look at this table suggests that much of the variation can be explained by three rules. First, other things equal the exporter's currency is preferred. For every country

**Table 10.2**
Invoicing of merchandise trade

|  | Share of domestic currency used to invoice: | | Share of exports to United States invoiced in dollars |
|---|---|---|---|
|  | Exports | Imports |  |
| Germany | 86.9 | 42.0 | 36 |
| Japan | — | — | 94 |
| France | 68.3 | 31.5 | 52 |
| United Kingdom | 73.0 | — | 44 |
| Italy | — | — | 68 |
| The Netherlands | 50.2 | 31.4 | 81 |
| Canada | — | — | 87 |
| Belgium | 47.7 | 25.4 | 78 |
| Sweden | 66.1 | 25.8 | 27 |
| Austria | 54.7 | 24.7 | — |
| Denmark | 54.0 | 24.0 | — |
| Finland | 15.5 | — | — |

Sources: Page (1977); Rao and Magee (1980).

for which data on both are available, a higher share of exports than imports is invoiced in domestic currency. Second, other things equal the currencies of large are used more than those of small countries. Thus Germany has the highest proportion of exports in domestic currency and a sizable fraction of imports in marks as well; the fraction of exports to the United States invoiced in dollars is noticeably high, even for countries which mostly invoice in home currency.

The third rule is that the yen is hardly used. As shown in the table, virtually all Japanese exports are invoiced in dollars. It is also true where data are available that the yen is much less used as an invoice currency in exports to Japan than Japan's size would lead one to expect. This may in part reflect a political decision on the part of Japan not to allow the yen to become an international currency.

In additional to these generalizations, we have one more observation: Raw materials trade, and with it most of LDC exports, is generally invoiced in dollars. McKinnon has proposed the terms "tradables I" and "tradables II" to describe the relevant distinction. Tradables I are differentiated manufactured products, typically produced by oligopolists and normally invoiced in exporting country currency—except, we might add, when the importer is large relative to the exporter, in which case the importer's currency is used. Tradables II are primary products, sold in a world market and normally invoiced in dollars.

Figure 10.3 shows a stylized version of the facts about choice of invoice currency. Four types of countries are distinguished: the United States, large

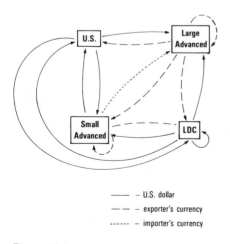

———  – U.S. dollar

— — –  exporter's currency

------  – importer's currency

**Figure 10.3**
Choice of currency in world trade

advanced countries, small advanced countries, and LDCs. An arrow indicates the direction of exports.[6] These then are our stylized facts about invoicing. What explains them? I would argue that they reflect essentially the cost of calculation.

Note that risk sharing by itself cannot explain the pattern of invoicing. The reason is that firms can always avoid exchange risk by entering the forward market and that the choice between invoicing in exporter and importer currency is simply a question of deciding who does the forward contract. (Even if no forward market exists, firms can "roll their own" forward contracts by international borrowing and lending.) Admittedly, forward contracting does involve some costs, but then it is on the "frictions" rather than on risk per se that we should focus.

The simplest explanation seems to be this. To deal with contracts denominated in foreign currency, one must be sophisticated about foreign exchange—and acquiring this sophistication has a real if hard-to-measure fixed cost. In the case of tradables I, the exporter is typically a firm selling a differentiated product. Its costs are mostly fixed in domestic currency, so its normal pricing strategy will be to keep the domestic currency price fixed. This being the case, it is natural that the firm should leave worrying about the exchange rate to the importer who has to deal with exchange markets as a matter of course in any case. The special case where a small country exports to a large country then falls into place. In small countries, everyone is obliged to be sophisticated about foreign exchange; in large countries nobody wants to worry about it.

Exporters of tradables II, by contrast, sell products whose prices depend very little on domestic factors. For them the easiest procedure—in the sense that each contract does not involve a simultaneous speculation on future exchange rates—is to have all contracts anywhere in the world written in the same currency, for which the international medium of exchange is the most natural.

Kindleberger has used the analogy between money and language to explain the role of the dollar; in this situation it fits very well. If I want to communicate with someone of a different nationality, one or both of us must invest in learning a second language. If she is from a large country and I from a small one, we will probably use her language; if we are both from small countries, we will both use some international language. If a Dutch business leader and a German business leader make an agreement, they will probably converse in German and quote prices in marks; if the Dutch business leader then deals with a Brazilian, the conversation will more likely be in English and the price in dollars.

This is a very loose argument, and we would not want to lean too hard on it. Nevertheless, we will push it just a bit further to suggest that international capital markets—especially under fixed rates—resemble tradables II in that bond prices are very much internationalized. LIBOR and the Chicago wheat price both are watched around the world, and in both cases this makes it convenient to denominate international contracts in dollars.

Is there anything in the unit-of-account role of the dollar that corresponds to the possibility of multiple equilibria in its medium of exchange role? In trade among the advanced countries, the choice of a unit of amount seems to be determined by fundamentals. The use of the dollar is comparable to the use of the mark; that is, the dollar plays no more of a role than the size of the United States entitles it to. Where there is an arbitrariness in the use of the dollar is in LDC/tradables II trade and, perhaps, in international lending. Here there is again a situation where the dollar is used because it is used, and its place could be taken by the mark or the yen.

## 10.4   The Dollar as an International Store of Value

Sterling and the Dollar as Banking Currencies

In 1913 working balances in sterling were held by banks and firms all around the world, reflecting in part the demand for sterling created by its other monetary roles, in part the economies of scale that made London the most efficient financial center. Thus settlement of trade contracts in sterling, servicing of sterling, denominated debt, and interbank transactions in sterling all required holding of sterling balances. The vehicle role of sterling made it more liquid than other currencies, and the scale of the London market made Lombard Street sterling balances an attractive proposition.

The dollar today holds a similar, but less striking, position. As we have seen, the dollar is dominant in interbank markets, still acounts for most international lending, and plays a disproportionate though not dominant role in trade invoicing. Economies of scale also play a role—but in a more confusing way. Dollar balances can be held not only in New York but also in London, so the advantages of the dollar are not so much tied to the scale of activities in a particular geographical center as they are to the scale of activities in that currency. Nonetheless, these economies are real—imagine asking a London bank to offer a Eurodrachma account or a Euroescudo account, and the importance of having at least some minimum scale becomes apparent.

**Table 10.3**
The dollar as a store of value

|                                                                         | 1970 | 1973 | 1980 |
|-------------------------------------------------------------------------|------|------|------|
| Share of dollars in "offshore" holdings of European banks[a]            | 77.1 | 70.4 | 69.0 |
| Share of dollars in world foreign exchange reserves[b]                  | 75.6 | 84.5 | 73.1 |
| Share of pounds in world foreign exchange reserves[b]                   | 12.6 | 5.9  | 3.0  |
| "International currency" share in foreign exchange reserves[c]          | 88.2 | 84.5 | 73.1 |

a. BIS *Annual Report*.
b. This number includes dollars exchanged by members of the EMS for ECUs. See IMF,
*Annual Report* 1981, p. 69.
c. See text for explanation.

As a store of value, however, the dollar has one disadvantage prewar sterling did not have. This is the uncertainty caused by floating exchange rates. Uncertain exchange rates push wealth holders toward diversification, opposing the forces encouraging convergence on a single currency. The result has apparently been a gradual diversification away from the dollar since 1973. The first line of table 10.3 presents some evidence from the Eurocurrency markets, where a slow drift away from the dollar seems to have occurred.

### The Dollar as a Reserve Currency

Probably the most important reason for holding reserves in dollars is that the dollar is an intervention currency. This means that reserves initially accrue to central banks in dollars and must be converted to other currencies if the central banks want to diversify. It also means that reserves must be converted back to dollars to be used for intervention. For large countries such operations carry more than a transaction cost: Movements into and out of nondollar currencies amount to intervention in other countries' foreign exchange markets that are likely to be resented (the United States is used to it). Because of this political aspect, jointly floating European countries (in the snake and later in the EMS) have continued to hold reserves in dollars, not in each others' currencies, and they have often maintained crossparities by simultaneous buying and selling of dollars, not by direct swaps of European currencies.

Opposing these advantages of the dollar is the desire of central banks to diversify against exchange risk. As table 10.3 shows, the dollar's share of world foreign exchange reserves actually rose in the early 1970s, then declined. But in a sense this is misleading as a measure of "demonetization" of reserves because sterling was still a partial international money in 1970. The last line of the table adds the dollar and pound shares in 1970, but not afterward, to give a rough measure of the share of international money in reserves. It suggests a continual and substantial shift on the part of central banks toward less liquid but less risky portfolios.

## 10.5   Prospects for the Dollar's Role

Determinants of the Dollar's Role

The theory of international money sketched out in the preceding sections emphasized two kinds of influence on the choice of currency as international money and on the importance of its role. First, the currency of a country that is important in world markets will be a better candidate for an international money than that of a smaller country. Second, the use of a currency as an international money itself reinforces that currency's usefulness, so there is an element of circular causation. This circularity was clearest in the case of choice of a medium of exchange, where a given structure of payments—a type of market fundamentals—might be consistent with several different structures of exchange, because of the self-justifying effect of making a currency serve as vehicle.

It is this circularity that raises the most worries about the future prospects of the dollar. The troublesome possibilities are either that the dollar's fundamental advantages will drop to some critical point, leading to an abrupt unraveling of its international role, or that a temporary disruption of world financial markets will permanently impair the dollar's usefulness. These are not purely academic speculations, since they have precedent in the history of sterling's decline. The disruption of World War I led to a permanent reduction in sterling's role, while the gradual relative decline of Britain's importance in the world was reflected not in a smooth decline in sterling's role but in surprising persistence followed by abrupt collapse.

These possibilities are illustrated in figure 10.4. We assume that it is possible to define some index of the use of the dollar as international money (though we have emphasized that the different roles are at least partly separable). The *desired* use of the dollar as international money will then be an increasing function of the actual use, as illustrated by the curve *UU*. The position of this schedule depends on fundamentals, such as the relative size of the U.S. economy and the openness and efficiency of its capital markets, as well as the stability of exchange rates and thus the strength of the incentives for diversification. Given these fundamentals, however, there

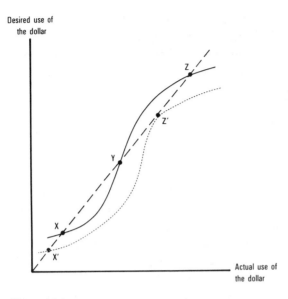

**Figure 10.4**
Possibilities for a collapse of the dollar's role

may be several equilibria. as illustrated. Even without a formal specification of dynamics, it seems clear that X and Z will be the locally stable equilibria here; Z might correspond to the current state of dollar standard with diversification, X to a multipolar world where the mark and yen serve as regional international currencies.

Suppose that the fundamental strength of the dollar were gradually to weaken (as it surely has). Then UU would shift downward. Initially the role of the dollar would also gradually decline, from Z to Z'. At that point, however, a critical level would have been reached; a small further decline in the fundamentals would produce an unraveling of the dollar's role. As it was used less, the desired use would fall, and the role of the dollar would decline to X' even without any further weakening in the fundamentals.

Alternatively, a temporary disruption of the system could shift the world from one equilibrium to another. It is depressingly easy to imagine scenarios; for example, a war scare in Europe. This could lead to capital flight and the imposition of exchange controls. If the controls lasted long enough they could break the habit of doing business in dollars, so that when they were lifted the world would end up at X instead of Z.

This may seem to be an extremely casual and oversimplified way to think about the future of the dollar. Oversimplified it certainly is; we would very

**Table 10.4**
Pax Brittanica versus Pax Americana

|  | United Kingdom, 1913 | United States, late 1970s |
|---|---|---|
| Share of world trade | 16[a] | 12.1[c] |
| Share of world output | 14[b] | 24.3[d] |
| Trade share of largest rival | 12[a] (Germany) | 11.5[c] (Germany) |
| Output share of largest rival | 36[b] (United States) | 10.1[d] (Japan) |

a. Exports plus imports, from Rostow (1978).
b. Industrial production, from Rostow (1978).
c. 1979 export figures, from *Report of the President on U.S. Competitiveness* (1980).
d. 1978 GNP figures, from *World Bank Atlas*.

much like to be able to treat the subject rigorously. But this analysis seems to be if anything more formal and less casual than most discussion of the international monetary system and monetary reform. And this analysis points to a useful way of framing the question of the future role of the dollar: Is the fundamental position of the dollar strong enough to sustain its world role?

## Is America Big Enough?

The question of whether the role of the dollar in sustainable should, in principle, be answered with a quantitative model. Unfortunately, this is not feasible. What we *can* do is to compare the position of the United States with that of the United Kingdom before the First World War, when sterling was the international currency to a much greater extent than the dollar has ever been. To the extent that the U.S. position is as strong or stronger, the continuation of a dollar-based international monetary system looks possible.

Table 10.4 presents some comparisons between the position of the United States in recent years and that of the United Kingdom at the peak of sterling's preeminence. The United Kingdom was the largest trading nation in 1913, by a small margin that was, however, bigger than the U.S. margin in the late 1970s. The U.K. domestic economy was, however, proportionately far smaller. Also the relatively large share of Germany in trade reflects its geographical position in Europe; outside Europe the United States still has a pronounced lead.

On the basis of these comparisons, then, there does not seem to be any reason why the dollar cannot continue to be the basic international money, indeed why it could not expand its role to something like that of sterling at its peak. There are, however, two features of the world which have changed—a less important one and a crucial one.

The less important aspect of the world that has changed is the increased relative importance of trade in manufactures as opposed to primary products. In McKinnon's terms, world trade has shifted from tradables II to tradables I. This in itself reduces the role of the center country's currency, since that currency is more likely to be used for the denomination and settlement of trade contracts in tradables II than tradables I.

The crucial difference of course is the advent of generalized floating with no end in sight. This creates incentives for diversification that reduce the usefulness of the dollar as a store of value. Perhaps this will be enough to tip the balance. If so, the dollar's role will unravel, not because of the relative decline of the United States but essentially because of the general problem of controlling inflation.

After the Fall

What would happen if the dollar's role were to decline sharply? There are really two questions here. The first is one of the transition. Would a decline in the dollar's role as a store of value, in particular, amount to a devastating run on the bank? Second, once the transition is accomplished. How much harm would the dethroning of the dollar do the world economy?

The important point to notice in discussing the transition is that the problem is *not* one of the United States having given the world paper in exchange for real goods and services. Very little of the "dollar" holding of the world is backed up by high-powered money; essentially it consists of short-term securities and bank deposits, many of the latter outside the United States. In principle then a change in the desired currency composition of liquid assets could be accommodated without any redistribution of wealth. Banks could convert their depositors' Eurodollar deposits into Euromark or European deposits at the current exchange rate; the Federal Reserve could buy up Treasury bills while selling mark-denominated securities. The currency transformation need not involve capital gains and losses to anyone.

Where the problem would arise is in the increased exposure of financial intermediaries to exchange risk. International banks borrow short and lend long, both at present mostly in dollars. A shift away from dollars would force a transition period during which the short borrowing and long lending are not in the same currency, posing obvious risks to the stability of the financial system. The example of Britain shows that the transition can be made—indeed the unraveling of the pound as an international money went along with continuing growth of London as a financial center. But it would not be a good idea to be too complacent.

What about the long-run costs? Replacing the dollar in all its roles, say, with the mark, would not seem to make much difference. A more likely outcome, however, is a multipolar system with the dollar, mark, and yen all playing some role as international money. The cost would be a loss of economies of scale. Transactions costs in the interbank market would be higher, as would the operating costs of international banks, but these costs are so low at present that even a huge proportionate increase would still be a small number. More important, perhaps, would be the increased difficulty of calculation in a world without a single international unit of account. But surely the use of three currencies to quote raw materials prices would be a far less important cost than what we have already experienced from inflation and floating exchange rates.

The moral then seems to be that it is not a collapsed but a collapsing role of the dollar that we should worry about.

# 11 Policy Problems of a Monetary Union

Over the past decade the major nations of Western Europe have decisively turned their back on flexible exchange rates and embarked on what seems to be a path toward ever-growing monetary integration. The adjustable-peg European Monetary System (EMS) has become increasingly credible over time, with realignments becoming smaller and rarer. And in the last few years the idea of a common European currency has moved with remarkable speed from intellectual plaything to realistic possibility.

The politics of this change in outlook are fairly apparent. First of all, disillusionment with the volatility of floating rates came sooner and stronger within Europe than elsewhere, partly because of the sheer size of trade flows within the region and partly because fluctuating exchange rates turn the management of European Community institutions, notably the Common Agricultural Policy, into an administrative nightmare. At a deeper level, monetary union is a natural political counterpart (though the economic logic is less clear) to other moves that attempt to use closer European economic integration to end the long stagnation of the European economy from the mid-1970s to the mid-1980s—that attempt, as the Brussels jargon has it, to "use the Community dimension to reinforce growth."

The first wave of the new drive to seek a solution to Eurosclerosis in greater European integration of course was the complex set of measures referred to as "1992." Whatever the ultimate success of 1992, it is a fairly uncontroversial initiative from the point of view of economic theory. Greater integration of markets brings gains that are well understood in principle, though poorly measured in practice. One may believe that the claims for 1992 are exaggerated—my own guess is that the Cecchini

Originally published in Paul DeGrauwe and Lucas Papademos (eds.), *The European Monetary System in the 1990's*, New York: Longman, 1990. Copyright © 1990 by the Centre for European Policy Studies and the Bank of Greece.

Report is overoptimistic by a factor of two or three—but the qualitative character of the gains is clear.

The push for closer monetary union represents the natural political continuation of 1992: Having achieved a stunning political success in their drive to eliminate barriers to trade in goods and services, the advocates of European economic union are looking for new frontiers to tear down. Yet from an economist's point of view trade integration and monetary union are very different kinds of action. The economics of international trade are relatively well understood (in principle, if not quantitatively), and the nature of the gains from trade, whether from comparative advantage, exploitation of scale economies, or increased competition are not controversial. The economics of international money, by contrast, are not at all well understood: They hinge crucially not only on sophisticated and ambiguous issues like credibility and coordination but on even deeper issues like transaction costs and bounded rationality. So the sudden enthusiasm for monetary union has carried us into largely uncharted territory.

This chapter presents a brief overview of some issues raised by European monetary union. The chapter takes the form of a somewhat rambling essay: I sketch out a few models. while trying to present as coherent a discussion as I can of the issues that at present defy formal modeling, and make no attempt to integrate the analysis into a coherent framework. The best defense I can offer is that monetary union is inherently a messy subject—and that becoming aware of that inherent messiness is the first part of wisdom in this field.

Although the title of the chapter refers to problems of policy under a monetary union, a substantial part is actually concerned with a somewhat different subject: The advantages and disadvantages of substituting a common currency for an adjustable-peg system of the kind that most of Western Europe already lives under. There are several reasons for spending a good deal of time on this question. First is that the issues of more or less fixed versus flexible exchange rates have already been the subject of a huge if not exactly conclusive literature, while the effects of going on from stable rates to an actual common currency have been less fully worked over. A second justification for focusing on the question of a common currency is that it is an idea whose time has apparently come, yet creation of such a currency is far from being a done deal. It seems particularly useful to review the issue now given that politicians are busy taking sides with very little basis in the scribbling of academics of this or any other year—the enthusiasm with which some have adopted the idea, and the dismay with which others regard it, are based more on gut reactions than on careful analysis. Finally, thinking about the costs and benefits of a common currency as compared with more modest schemes like EMS-style fixed rates helps us to think about what policies are needed to make either kind of system work.

The chapter is in six sections. Section 11.1 addresses some general "philosophical" issues regarding monetary economics in general and monetary union in particular. Section 11.2 reviews the traditional optimal currency argument, which applies both to the question of whether to form a monetary union and the question of whether to take the final step to a common currency. Section 11.3 and 11.4 examine some more newfangled arguments involving coordination and credibility. Section 11.5 briefly examines whether monetary union also demands coordination of fiscal policies. Section 11.6 presents a different argument regarding monetary union, which links it to the imperatives of political integration.

## 11.1  Money and Monetary Union: Some General Considerations

I want to begin the discussion in this chapter with two "philosophical" points. The first is that monetary economics, in general, and the economics of international monetary arrangements, in particular, cannot be addressed using presumptions from our usual economic rules of thumb. The second is to stress the importance of defining the alternatives to be discussed: I want to argue that the most interesting alternatives are floating rates, an adjustable-peg system, and a common currency.

Let me start with the question of how to think about monetary economics. Most of what economists think they know comes from microeconomic theory, and in particular from the model of frictionless, competitive general equilibrium. From this model comes the general presumption that markets work, that government interference reduces welfare unless there is a clear-cut market failure. For many policy issues the presumptions of simple microeconomics give clear guidance. Unfortunately, in monetary economics, almost by definition, standard microeconomic presumptions are of little help. Simple microeconomics assumes an absence of frictions; monetary economics is precisely about frictions and the institutions that are devised to cope with them.

Consider the main roles of money. Although the traditional Jevons classification gives four roles of money—medium of exchange, unit of account. store of value, standard of deferred repayment—it is the first two that are essential. Yet neither role makes sense in the kinds of models that underlie most of our policy judgments. A medium of exchange is needed to reduce transaction costs, yet standard economic models do not allow for transaction costs, and indeed even the most sophisticated models have trouble incorporating such costs in a coherent way. The role of money as a unit of account presumes that people need a shortcut for making economic calculations—that they cannot keep the whole vector of relative prices in their heads. This is reasonable enough. Yet once we allow for the possibility that people cannot use all the information they have, we are into the world of bounded rationality, a difficult area where we know that many of the standard presumptions of economics need to be questioned.

Now admittedly there have been a number of efforts on the part of economists to incorporate money in a systematic way into their models—typically through approximate ways of representing the medium of exchange function, such as the so-called Clower constraint that requires that individuals have cash in advance of any purchase. These models provide little useful guidance for evaluating international monetary arrangements, however, for two main reasons. First, as nearly all of their creators would admit, they are incomplete: At best they give a stylized account of the role of money as medium of exchange, but they have nothing to say about its unit of account role. Since both the costs and benefits of monetary unions depend crucially on the role of national versus multinational standards as units of account, this is a vital omission. Second, formal analyses of money nearly always assume that use of a single currency is imposed by fiat of a single government. This assumption looks like a reasonable approach for many purposes, but unfortunately it immediately takes many of the issues concerning monetary union off the table. So there is not much guidance to be had in standard economic theory for the key monetary issues facing Europe.

My point in proclaiming our ignorance is to emphasize that economic theory does not give us any simple presumptions about monetary unions. In particular, one cannot appeal to any presumption in favor of free markets. For one thing, in the inherently second-best world of monetary arrangements there is no reason to assume that markets get it right; for another, alternative international monetary arrangements may be equally well characterized as free market (or unfree market). Which is more nearly a free-market system: flexible exchange rates, fixed exchange rates, or a common currency? The answer is not obvious, and even if we could decide on some ranking of freeness, no policy conclusion would follow.

Let me turn next to the question of what alternatives we should discuss. This chapter could make a number of comparisons: fully flexible rates versus target zones, or absolutely fixed rates versus adjustable pegs, and so on. I would argue, however, that for Europe right now the interesting issues are the comparison between flexible rates, an adjustable-peg system and a common currency.

The first reason that these are the interesting choices is that within Europe these are the choices currently on the table. The United Kingdom is still debating whether to join the exchange rate mechanism of the EMS; for the rest of Europe the longer-term question is whether that mechanism evolves into something more.

One might of course want to discuss intermediate choices: Why not discuss the desirability of British "shadowing" of the European currency unit (ECU), or of a transition of the EMS from adjustable pegs to more rigidly fixed rates? The answer, on one hand, is that I do not believe that a target zone and an adjustable peg are very different in their economic impact; as recent research has shown, target zones tend to stabilize exchange rates toward the middle of the band while they are credible, and to be subject to speculative attacks just like fixed rates when they are not. On the other hand, I would argue that the case of an adjustable-peg system is more fundamental than that of a totally fixed system, at least as long as we have a comparison with a common currency on the table. Any system of national currencies is, potentially, one in which exchange rates *could* change. This possibility might not be exercised very often, but the possibility of realignment is one of the crucial differences.

This concludes the philosophical setup of the chapter. Now we can proceed on to the analysis.

## 11.2   The Optimal Currency Area Approach

The traditional starting point for discussion of issues concerning monetary union has been via the so-called optimal currency area approach. In more recent discussion new ideas concerning policy coordination and credibility have become more fashionable. However, the optimal currency area approach is still very useful as a first step, and probably more fundamental. Thus as a way of organizing our thoughts, it is important to review it.

The basic optimal currency area argument may be illustrated by imagining that Europe consists of only two countries, France and the Federal Republic of Germany (FRG). Let us imagine that these countries have some difference in their export mix—say, France exports cheese, the FRG wurst. And let us also suppose that the world market is subject to occasional shocks that shift the relative demand for cheese and wurst.

Should France and the FRG maintain separate currencies? If so, should the exchange rate between these currencies be fixed, or should it be allowed to float? Let us consider these questions in reverse order.

The basic argument for allowing the exchange rate to float is that it eases the process of adjustment to shocks. Suppose that the world relative demand for cheese falls, necessitating a fall in the relative price of French goods and labor. Then it will ordinarily be easier for this change in relative prices to be accomplished via a decline in the French franc (FF) against the Deutsche mark (DM) than via some combination of inflation in the FRG and deflation in France. In particular, if prices and wages are sticky, changing the exchange rate avoids the necessity for a French recession. So allowing the exchange rate to float has obvious macroeconomic advantages.

It might seem that these same advantages could be achieved in a discretionary fashion even within a currency union (but not with a common currency) by having a rate that is fixed by the central banks but adjusted when necessary. The problem with such a system is that it is subject to speculative attacks when the market thinks an exchange rate change may be in prospect. To limit such attacks, the central banks must try to make credible their commitment not to change parities too often, and the attempt to retain credibility will inhibit their ability to make exchange rate adjustments. This problem should not be overstressed: An adjustable-peg system can work and need not forsake all the advantages of exchange rate flexibility, but because of the need for credibility it tends to become less effective at smoothing macroeconomic adjustment than a pure float.

Returning to our example, what are the disadvantages of floating? The answer is that they are microeconomic. Fluctuating exchange rates will impose costs due to uncertainty;[1] these costs will be larger if the exchange market is speculatively inefficient, producing excess volatility (and all available evidence suggests that this is in fact the case). Essentially a floating exchange rate will tend to degrade the unit of account function of both national moneys.

A transition from floating to fixed rates then would impose a cost—increased difficulty in adjusting relative prices—and a benefit—decreased uncertainty and confusion about the values of national moneys. Notice that both the cost and the benefit depend on the unit of account function of money: the tendency of firms to set prices that are sticky in nominal terms, on one side, and the importance of a stable standard in calculations, on the other. But the unit of account function of money is essentially a bounded rationality issue, so that even in this most simple exercise in international monetary economics we are in deep theoretical waters.

% of GNP

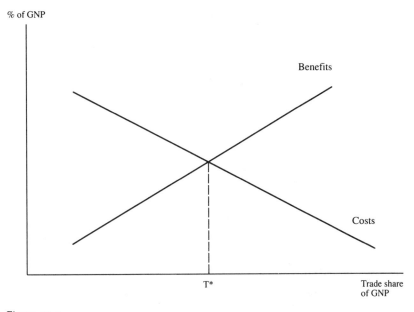

Benefits

Costs

T*                                                                   Trade share
                                                                     of GNP

**Figure 11.1**

This means that the next step, which is the elaboration of the conditions under which a fixed rate is desirable is highly speculative. Nonetheless, the optimal currency approach makes the plausible assertion that a fixed rate is more desirable, the more closely linked are the two economies. The argument is illustrated in figure 11.1. On the horizontal axis we have the trade between France and the FRG, as a share of European gross national product (GNP); on the vertical axis, the costs and benefits of forming a monetary union. The benefits curve is drawn as an upward slope and the cost curve as a downward slope.

The upward slope of the benefits curve may be justified by the argument that the benefits from reducing exchange rate uncertainty, and any consequent effect of a monetary union in enhancing the unit of account function of each country's money, will be larger as a percentage of GNP, the larger the share of international trade in GNP. This seems fairly obvious, even though we do not have any idea how large these benefits may actually be.

The downward slope of the cost curve may be justified by two arguments. One is fairly concrete: The size of required price adjustments to accommodate any given external shock is likely to be smaller, the larger the initial trade is within the monetary union. Consider the effect of a simultaneous rise in demand for wurst and decline in demand for cheese that worsens

France s trade balance with the outside world by 1 percent of its GNP, with a corresponding improvement in the FRG's balance. To offset this shock, France would have to improve its balance with the FRG by an amount equal to 1 percent of its GNP; this would have to be accomplished through a decline in French relative wages and prices that makes French goods more competitive vis-à-vis German. Clearly the size of the required fall in wages would be less if French exports to the FRG are initially 20 percent of GNP than if they were initially only 1 percent. For any given Phillips curve then the cost of accommodating the shock without changing the FF–DM exchange rate would be less the more trade there is between France and the FRG.

The other, somewhat vaguer reason for downward-sloping costs lies in the effect of large-scale trade on the adjustment of prices and wages themselves. If France has extensive trade with the FRG, it becomes possible for French wages to be explicitly or implicitly indexed to the DM, so exchange rate adjustment would become ineffective in any case. That is, depreciation of the FF would not succeed in lowering relative French wages and prices, it would simply cause French inflation. The crossing-point of the curves then defines the critical level of integration: If trade exceeds the level $T^*$, a fixed rate system is preferable to floating.

Many discussions of optimal currency areas add a further observation that the degree of factor mobility makes a difference. Suppose that labor moves easily and freely between the FRG and France. Then when the demand for cheese falls, French workers could move to the FRG and start making sausage. This would reduce both the need for wage adjustment and the costs of incomplete adjustment, lowering the costs of a fixed rate system and thereby making it more desirable.

The thought experiment conducted here considers whether two given countries should form a monetary union. If one could measure the costs and benefits involved, however, the exercise could be turned around to ask how the world should optimally be carved up into currency areas. Assuming that the optimal size of such an area is less than the whole world but bigger than the typical country, such areas would consist of regional blocs of countries that do much of their trade with each other, such as Western Europe, North America, and perhaps the western Pacific.

Unfortunately, the assumption that the optimal currency area is intermediate in size between a large country and the world is not based on any real evidence. We actually have no particular reason to suppose that Europe is the right size for a monetary union. At one extreme one could claim that the whole world constitutes the optimal currency area. This is a fairly popular position at the moment, under the influence of global monetarists like McKinnon, and it is also a safe position, since it is not going to happen.

The contrary positon is near-heresy in the current political climate, but it is perfectly possible to make a case that Europe is too large for monetary union to be desirable. We might note the following points: First, the large countries of Europe do not do all that much trade with each other; the average intra-Community trade of the four major economies is only 15 percent of GNP, less than Canada's trade with the United States, yet Canada has not made a monetary agreement a priority. Second, exchange rate changes are hardly ineffective at changing relative wage rates within Europe—one need only look at the United Kingdom's roller-coaster competitiveness from the mid-1970s to the mid-1980s as a demonstration. Third, labor mobility among the European nations is hardly enough to provide much of an alternative to exchange rate adjustment.

But if Europe is not an optimal currency area, why should we think that the United States constitutes one? Well, maybe it does not. Would not it have been helpful at some time in the recent past to have been able to devalue the midwestern dollar? The idea of floating rates within the United States seems absurd, and not simply because the United States has much higher internal factor mobility than Europe. However, the reasons why It seems absurd probably stem more from issues of political symbolism than from any solid evidence that the costs would exceed the benefits.

The optimal currency area concept is very far from giving an operational guide to policy. Nonetheless, it is useful as a way of organizing our thoughts, and at least of revealing what we do not know. It can also be modified quite easily to consider the next question, that of comparing a fixed rate system with a common currency.

A transition from an adjustable-peg system like the EMS to a common currency would generate a concrete, if rather mundane, benefit: the elimination of foreign exchange transaction costs. It would also generate some further unit-of-account-type gains by removing residual uncertainty. On the other hand, adoption of a common currency would remove any remaining flexibility. imposing another cost.

The saving on transaction costs ought not be dismissed, even though it sounds rather boring. Admittedly transaction costs in the interbank market for foreign exchange, on which financial institutions swap funds, are negligible. Firms engaging in international trade, however, to say nothing of tourists and business travelers, must buy foreign exchange retail, paying a spread of 2 to 3 percent.

Is this a significant number? If one has in mind some spectacular payoff to the creation of a common currency, then the answer is no. However, the costs of transacting foreign exchange in Europe are of a roughly similar scale to typical estimates of those costs of crossing borders (delays, administrative costs, etc.) that 1992 is supposed to eliminate. It is widely hoped that eliminating border costs will bring indirect benefits through industry rationalization and increased competition that exceed the direct savings on transport itself. So a common currency would in this mundane way be comparable to the border-eliminating measures of 1992 as a force for European growth.

These gains from reduced transaction costs obviously depend on the scale of trade; in a less clear-cut way, the unit-of-account gains probably do the same. On the other hand, the costs of eliminating the option of exchange rate realignments will once again be less, the larger is trade. So the cost–benefit diagram for the transition from monetary union to common currency will look the same as that for transition from flexible rate to monetary union. Presumably the size of the optimal area for Common currency will be smaller than that for more modest monetary union, so (if the sizes are the right order of magnitude) the optimal world will have a hierarchy of common currency areas organized into currency blocs that in turn float against one another.

This then is the traditional optimal currency area approach. In my view, it still captures the most fundamental considerations. In recent discussions, however, other issues—notably those of coordination and credibility—have come to play an increasingly important role. This partly reflects intellectual fashion (this is the age of game theory) and partly the particular context of the EMS in the 1980s. My guess is that when the dust has settled, the old optimal currency area approach will still occupy center stage, while these new approaches will look oversold and dated. However, it is worth spending at least a little time on these newer issues.

## 11.3   Coordination and the Central Bank's Role

Twenty years ago advocates of floating rates argued that they would allow nations to pursue independent monetary policies. It has become apparent since then that the independence of nations under floating rates is much less than imagined and that indeed there are important issues of coordination. Somewhat ironically monetary union is now being advocated by some as a way of resolving coordination problems that arise under floating rates. In the simplest version of this story, countries under floating rates have an incentive to engage in beggar-thy-neighbour disinflation: By pursuing a tight monetary policy, any individual country, can appreciate its currency and thereby achieve a rapid reduction in inflation. Unfortunately, if all countries try to do this, they will find that they have chosen a deeper recession than they would have faced with the true collective inflation–output trade-off.

Fixed rates eliminate this problem by imposing the necessity of coordinated monetary policies. However, coordination does not become magically generated by the decision to fix rates. Some additional rules of the game are needed, and what we have learned is that in essence what is needed is the designation of someone as central banker.

This may seem like too flat a statement. At the level of pure economic analysis, all that we can say for sure is that a system of fixed exchange rates requires coordination of monetary policies. The famous $N - 1$ problem, which points out that there is one less exchange rate than there are currencies, makes the need for some agreement on who does what into a kind of theorem. This need could in principle be met by some kind of symmetrical coordination of policies. Indeed the EMS is a symmetric system on paper. In practice, however, symmetry is not what results. It is now widely accepted that fixed rate systems, when they work, almost always do so in part because one national central bank takes on the implicit role of central banker to the system as a whole.

It is arguable that even the classical gold standard in its last decades was really a Bank of England standard; it is much more apparent that Bretton Woods gave central monetary authority to the Federal Reserve despite an apparent external discipline imposed by the role of gold. The EMS, however, provides the most instructive case: A system that is fully symmetric at a formal level is generally regarded as a German monetary area at a practical level.

The reasons for German preeminence are now familiar: Since the FRG is the most credibly anti-inflationary of the major European economies, it is useful for other nations to follow the FRG's lead as a way of borrowing credibility—a bit of policy slipstreaming that is helped by the lucky coincidence that the economy with the sternest managers is also the largest. What is particularly interesting is the way that this strongly asymmetric system is entirely implicit, a matter of latent rather than manifest function. This difference between formal structure and practical outcome has turned out to be useful to all concerned; one of the main difficulties with a move to a common currency might be that the ability to cloak reality would be reduced, as I will show in section 11.4. For now, however, I simply note that the difference between implicit roles that flourishes under the EMS could not continue with a common currency, for no ambiguity about who the central bankers really are can the tolerated when fixed rates are replaced by a common currency.

The point that a common currency requires explicit designation of a single central bank is pretty obvious, but it may be worth spending a little time emphasizing why. In much recent work on monetary economics, issues of seigniorage are greatly overplayed, largely because it is something we know how to model. The need for a central bank. however, is one of those issues in which the problem of seigniorage really does play a key role.

Imagine that a group of countries were to try to form a currency union without establishing a common central bank so that each national bank would have the right to issue Community money. Evidently there would be an externality. Each bank's credit creation would generate seigniorage for itself, while generating inflation that falls on all countries. The result would be a bias toward excessive inflation.

Of course externalities of this kind are common in many international contexts, including pure floating, and countries often manage to live with them or make rough accommodations that manage them well enough. However, the conflict over seigniorage among members of a monetary union would be much worse than the usual coordination problem for one key reason. This is that size inequalities, which usually reduce coordination problems, would in this context greatly worsen them. When we consider problems of international policy coordination, we usually conclude that the existence of a dominant player—an FRG versus Greece situation—tends to resolve the issue because the small player ends up following the large player's lead. This general point is sometimes grandly dubbed the theory of hegemonic stability. In a currency union without a central bank, however, the situation would be reversed. Small players would be aggressive in creating money, swamping the big players. The reason is that the small players would find that the benefits of an additional real ECU of seigniorage are just as large for them as for the big players, while the costs of an additional point of inflation are much less.

A simple algebraic example may help make the point. Consider a currency union consisting of two countries that retain independent central banks. One country has a population $n_1$: the other a smaller population $n_2$. Assume for simplicity that the countries are very similar except for the difference in their populations, with each having a per capita real demand for money $m$ (assumed inelastic with respect to the rate of inflation), and with each bank having the objective function

$$W = r - \beta\pi^2, \tag{1}$$

where $r$ is per capita seigniorage and $\pi$ the rate of inflation. It is straightforward to show that the rate of inflation in this imaginary union will be

$$\pi = \frac{n_1 r_1 + n_2 r_2}{m(n_1 + n_2)}. \tag{2}$$

Now suppose that each country were to try to choose a level of seigniorage, taking the other country's level as given. Then the first-order conditions would be

$$\pi = \frac{n_1 + n_2}{\beta n_1} \tag{3}$$

for the first country, and

$$\pi = \frac{n_1 + n_2}{\beta n_2} \tag{4}$$

for the second.

Clearly we have a problem. The second country, with its smaller population, will try to collect seigniorage up to the point where inflation reaches a higher level than the larger country will tolerate. A literal interpretation of this model is that the large country would try furiously to pull money out of the system while the small country pushes it in as fast as its printing presses allow; a realistic interpretation is that if the central banks of Greece and the FRG were both to have the right to print ECUs, Greece would abuse the privilege and quickly drive the FRG out of the system in disgust.

The essential difference from a system of fixed exchange rates is that under that system Greece cannot hope to extract seigniorage from the population of the FRG. With a common currency, however, the weakness of a bank's home turf would not impair the value of its notes, and so the usual leader-follower relations would break down.

So a common currency requires explicit designation of a central bank. This is a major difference from a fixed exchange rate system where national currencies are retained because the central banking role may remain implicit under such systems. Under Bretton Woods the Federal Reserve effectively acted as central banker to the world, in a way that was only half acknowledged by the formal system; under the EMS the Bundesbank has come to play the central role in a wholly unlegislated way. With a common currency, however, the designation of a central bank would have to be a formal process. As I will argue below, this will normally change the outcome, quite possibly in an undesirable way.

## 11.4   Credibility

The EMS is now widely regarded as having done as well as it has because it is a device that allows less self-controlled countries to take a ride on German credibility. This is by way of a caricature, but it is sufficiently valid to serve as a useful way of approaching the problem. Let us review the argument briefly and then ask two questions: Is the success likely to persist in a future era when other nations do not need to assume Teutonic coloration as badly? And would this credibility-enhancing function be enhanced or worsened by a move to a common currency?

The credibility argument can be stated in brief using a version of a now standard model. Suppose that each European nation is able to choose its rate of inflation $\pi$, given an expected rate of inflation $\pi^E$ already built into wage contracts. Suppose also that each country has a loss function that penalizes it for deviations from target levels of employment and inflation. Employment, however, depends on the deviation of actual inflation from that expected, and we assume that each country has a target employment that is higher than the "natural rate" that results when actual and expected inflation are equal. Then a quadratic version of such a loss function would be

$$L = (\pi - \pi^E - \alpha)^2 + \beta \pi^2,$$

where the constant term $\alpha$ captures the desire of the government to achieve higher employment than the natural rate and $\beta$ is a measure of distaste for inflation.

A country trying to minimize this loss function ex post, that is, given $\pi^E$, will choose $\pi$ so that

$$\pi = \frac{\alpha}{1 + \beta} + \frac{\pi^E}{1 + \beta}.$$

If wage-setters know this, however, they will set wage contracts based on an expected $\pi$ that is then validated by the government. The end result is that the government fails to achieve its goal of raising employment above its natural rate and pays a price in inflation for its known desire to do so.

The equilibrium is shown in figure 11.2. For each of the several governments there, we show a reaction function of $\pi$ as determined by $\pi^E$. Equilibrium in each case is where the reaction function crosses the 45-degree line. For Italy the equilibrium is at point $I$; for Germany, which we

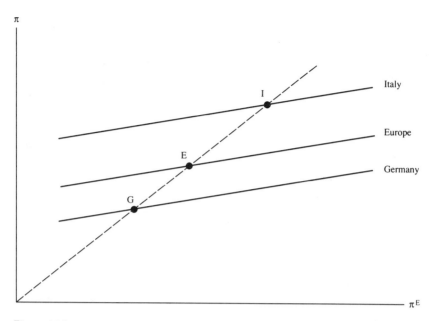

**Figure 11.2**

suppose has either more modest goals for employment, greater distaste for inflation or both, at point G. (Disregard the schedule labeled Europe for the moment.) In this kind of model then the willingness to sacrifice to obtain low inflation achieves its end without the need actually to pay the costs. A government can therefore gain from anything that enhances its anti-inflationary credibility.

The now standard argument for the EMS is apparent. Suppose that the Italians, by making some kind of moral commitment to the EMS, are able credibly to promise to match German inflation performance. Then they obtain the German expected rate of inflation and are able to achieve the superior German result. at point G.

This is clearly an overstated argument. It places more weight on rationality in price determination than the evidence warrants and ignores the costs of loss of flexibility. Nonetheless, it allows us to approach the remaining issues: Will this argument remain valid as the FRG's special role fades? And will it be reinforced or weakened under a common currency?

There is no simple answer to the first question. One cannot expect the FRG always to be a monetary paragon. If the system depends ultimately on the implicit German role, it will eventually be in trouble. Among the reasons that Bretton Woods fell apart was that the United States went from being a pillar of responsibility on which other countries could lean to a source of imported inflation; the FRG will not always be as German as it is now. However, Europe is somewhat different from the Bretton Woods group of nations in that it is more symmetric. If there comes a day when the FRG has an inflation problem and France does not, they could conceivably reverse roles, since Germany is not overwhelmingly the largest European economy.

Indeed one could argue that the EMS, which may eventually contain four roughly equal-sized economic powers, could in time develop into a system in which there is de facto competition for the hegemonic role. In this case the national central bank perceived as having the most conservative monetary policy would tend to emerge as the de facto European central bank, but with that status always provisional.

Now for the next question: Would credibility be better or worse under a common currency?

At first sight one might think that it would necessarily be better, since commitment to fixed rates is always provisional as long as national currencies remain; a fixed rate system is always in some sense still an adjustable peg. Establishment of a common currency is a more credible commitment than a mere promise to stabilize exchange rates. It is not easy to opt out of a common currency, as Panama has found; nor is it easy to impose capital controls or otherwise seek monetary independence.

Yet there is an alternative argument that suggests to me that a common currency might provide less credibility as an anti-inflationary device than an EMS-type system. The reasons are as follows: Under the apparent symmetry of the EMS, it is possible for the inflation-prone countries to sacrifice their monetary independence implicitly, without any formal political humiliation. With a formal designation of a central bank, this would no longer be possible, and the views of the inflationary nations would have to be reflected—whether they like it or not. Thus the credibility of the system would actually be less.

Consider figure 11.2 again. Suppose that the FRG and Italy form a monetary union and that the central bank reflects the views of both. Then the European central bank's reaction function would lie intermediate between the German and Italian schedules, leading to an outcome at $E$ that is better than Italy under floating rates but worse than the common outcome at $G$ under fixed rates!

This is clearly too extreme a result. It comes from a model in which there is never any reason to want a more expansionary monetary policy ex ante, in which a central bank that is indifferent to employment does just as well in terms of employment as one that makes employment a priority and achieves this result with lower inflation. A more realistic model would allow some role for active stabilization policy, and in this model Italy might prefer to have a seat on the central bank's board, even though that bank's credibility might suffer slightly as a result. I have also neglected the point that Italy might have problems being fully credible in its commitment to stabilize its exchange rate.

Nonetheless, the basic result that everyone's credibility might actually be worse with a common currency than with mere fixed rates may serve as a useful corrective to excessive enthusiasm about a European currency.

## 11.5  Fiscal Policy

An issue that has arisen both from 1992 and from movements toward monetary unification is whether a highly integrated economy requires fiscal as well as monetary and trade policy coordination. This is a heated issue; it may be useful to throw some cold water on the subject.

The basic case for coordination of fiscal policy is similar to the general case for policy coordination: It is based on externalities between the major nations. Consider the following example: A group of countries has established a credible monetary union; never mind, for the moment, who acts as central banker. Suppose also that despite the existence of some kind of union central banker, it is true both that countries have individual current account targets and that fiscal policy is an essential tool of stabilization policy. Then there will be a potential deflationary bias in the system. Each country will be tempted to follow a tight fiscal policy in pursuit of a current account surplus, but the collective result of these policies will be low output for everyone without much current account improvement.[2] Thus it becomes necessary to have coordination of fiscal as well as monetary problems.

How reasonable is this concern? I am sceptical on one theoretical and two practical grounds. The theoretical question is, What happened to monetary policy? The argument here depends on the Keynesian view that a sufficiently expansionary fiscal policy is needed to achieve a desired level of demand. As long as someone is playing the central bank role, however, there is no particular reason why monetary policy cannot do the job instead. Since it is aggregate demand for the whole of Europe, not local demand, that is the issue, it is hard to see why the level of fiscal stimulus matters very much.

As a practical matter, what stands out first is that the active use of fiscal policy for stabilization purposes has become fairly rare in any case in the last decade. So it is hard to see why it should suddenly become a major issue for European monetary union. Furthermore there is the always useful comparison with the United States, with its federal system: If fiscal coordination is so important, why has the United States found it unnecessary to police state and local budgets? On the whole, the case for fiscal coordination seems much weaker than that for monetary coordination, and it is hard to work up much enthusiasm for it.

## 11.6   Monetary and Political Union

The discussion presented so far does not convey an overwhelming case for European monetary union, still less for creation of a European common currency. The theory of optimal currency areas suggests that a monetary union should take place when the relevant countries are very closely integrated, to the point where the costs of forgoing exchange rate flexibility are small and the costs of uncertainty about rates large. Europe is still arguably too large and poorly integrated to fit the criteria. That same theory suggests that optimal areas for common currencies are smaller than optimal areas for fixed rates, so a fortiori the case for a common European currency is questionable.

Nonetheless, creation of a common European currency is strongly advocated by many of Europe's political èlite. for reasons that have little to do with economics. And they are probably right in their advocacy. Monetary union may well be a necessary counterpart of closer European political unity, whether or not it is actually the best thing from a strict economic point of view. I have previously noted that while a reasonable economic case can be made for having regional currencies inside the United States that can be realigned against one another, this idea seems absurd. The time has now come to sketch out why it seems impossible, and correspondingly why Europe may need a common currency.

Suppose that we make the following argument: A unified polity requires full freedom of movement of goods, services, and people. Historically governments have acted in ways that suggest that easy movement across the polity is a crucial aspect of political identity: Examples include the practice of charging a flat postal fee for domestic mail, regardless of distance, and the often costly construction of transportation routes that follow political rather than national geography (e.g., the Canadian railway system).

If freedom of economic movement is a crucial symbol of political unity, then part of this freedom is the ability to use as legal tender in all parts of a polity the same currency that one uses elsewhere. It is a powerful symbol of Canadian existence that a resident of Vancouver can use dollars in Montreal but not in Seattle; there would not be much of a Canadian identity left if this was otherwise.

Now one might imagine that European currencies could circulate side by side, with DM legal tender in France and FF the same in the FRG. This would, however, raise two problems. If the currencies really were accepted equally, we would have the competitive seigniorage problem discussed in section 11.3. More likely, however, the most widely used currency would tend to crowd out the others through a cumulative process. So Europe would end up with a single currency anyway. Clearly it would be politically necessary in this case that the currency be issued by a community rather than a national bank.

Now the argument that in free currency competition Europe would tend to converge on a single currency may seem to demonstrate to many readers that Europe is an optimal currency area—after all, that is the free-market outcome. Here, however, the philosophical points of section 11.1 apply. Given the inherent second-best nature of monetary economics, free-market outcomes have no special appeal: The market is not always right. It is perfectly possible that market forces may lead to the existence of too few currencies in the world. I find it quite reasonable to guess that Europe is too large, diverse, and poorly integrated to benefit economically from a single currency. I also think that a single currency for Europe is an excellent idea. Economic efficiency is not everything. A unified currency is almost surely a necessary adjunct of European political unification. and that is a more important goal than the loss of some flexibility in adjustment.

# Notes

## Chapter 1

1. Feldstein's exposition was the one that brought the link between budget and trade deficits to public attention. But this thesis was suggested by many people, so no one individual can claim sole responsibility.

2. Which is no doubt why other supply-siders have attacked Roberts's views as "dangerous" and "demand-side in origin." See "Supply-Siders Suffer a Decline in Demand for Their Policy Ideas," *Wall Street Journal*, August 18, 1987.

3. One possible way to expand the role of money is to suppose that the tight U.S. money of 1980–82 generated a speculative belief in a permanently strong dollar that the subsequent monetary easing somehow failed to dispel. Although this is a pretty much untestable hypothesis, I have some sympathy with it. It helps explain both why the dollar rose to levels that were higher than real interest rates could justify (Krugman 1985c) and why so much of the decline in national saving was financed by capital inflows.

4. In a standard Mundell-Fleming model this differential growth with a constant exchange rate could be accomplished through a monetary-fiscal max. Assume, for example, that the U.S. engages in fiscal contraction while the rest of the world keeps its fiscal policy unchanged. Then the desired combination of foreign growth with constant U.S. output and a stable exchange rate could be achieved by assigning U.S. monetary policy the task of maintaining constant U.S. employment while foreign monetary policy is used to peg the exchange rate. It is straightforward to show that to accomplish these goals, the U.S. money supply would have to expand (because world interest rates fall, increasing money demand) but that the reat of the world's money needs to expand by more (because it must support not only the increase in demand due to lower interest rates but also an expansion in income).

5. The IMF's 1987 *World Economic Outlook* finds that "the degree of cyclical slack in [the industrial] countries is comparatively small at the present time." Japan, France, and the United Kingdom are estimated to have negligible ability to expand their economies without generating inflationary pressures; Germany to have only about three percentage points of GNP gap. Only Canada and Italy are believed to

have excess capacity exceeding 4 percent. (See *World Economic Outlook*, 57–58.) One may question these estimates, especially the pessimistic view for Europe. However, for at least the medium term the crucial point is that policymakers in the major countries are at least this pessimistic, if not more so. The Germans, for example, do not believe that they have even as much room to expand as the IMF does. Thus the idea that rapid growth in the surplus countries can be expected to do much to close external imbalances is simply unrealistic.

6. Or a rise in domestic output if there is excess capacity, but the implicit model of those who deny favorable effects from devaluation is one in which monetary shocks cannot induce output expansion.

7. For a recent survey of results, see Bryant and Holtham (1987); also see Krugman and Baldwin (1987). There are several major sources of uncertainty about how far the dollar would have to fall to achieve current account balance. For one thing, exchange rates have been well away from equilibrium levels for almost the whole of the 1980s, so it is difficult to disentangle exchange rate effects from other factors, such as changes in the U.S. technological position, the rise of East Asian NICs, or the debt crisis, that might have altered the equilibrium rate. Further there are some major anomalies in recent behavior, notably in pricing, that suggest some kind of structural change and cast doubt on the reliability of all econometric estimates. See, in particular, Mann (1987).

## Chapter 3

1. Ideally we should use the ratio of domestic to foreign growth, but I was not able to reconstruct the "foreign" growth for the Houthakker-Magee sample. In the analysis of post-1970 data later in this chapter the correct ratio is used.

2. A more elaborate formulation of how technological catch-up can progressively worsen the terms of trade of the country being caught up to is offered in Krugman (1985), which in turn draws heavily on Dornbusch, Fischer, and Samuelson (1977).

3. I ignore the question of how consumption is allocated intertemporally. For the sake of argument, suppose that there is no capital mobility and that we ignore investment. Then at each point in time, people simply maximize their instantaneous utility subject to their current income. Adding investment and capital flows will complicate the picture a little, but not much.

## Chapter 4

1. This result was brought to my attention by Stephen Salant. A brief discussion of speculative attacks on goverment resource stocks is contained in Salant and Henderson (1978).

2. The reason for making this assumption is that it rules out international interest payment, allowing us to identify the current account with the trade balance.

3. Note that I am making a clear distinction bewteen stocks and flows; in any instant asset holdings are not affected by current saving.

4. A more general assumption would be "rational expectations," allowing for the existence of uncertainty. The special case of perfect foresight is easier to work with, however, and sufficient for present purposes.

5. The proof runs as follows: Just before reserves were exhausted, they must have been falling. If we can show that at the point at which $OX$ crosses $SS$ reserves are rising, we know that the position at the moment of exhaustion must be one at which wealth is larger and hence private saving less—that it lies to the right of the intersection. But consider the magnitude of saving where the lines cross. Under *flexible* rates the intersection is the point at which inflation is zero, implying that investors are willing to add real balances at a rate just matching the government deficit. That is,

$$\dot{m} = G - T = L(0)S + L_1 m \cdot \dot{\pi}.$$

But $\dot{\pi} > 0$ because the share of domestic money in wealth is falling. So

$$L(0)S - (G - T) > 0.$$

But under *fixed* rates, $\dot{R} = L(0)S - (G - T)$. So $\dot{R} > 0$ at the intersection of $OX$ with $SS$.

6. The intersection of $TT$ with the horizontal axis corresponds to the intersection of $OX$ with $SS$ in figure 4.5. But as argued in note 5, that intersection takes place at a level of wealth for which $\dot{R} > 0$.

## Chapter 6

1. Dumas and Delgado (1990) argue that since the tangency condition in these models does not arise from optimization, it really should not be called "smooth pasting." This seems a semantic point, and in any case the terminology has already become so common that it really cannot be undone.

2. The equilibrium proposed here is similar, albeit with a rather different justification, to the solution to the gold standard paradox proposed by Delgado and Dumas (1990).

## Chapter 8

1. If there is no uncertainty about the future, it is always in the interests of creditors to forgive debt down to the level at which it will be repaid. In this case any secondary discount would constitute a case for debt forgiveness. Unfortunately, this is not the case when the future is uncertain.

2. Debt buy-backs at a discount were actually quite common in the 1930s. See Portes (1987).

3. This is not quite right because the secondary-market price of the debt will change as a result of the buy-back, and the amount purchased will depend on the post-buy-back equilibrium price, not the pre-buy-back one. For a marginal change, however, this makes no difference, and by focusing on the total returns to creditors, we bypass the problem in any case.

4. The same qualification as in note 3 applies: The price at which the bonds trade for old debt will be the postsecuritization discount, which changes as a result of the action itself. But the analysis is exactly right for marginal changes, and the key point of total returns to creditors is correct.

## Chapter 10

I would like to thank Peter Kenen for helpful suggestions.

1. Kindleberger (1981) treats the denomination of loans in dollars as a seventh role, that of "standard of deferred repayment." I prefer to regard this as a particular case of the "invoice" role.

2. An ingenious and suggestive model along these lines of the emergence of a domestic medium of exchange is Jones (1976).

3. If the structure of payments is not bilaterally balanced, the model becomes much more complicated. It becomes possible that some payments are made indirectly through the vehicle currency; this "partial indirect exchange" will be associated with a systematic difference between the direct exchange rate and the cross rate. For an unfortunately unreadable analysis, see Krugman (1980).

4. Cohen (1971, 60) quotes A. C. L. Day: "In general the more connexions a country has and the stronger they are, the more connexions [it] is likely to attract. This meant that because Britain had very extensive trading ... connexions, sterling would be all the more useful to a country which choose to use it; and as more people came to use it, sterling would be all the more attractive as a means of international payment to everyone."

5. This account is drawn from Yeager (1976) and Cohen (1971).

6. This scheme is essentially that offered by Magee and Rao (1980).

## Chapter 11

1. It is sometimes thought that the costs of exchange rate uncertainly are summarized by the effect of exchange risk in discouraging international trade and investment. It is then argued that the absence of any clear negative effect of exchange rate volatility on trade volumes shows that the costs have been negligible. However, the effects of uncertainty may take other forms than simply adding risk. Uncertainty may make investment decisions sluggish in response to cost changes because of the option value of waiting and seeing; or it may lead firms to construct excess capacity, to take advantage of exchange rate swings; or it may simply degrade the quality of decisions. So the fact that trade has continued to grow despite volatile exchange rates tells us little about the actual costs of that volatility.

2. Daniel Cohen and Charles Wyplosz have suggested a reverse scenario. In their version members of a monetary union are indifferent to the effect of their policies on current balances inside the union, and therefore follow fiscal policies that lead to a larger-than-optimal current deficit of the union against the rest of the world. While the logic of the model given the assumptions is impeccable, I am not persuaded that this is a realistic characterization of the problem.

# References

Bailey, N. 1983. A safety net for foreign lending. *Business Week*, January 10.

Bertola, G., and R. Caballero. 1990. Target zones and realignment. Mimeo. Princeton.

Bhagwati, J. 1958. Immiserizing growth: A geometrical note. *Review of Economic Studies* 25: 201–205.

Bhagwati, J. 1969. International trade and economic expansion. In *Trade, Tariffs, and Growth*. Cambridge: MIT Press.

Blanchard, O., and L. Summers. 1984. Perspectives on high world real interest rates. *Brookings Papers on Economic Activity* no. 2.

Branson, W. 1985. Causes of appreciation and volatility of the dollar. In *The US Dollar—Recent Developments, Outlook, and Policy Options*. Kansas City: Federal Reserve Bank.

Brock, W. A. 1975. A simple perfect foresight monetary model. *Journal of Monetary Economics* 1 (April), 133–150.

Brookings Institution. 1987. Workshop on the US current-account imbalance: Comparative tables and charts. *Brookings Discussion Papers in International Economics* no. 58.

Bryant, R., and G. Holtham. 1987. The external deficit: Why? Where next? What remedy? *Brookings Review*, 5, 28–36.

Bulow, J., and K. Rogoff. 1986. A constant recontracting model of sovereign debt. Mimeo. Stanford University.

Bulow, J., and K. Rogoff. 1988. The debt buyback boondoggle. *Brookings Papers on Economic Activity*.

Claessens, S., I. Diwan, K. Froot, and P. Krugman. 1989. The art of the deal: An Analytical Overview of Market-Based Debt Reduction Schemes. Draft report prepared for the World Bank.

Cline, W. R. 1983. *International Debt and the Stability of the World Economy*, Policy Analyses in International Economics, no. 4 Washington: Institute for International Economics. September.

Cohen, B. J. 1971. *The Future of Sterling as an International Currency.* London: Macmillan.

Delgado, F., and B. Dumas. 1990. Monetary contracting between central banks and the design of sustainable exchange-rate zones. NBER Working Paper no. 3440.

Dixit, A. 1989. Entry and exit decisions under uncertainty. *Journal of Political Economy* 97: 620–638.

Dixit, A., and J. Stiglitz. 1977. Monopolistic competition and equilibrium product diversity. *American Economic Review* 67: 297–308.

Dornbusch, R. 1976. Exchange rate expectations and monetary policy. *Journal of International Economics* 6 (August): 231–244.

Dumas, B. 1988. Pricing physical assets internationally. NBER Working Paper no. 2569.

Eaton, J., M. Gersovitz, and J. Stiglitz. 1986. The pure theory of country risk. *European Economic Review* 30, 3: 481–513.

Feldstein, M. S. 1986. International debt service and economic growth: Some simple analytics. NBER Working Paper no. 2138.

Feldstein, M. S., and H. C. 1980. Domestic saving and international capital flows. *Economic Journal* 90: 314–329.

Flood, R., and P. Garber. 1983. A model of stochastic process switching. *Econometrica* 51: 537–551.

Flood, R., and P. Garber. 1984. Collapsing exchange rate regimes: Some linear examples. *Journal of International Economics* 17: 1–13.

Flood, R., and P. Garber. 1989. The linkage between speculative attack and target zone models of exchange rates. NBER Working Paper no. 2918.

Frankel, J. 1986. International capital mobility and crowding-out in the US economy: Imperfect integration of financial markets or of goods markets? In R. W. Hafer (ed.), *How Open is the US Economy.* Lexington, MA: Lexington Books.

Friedman, M. 1953. The case for flexible exchange rates. In *Essays in Positive Economics.* Chicago: University of Chicago Press.

Froot, K., and M. Obstfeld. 1989a. Exchange rate dynamics under stochastic regime shifts: A unified approach. NBER Working Paper no. 2835.

Froot, K., and M. Obstfeld. 1989b. Stochastic process switching: Some simple solutions. NBER Working Paper no. 2998.

Girton, L., and D. W. Henderson. 1976. Central bank operations in foreign and domestic assets under fixed and flexible exchange rates. Federal Reserve Board International Finance Discussion Paper no. 83. May.

Goldstein, M., and M. Khan. 1985. Income and price effects in foreign trade. In R. W. Jones and P. B. Kenen (ed.), *Handbook of International Economics.* Amsterdam: Elsevier.

Gordon, R. 1986. US fiscal deficits and the world imbalance of payments *Hitotsubashi Journal of Economics* 27: 7–41.

Grassman, A. 1973. A fundamental symmetry in international payment patterns *Journal of International Economics* 3: 105–116.

Grilli, V. 1989. Managing exchange rate crises: Evidence from the 1890s. *Journal of International Money and Finance*, forthcoming.

Harrison, M. 1985. *Brownian Motion and Stochastic Flow Systems*. New York: Wiley.

Houthakker, H., and S. Magee. 1969. Income and price elasticities in world trade. *Review of Economics and Statistics* 51: 111–125.

Johnson, H. 1955. Economic expansion and international trade. *Manchester School of Economics and Social Studies* 23: 95–112.

Johnson, H. 1958. *International Trade and Economic Growth: Studies in Pure Theory*. London: Allen and Unwin.

Jones, R. 1976. The origin and development of media of exchange. *Journal of Political Economy* 84: 757–776.

Kindleberger, C. 1981. *International money*. London: Allen and Unwin.

Kouri, Pentti J. K. 1976. The exchange rate and the balance of payments in the short run and in the long run: A monetary approach. *Scandinavian Journal of Economics* 78: 280–304.

Krugman, P. 1979. A model of balance of payments crises. *Journal of Money, Credit, and Banking* 11, 3 (August).

Krugman, P. 1980. Scale economies, product differentiation, and the pattern of trade. *American Economic Review* 70: 950–959.

Krugman, P. 1980. Vehicle currencies and the structure of international exchange. *Journal of Money, Credit, and Banking* 12: 513–526.

Krugman, P. 1985a. Fiscal policy, interest rates, and exchange rates: Some simple analytics. Mimeo. MIT.

Krugman, P. 1985b. International debt strategies in an uncertain world. In J. Cuddington and G. Smith (eds.), *International Debt and the Developing Countries*. Washington: World Bank.

Krugman, P. 1985c. Is the strong dollar sustainable? In *The US Dollar—Recent Developments, Outlook, and Policy Options*. Kansas City: Federal Reserve Bank.

Krugman, P. 1985d. Prospects for international debt reform. In *International Monetary and Financial Issues for the Developing Countries*. Geneva: UNCTAD.

Krugman, P. 1987. Trigger Strategies and Price Dynamics in Equity and Foreign Exchange Markets. NBER Working Paper no. 2459.

Krugman, P. 1988. Financing vs. forgiving a debt overhang. *Journal of Development Economics* 29: 253–268.

Krugman, P. 1989. Target zones with limited reserves. Mimeo. MIT.

Krugman, P. 1991. Target zones and exchange rate dynamics. *Quarterly Journal of Economics.*

Krugman, P., and R. Baldwin. 1987. The persistence of the US trade deficit. *Brookings Papers on Economic Activity* no. 1.

Kubarych, R. 1978. *Foreign Exchange Markets in the United States.* New York: Federal Reserve Bank.

McKinnon, R. 1979. *Money in International Exchange.* Oxford: Oxford University Press.

McKinnon, R. 1984. *An International Standard for Monetary Stabilization.* Washington: Insitute for International Economics.

McKinnon, R., and K. Ohno. 1986. Getting the exchange rate right: Insular versus open economies. Presented at American Economic Association meetings, New Orleans, December.

Magee, S., and R. Rao. 1980. Vehicle and non-vehicle currencies in international trade. *American Economic Review Papers and Proceedings* 70: 368–373.

Mann, C. 1987. Exchange rates and import prices. Presented at NBER Summer Institute in International Economics. August.

Marris, S. 1985. *Deficits and the Dollar: The World Economy at Risk.* Institute for International Economics Policy Study in International Economics no. 14.

Miller, M., and P. Weller. 1989. Solving stochastic saddlepoint systems: A qualitative treatment with economic applications. CEPR Discussion Paper no. 308.

Mundell, R. 1962. Capital mobility and stabilization policy under fixed and flexible exchange rates. *Canadian Journal of Economics and Political Science* 29: 475–485.

Mundell, R. 1987. A new deal on exchange rates. Presented at the MITI symposium "The Search for a New Cooperation." Tokyo. January.

Page, S. A. B. 1977. The currency of invoicing in merchandise trade. *National Institute Economic Review* 81: 77–81.

Portes, R. 1987. Debt and the Market. Unpublished. Presented at the Group of Thirty Plenary Meeting, New York. September.

Roberts, P. C. 1987. The dollar "crisis" changes its spots. *Wall Street Journal,* January 23.

Rostow, W. W. 1978. *The World Economy: History and Prospect.* Austin: University of Texas Press.

Sachs, J. D. 1984. *Theoretical Issues in International Borrowing.* Princeton Studies in International Finance, no. 54. Princeton University. July.

Sachs, J. D. 1986. The debt overhang problem of developing countries. Presented at the conference in memorial to Carlos Díaz-Alejandro. Helsinki. August.

Salant, S. W., and D. W. Henderson. 1978. Market anticipation of government policy and the price of gold. *Journal of Political Economy* 86 (August): 627–648.

Swoboda, A. 1969. Vehicle currencies in the foreign exchange market: The case of the dollar. In Robert Z. Aliber (ed.), *The International Market for Foreign Exchange*. New York: Praeger.

Wakasugi, R. 1987. Attack the problem at its source. *Look Japan*, July, p. 3.

Williamson, J. 1985. *The Exchange Rate System*. Washington: Institute for International Economics.

Williamson, J. 1988. *Voluntary Approaches to Debt Relief*. Washington: Institute for International Economics.

Yeager, L. 1976. *International Monetary Relations: Theory, History, and Policy*. New York: Harper and Row.

# Index